Salesforce Lightning Reporting and Dashboards

Create, customize, and manage your Salesforce reports
and dashboards in depth with Lightning Experience

Johan Yu

BIRMINGHAM - MUMBAI

Salesforce Lightning Reporting and Dashboards

First published: August 2017

Production reference: 1020817

Published by Packt Publishing Ltd.
Livery Place
35 Livery Street
Birmingham
B3 2PB, UK.

ISBN 978-1-78829-738-7

www.packtpub.com

Credits

Author
Johan Yu

Reviewers
Chamil Madusanka
Tom Blamire

Commissioning Editor
Merint Mathew

Acquisition Editor
Karan Sadawana

Content Development Editor
Siddhi Chavan

Technical Editor
Tiksha Sarang

Copy Editor
Stuti Srivastava

Project Coordinator
Prajakta Naik

Proofreader
Safis Editing

Indexer
Francy Puthiry

Production Coordinator
Nilesh Mohite

Foreword

Before you dive into Johan's amazing book about Salesforce technology, I want to invite you to be a part of something special. We are in the midst of a major shift, and we're leaning into it with the full power of Salesforce. Our mission is to empower people to blaze their own trails, as well as to motivate and educate everyone in our community with how we live our values of trust, growth, innovation, and equality.

If you're reading this book, you are a Trailblazer and have more power than ever to make positive changes happen in your companies, communities, and careers. Doing well and doing good is about the power of working together to help companies be better for their customers, and businesses and to be major drivers of change. We want every individual to realize their full potential in their careers and lives. With this shift, we can generate hundreds of billions of dollars in GDP, create millions of new jobs, and help new Trailblazers learn the skills they need to succeed.

I'd like to introduce you to a few of the concepts that are central to this shift and core to our community: Ohana, Trailblazer, and Equality.

Ohana: This is defined broadly as "family" in Hawaiian, but at Salesforce, it means to connect, collaborate, learn, and have fun together. As one Salesforce Ohana, we all need to be Trailblazers, moving forward together on the same trail with the intentional purpose of delivering customer success and a path into the Salesforce economy. This, in turn, will generate hundreds of billions of dollars in GDP, create millions of new jobs, and help new Trailblazers learn the skills they need to succeed.

Trailblazer: This is a pioneer; an innovator; a lifelong learner; a mover and shaker; a leader who leaves a path for others to follow; and, most importantly, someone who inspires and drives change, and is committed to making the world a better place. This is all about being your best through a constant commitment to learning and giving back--and that's what this community is all about.

Equality: At Salesforce, works together with our whole Ohana--our employees, customers, partners, community organizations, and the whole tech industry--to build a path forward to equality for all. We are taking action across four key pillars: equal pay, equal opportunity, equal education, equal rights.

Let me leave you with this--ask yourself what will you learn this year? What will you teach? Will you be a mentor or a mentee? What's the Salesforce path you want to follow? I encourage you to BE BOLD in your life, career, and community--be a part of this amazing shift!

Erica Kuhl
Vice President, Community - Salesforce

About the Author

Johan Yu has more than 19 years of experience working in the IT sector across MNCs and at a leading Salesforce consulting company in the Asia-Pacific region. He has spent more than 12 years working with Salesforce technology, starting his career as a developer, team leader, and technical manager, among many other challenging roles.

Based in Singapore, Johan holds 12X active Salesforce certifications, ranging from Administrator to Architect/Designer certifications. In his spare time, he enjoys writing blogs and answering questions in the Salesforce Success Community.

In May 2014, Johan became the first Salesforce MVP, not only from Singapore, but also from Southeast Asia. He is also the leader of the Salesforce Singapore User Group and is keen to help members solve issues related to configuration, implementation, and adoption, until more technical issues arrive.

First of all, I am grateful to Almighty God for enabling me to complete this book. After living and breathing with Salesforce technologies for more than a decade, it's a miracle and my happiest moment to write my second book on Salesforce. I would like to thank the creator of Salesforce for the invention of such a great technology. Thanks to the Salesforce MVP family and the entire Salesforce team for building a great Salesforce community around the world #ohana. I wish to express my sincere gratitude to my reviewers, Chamil Madusanka and Tom Blamire, for completing the review and feedback of this book. I would also like to thank the whole Salesforce Singapore User Group family; my co-leaders; my buddies Vladimir Vujatovic, Chrisila Low, and Raphael Fraga for the dedication to the community; and many Salesforce User Group leaders around the world--I can't name each of you. Another big thanks to the team at Packt for their guidance and support which made this book happen. I would also like to thank my employer, church, family, and friends. Thanks to Ps Jacub Suria and Ps Yenny Sari, Minister of the Indonesian Family Church, Singapore, for the down-to-earth kindness and passion in giving all of us sermons and tasty food! Lastly, huge thanks and love to my wife, Novida Lunardi, for being a part of my life--her understanding, continued support, and encouragement helped me get this book completed.

About the Reviewers

Chamil Madusanka is a Salesforce.com certified Force.com developer. He has been working with Salesforce.com related technologies since 2011. He works as a developer on many custom applications built on Force.com and has also trained end users and new Salesforce developers at his current company, Dazeworks Technologies Pvt Ltd., and former companies, Sabre Technologies (Pvt) Ltd and attune Lanka Pvt. Ltd. He has authored *Visualforce Developer's guide* and *Learning Force.com Application Development* with Packt.

He is an active member of the Force.com community and contributes through various channels. He is passionate about Force.com and shares his knowledge of Force.com technologies through his blog. He is a super-contributor on the Force.com discussion board and shares his knowledge and experience on the topic by providing effective answers to developer questions. He is the initiator and organizer of the Sri Lanka Salesforce Platform Developer User Group. His contribution to the Sri Lanka Salesforce community has led to an increase in Salesforce competency in Sri Lanka.

Chamil completed his BSc in Computer Science from the University of Colombo School of Computing (UCSC), Sri Lanka and MBA in Management of Technology from the University of Moratuwa, Sri Lanka. His areas of interest include cloud computing, Innovation & R&D, Semantic Web technologies, and ontology-based systems. Hailing from Polonnaruwa, an ancient city in Sri Lanka, he currently resides in Gampaha in the Western province of Sri Lanka. His interests include reading books and blog posts related to technology and playing cricket. He can be reached via Twitter at @chamilmadusanka, Skype at chamilmadusanka, and email at chamil.madusanka@gmail.com.

I would like to thank Johan (the author), and Packt for giving me this opportunity and I would like to thank my family for their support during the time I was reviewing this book.

Tom Blamire is a dedicated Salesforce administrator and evangelist who accidentally fell into Salesforce in 2014. He has come from an office administration background, working in various industries, and tries to apply that knowledge and skillset to every organization he has worked in.

I would like to thank Johan for initially asking me to be a part of this amazing adventure; my GIF Squad colleagues, Amy, Ben, Stuart, Pat, Bill, Justice, Stacey, Monica, Melinda, and Sam for their continued support, loyalty, inspiration, and dedication to the cause; Marc Benioff and Parker Harris for making the greatest platform on earth and helping change the lives of so many people for the better; the Salesforce Success Community, Trailhead, and Awesome Admin Jobs Team for doing what you do on a day-to-day basis and constantly supporting the #salesforceohana; Tony Prophet and team for helping to make the world a more educated and less critical place to be; and, most importantly, thank you to my wife and unborn son for everything, as without you, life would be a dark and empty place to be.

www.PacktPub.com

For support files and downloads related to your book, please visit www.PacktPub.com.

Did you know that Packt offers eBook versions of every book published, with PDF and ePub files available? You can upgrade to the eBook version at www.PacktPub.com and as a print book customer, you are entitled to a discount on the eBook copy. Get in touch with us at service@packtpub.com for more details.

At www.PacktPub.com, you can also read a collection of free technical articles, sign up for a range of free newsletters and receive exclusive discounts and offers on Packt books and eBooks.

https://www.packtpub.com/mapt

Get the most in-demand software skills with Mapt. Mapt gives you full access to all Packt books and video courses, as well as industry-leading tools to help you plan your personal development and advance your career.

Why subscribe?

- Fully searchable across every book published by Packt
- Copy and paste, print, and bookmark content
- On demand and accessible via a web browser

Customer Feedback

Thanks for purchasing this Packt book. At Packt, quality is at the heart of our editorial process. To help us improve, please leave us an honest review on this book's Amazon page at `https://www.amazon.com/dp/1788297385`.

If you'd like to join our team of regular reviewers, you can e-mail us at `customerreviews@packtpub.com`. We award our regular reviewers with free eBooks and videos in exchange for their valuable feedback. Help us be relentless in improving our products!

Table of Contents

Preface

This book is for Salesforce administrators, business users, and managers who use Salesforce Lightning Experience in their daily work or to analyze data in Salesforce. It covers all items related to reporting and dashboards in Salesforce Lightning Experience. This book will benefit business users, who will gain knowledge ranging from creating basic reports to advanced report and dashboard configuration. Administrators will learn the entire concept of reporting and dashboards, object models, permissions related to reports and dashboards, report storage, and reporting on historical data.

Reports and dashboards are among the most powerful and easy to use features in the Salesforce platform, including Sales Cloud, Service Cloud, and Force.com, where business users are able to create and customize reports and dashboards as needed in minutes.

Business users should have basic knowledge, or should be using Salesforce in their daily work, such as logging in to the system, navigating through the Salesforce Lightning environment, creating and editing data, and running reports in Salesforce. Admin users should have basic knowledge of customizing Salesforce, such as the Setup menu, tabs, user profiles, permission sets, and standard and custom objects.

What this book covers

Chapter 1, *Fundamentals of Salesforce Reports and Dashboards*, provides a basic overview of the Salesforce Lightning Experience, object model, Setup menu navigation, and navigating reports and dashboards.

Chapter 2, *Concepts and Permissions in Reports and Dashboards*, talks about the relationship between data visibility and result in a report generated, continues about report and dashboard storages, and permissions for reports and dashboards.

Chapter 3, *Implementing Security in Reports and Dashboards*, discusses how to secure and limit accessibility to the reports and dashboards stored in Salesforce.

Chapter 4, *Creating and Managing Reports*, covers the basic skills in required to create a new report, ranging from selecting a report format, adding filters to the report, and hands-on creation of simple report.

Chapter 5, *Understanding Report Types*, explains the report type as the foundation of the report which will also determine the availability of objects and fields, including data in the generated report. This chapter share about the standard report types, including creating custom report types.

Chapter 6, *Advanced Report Configuration*, discusses categorizing data in reporting using bucket fields and custom summary formulas.

Chapter 7, *Adding Charts in Reports and Pages*, talks about the types of charts available in the report for Lighting Experience, adding a chart to the report, and also using the same chart on the record page.

Chapter 8, *Working with Reports*, covers working with reports and items available under the Reports tab, the report folder, and things that can be configured after running a report.

Chapter 9, *Building Dashboards in Lightning Experience*, covers opening and searching for dashboards, and navigating, building, and refreshing dashboards and the components in them.

Chapter 10, *Learning Advanced Dashboard Configuration*, explains the advanced functionalities in dashboards, including dashboard filters, dynamic dashboards, drilling down, and getting additional dashboards from AppExchange.

Chapter 11, *Advanced Tips and Tricks for Reports and Dashboards*, covers collaboration in reports and dashboards, filtering reports using URL parameters, Field History Tracking, and setting up Reporting Snapshot.

Chapter 12, *Dashboards and Reports in the Salesforce1 Mobile App*, shows you how to access reports and dashboards on the go, using the Salesforce1 mobile app, including offline access without the internet.

What you need for this book

The best approach to get the most of this book is to get hands-on experience of all the exercises. You will need the following:

- A Salesforce account. You are advised to use the Enterprise edition or above. However, for the purposes of testing and learning, a Sandbox instance and Developer edition are good enough.
- A web browser.
- An internet connection.

- A computer.
- A mobile phone--iOS or Android.

Who this book is for

This book is written for business analysts, reporting analysts, sales representatives, sales operations, and Salesforce administrators. This book is also for users who want to learn about Salesforce reporting and dashboards in depth using Lightning Experience. You will gain knowledge of items related to reports and dashboards in Salesforce, starting from creating basic reports and customizing them, and moving up to the most advanced reports and dashboards in Salesforce Lightning Experience.

Conventions

In this book, you will find a number of text styles that distinguish between different kinds of information. Here are some examples of these styles and an explanation of their meaning.

Code words in text, database table names, folder names, filenames, file extensions, pathnames, dummy URLs, user input, and Twitter handles are shown as follows: "Create an Account report and use the `No of Won Opportunity` field as the report filter."

Any command-line input or output is written as follows:

```
SELECT Id FROM Report USING SCOPE allPrivate WHERE OwnerId =
'00541000001cTYgAAM'
```

New terms and important words are shown in bold. Words that you see on the screen, for example, in menus or dialog boxes, appear in the text like this: "Navigate to the **Reports** tab and click **New Report** button."

 Warnings or important notes appear like this.

 Tips and tricks appear like this.

Reader feedback

Feedback from our readers is always welcome. Let us know what you think about this book-what you liked or disliked. Reader feedback is important for us as it helps us develop titles that you will really get the most out of. To send us general feedback, simply e-mail feedback@packtpub.com, and mention the book's title in the subject of your message. If there is a topic that you have expertise in and you are interested in either writing or contributing to a book, see our author guide at www.packtpub.com/authors.

Customer support

Now that you are the proud owner of a Packt book, we have a number of things to help you to get the most from your purchase.

Downloading the color images of this book

We also provide you with a PDF file that has color images of the screenshots/diagrams used in this book. The color images will help you better understand the changes in the output. You can download this file from https://www.packtpub.com/sites/default/files/down loads/SalesforceLightningReportingandDashboards_ColorImages.pdf.

Errata

Although we have taken every care to ensure the accuracy of our content, mistakes do happen. If you find a mistake in one of our books-maybe a mistake in the text or the code-we would be grateful if you could report this to us. By doing so, you can save other readers from frustration and help us improve subsequent versions of this book. If you find any errata, please report them by visiting http://www.packtpub.com/submit-errata, selecting your book, clicking on the **Errata Submission Form** link, and entering the details of your errata. Once your errata are verified, your submission will be accepted and the errata will be uploaded to our website or added to any list of existing errata under the Errata section of that title. To view the previously submitted errata, go to https://www.packtpub.com/book s/content/support and enter the name of the book in the search field. The required information will appear under the Errata section.

Piracy

Piracy of copyrighted material on the Internet is an ongoing problem across all media. At Packt, we take the protection of our copyright and licenses very seriously. If you come across any illegal copies of our works in any form on the Internet, please provide us with the location address or website name immediately so that we can pursue a remedy. Please contact us at copyright@packtpub.com with a link to the suspected pirated material. We appreciate your help in protecting our authors and our ability to bring you valuable content.

Questions

If you have a problem with any aspect of this book, you can contact us at questions@packtpub.com, and we will do our best to address the problem.

1

Fundamentals of Salesforce Reports and Dashboards

This chapter will give you a general overview of the Salesforce cloud technology including the benefits of the Cloud Platform, the introduction of Salesforce Lightning Experience, extending Salesforce beyond **Customer relationship management (CRM)**, and navigating Salesforce reports and dashboards. We will also touch on the Salesforce architecture, Setup menu, and Lightning Experience user interface.

This chapter contains information that applies to both business users and Salesforce system administrators. Some topics in this chapter discuss features specific for the system administrator, but the business user might find it interesting to have a better understanding of the Salesforce architecture.

Throughout the book, we will provide notes and tips to help you to understand Salesforce technology easily. In the next few chapters, we will look at various skills to build advanced reports and dashboards, which suit your business requirements in Lightning Experience. Hands-on activities will be part of most chapters, while creating reports and dashboards will be covered in `Chapter 4`, *Creating and Managing Reports* and onward.

The following topics will be covered in this chapter:

- An overview and the benefits of Salesforce
- Salesforce Lightning Experience
- The Salesforce object model
- Navigating to the Setup menu
- Navigating to reports and dashboards

An overview and the benefits of Salesforce

Salesforce is an enterprise, web-based platform which can be accessed from anywhere, anytime, and on any device as long as your device is connected to the Internet. It is a cloud application, so you do not need to purchase any server/hardware, operating system, or database to use it. If you haven't already used the Salesforce platform, it is a web-based application like Gmail or Yahoo, but more than that, it allows you to configure and customize the application to suit your own business needs.

When you sign up for Salesforce, either the free developer edition or the paid version, you will be provided with an organization--a software environment. The hardware, operating system, and database are shared among all Salesforce customers within the same instance. All customers within the same instance will be in the same release. Salesforce has three feature releases every year.

You can imagine it as an apartment building block shared by many residences. In this multi-tenant environment, each organization's data, configuration, and users are completely isolated, and are not accessible by any other organization. So, when you configure your Salesforce organization, the metadata changes are only for your organization. The same is true for data; it is accessible only by your registered users.

If you've heard about cloud computing, Salesforce is a **SaaS (Software as a service)** model, which means that you only need to configure Salesforce to start using it. Salesforce provides everything you need to run your business--the object model, business rules, workflow and automation, page layout, report and dashboard, and so on. You just need to configure them as per your business needs. Salesforce also has its own Java-like programming language called **Apex,** and HTML-like visual markup language called **Visualforce** page for custom user interface design.

Since Salesforce's team takes care of the infrastructure, maintenance, software upgrades, backup, and performance, this benefits companies, as it brings down the IT and resources costs. As a Salesforce subscriber, you just need to support your users, and implement your business processes in the platform.

When Marc Benioff started Salesforce.com from his apartment in San Francisco back in 1999, Salesforce.com was intended to be a CRM application only, but as the platform grew and became more robust, it was extended as Force.com Platform, where you can build any kind of application beyond CRM, or get an app from **AppExchange,** the app marketplace for the Salesforce platform. AppExchange is similar to the App Store for iOS devices, or Google Play Store for Android devices. AppExchange is the app store (free and paid) for the Salesforce platform.

The following are a few cloud products offered by Salesforce right now:

- **Sales Cloud**: Sales Cloud automates your sales process
- **Service Cloud**: Service Cloud delivers an evolutionary customer service process
- **Marketing Cloud**: Marketing Cloud gains from digital marketing automation
- **Community Cloud**: Community Cloud connects with your customer and partner
- **Wave Analytic**: Wave Analytic delivers analytics for business users and analysts
- **App Cloud**: App Cloud allows you to build an app for your business needs
- **IoT Cloud**: IoT Cloud is to store and process **Internet of Things (IoT)** data for connected devices
- **Commerce Cloud**: The Commerce Cloud enables you to build a unified shopping experience

As Salesforce keeps acquiring and building new products, the preceding list may change anytime.

In short, these are the advantages of using Salesforce as compared to other on-premise applications:

- Faster implementation schedule
- Lower maintenance cost, since you don't have to buy or support in-house servers, and maintain resources for it
- Scalability and robustness
- Secure and high performance
- Easy to expand the functionality using prebuilt solutions from AppExchange
- Accessible from desktops, laptops, tablet, and mobile apps
- Enterprise-level grade application for small and medium business

Salesforce Lightning Experience

Lightning Experience is a modern, fast, and beautiful user interface designed to help your sales users to be more productive and efficient. It is built with a sales-centric mindset, focusing on helping sales representatives work more naturally on a daily basis. With Lightning Experience, your users will get an intuitive and intelligent user interface.

Lightning Experience is built with proven Salesforce1 Mobile App technology. Your sales representatives already use mobiles to enter prospective customers, log tasks and notes after client meetings, run reports and dashboards, and more. All this cool stuff from the mobile experience is being brought into the computer web browser by Lightning Experience.

Let's get the right term

On many occasions, Lightning Experience is simply referred to as Lightning, although there are many items in the Salesforce platform which start with the word "Lightning", such as Lightning Login, Lightning App Builder, Lightning for Outlook, Lightning Components, Lightning Sync, and so on. Some of them are applicable in Lightning Experience only, but some others will work in both Lightning Experience and older Classic user interfaces, for example, Lightning Sync is used to sync your user contacts and events between your email server with Salesforce.

Just to make it clear, when you meet someone from the Salesforce community, and he asks if you are on lightning, most probably, he is referring to Lightning Experience. To get the term right, it is Lightning, not Lightening or Lighting.

What was before the Lightning Experience?

If you noticed, we mentioned the term classic user interface in the *Let's get the right term* section. Yes, that is the one--Salesforce Classic had been serving well for many years before Lightning Experience was introduced. Salesforce Classic still exists, and is widely used by many customers, but mostly, the new features introduced by Salesforce in recent releases are only applicable for Lightning Experience.

If you are still with Classic, Salesforce urges you to migrate to Lightning. Why do I use the term migrate? Because the user interface is totally different, and some of your existing customizations may not work, such as the JavaScript button built by your Salesforce partner or your IT team. You should consult with your Salesforce Success Manager, partners, or IT before making the decision.

Because the user interface is totally different from Classic, your user manual, training video and material, and so on, need to be updated, so plan this journey with proper project management to roll out Lightning Experience.

Let's turn the Lightning Experience on

This section is intended for system administrators who still operate in Salesforce Classic--only system administrators will have the permission to enable Lightning Experience. If you are on Lightning Experience already, you can skip this section.

Let's have a quick hands-on exercise on how to enable Lightning Experience:

1. Click on **Setup** to navigate to the setup menu, and then click on **Lightning Experience** in the top-left menu:

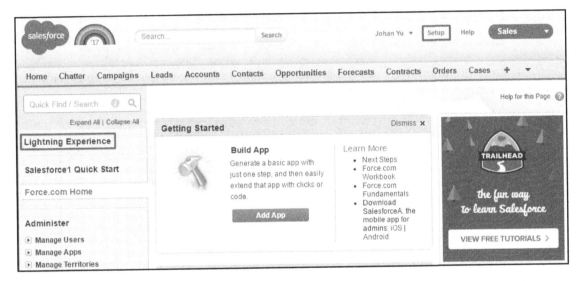

2. Scroll down to the bottom of the page, look for **Lightning Experience**, then switch to enable it:

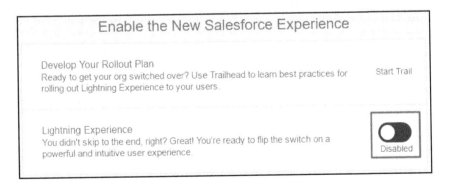

3. Click on **Finish Enabling Lightning Experience** to confirm:

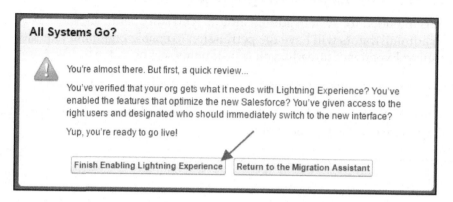

4. Once Lightning Experienced is enabled, notice that the switch turns to green with the label changed to **Enabled**:

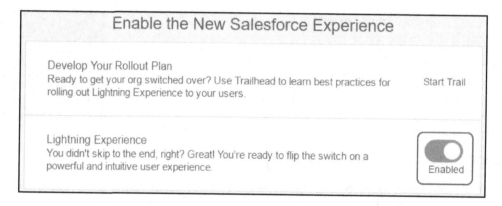

5. Click on your name in the top-right corner; you will notice that a new menu, **Switch to Lightning Experience**, is added, as shown in the following screenshot:

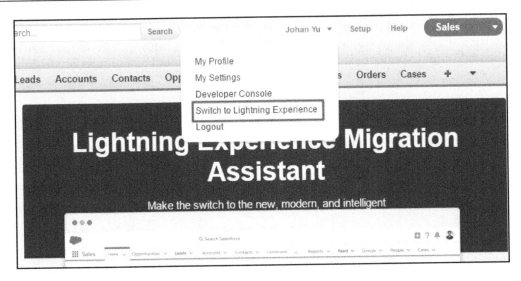

6. Done! Now click on **Switch to Lightning Experience** from the menu to start exploring the modern Lightning Experience.

7. This hands-on exercise will allow you, as a system administrator (including other system administrators), to try and explore Lightning Experience for your organization. Your normal users will not see the new menu, **Switch to Lightning Experience**, until you configure it for them.

8. To enable Lightning Experience for your business users, as a system admin, you have the option to enable it by Profile (for all the users in that Profile) or by Permission Set (to assign on the user by user basis).

9. To enable by Profile, click on **Edit** on the Profile, scroll down to the **Administrative Permissions** section, and look for **Lightning Experience User** permission; enable it, then save the Profile.

10. To enable by Permission Set, the same permission **Lightning Experience User** is assigned to specific users who need to switch to Lightning Experience.

It is best practice for a system admin to evaluate Lightning Experience before he/she (system admin) enables it for all Salesforce users, and find the gap for the functions that may not work when you switch to Lightning Experience. Before enabling Lightning Experience users, another best practice is to enable it just for a group of pilot users, get their feedback when using Salesforce as part of the daily job. Permissions Set would be the option if the users have a different type of Profile.

Salesforce provides a tool to help you check your organization's readiness for Lightning Experience. Click on the **Evaluate** link under **Check Your Lightning Experience Readiness** from the Lightning Experience setup menu. Salesforce will email a readiness report to you.

Switch to Lightning Experience

Once Lightning Experience is enabled and permission assigned, click on **Switch to Lightning Experience** after clicking on your name, as seen in the following screenshot:

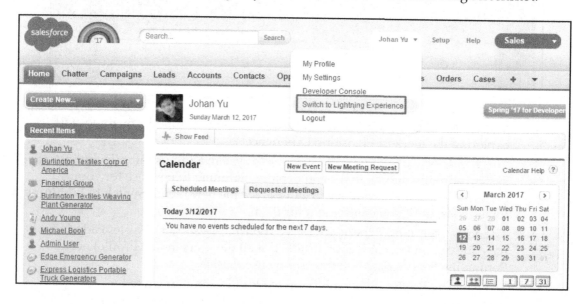

Here is a screenshot of the modern Salesforce Lightning Experience:

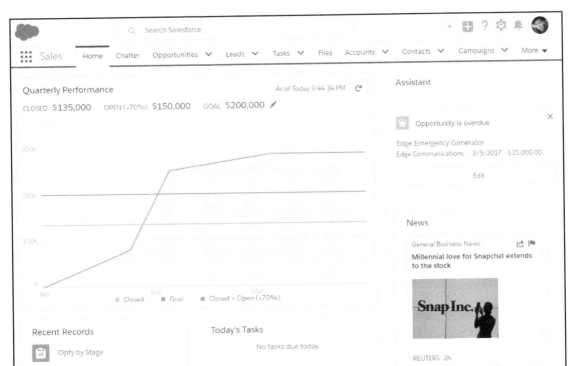

Notice that the user interfaces of the Classic and Lightning Experience are totally different; if you still see a bluish background around the tab menu, you are in the Classic interface. Follow the *Let's turn the Lightning Experience on* section to enable it, or contact your system administrator to enable this for you.

 All navigations and screenshots for this book will be in the Lightning Experience interface only.

As of now, not all features from Classic are available in Lightning Experience; you may need to switch back to Classic when needed. For example, Recycle Bin is not available in Lighting Experience. To switch back to Classic, click on your photo, then click on **Switch to Salesforce Classic**. You can use the same path to switch back to Lightning Experience:

 The Summer '17 release offers the ability for admin to remove the switcher for a user to go back to Classic. If you are not the system admin, reach out to your system admin, but if you are the system admin, there is a new permission that controls this-- it is called **Hide Option to Switch to Salesforce Classic** in Profile.

The Salesforce object model

No matter what the user interface, Classic or Lightning Experience, the backend database is the same. You will see the same data in Classic or in Lightning Experience, or even from the Salesforce1 Mobile App. All reports and dashboards which can be built are based on the object model implemented in your Salesforce organization, from objects relationship, down to the field type level. It's crucial for you to know this as a basis, before learning to build advance reports and dashboards.

This section will discuss the object model in Salesforce. Objects are a key component in Salesforce. They allow you to store your data. Similar to a table in the database, an object comprises several fields to store data. You can set some fields as mandatory, while some other fields will be automatically populated by the system, such as **ID**, **Created Date**, **Created By**, **Last Modified Date**, and **Last Modified By**.

You can illustrate an object as a table, field as a column in the table, and record as a row in the table. In the following table, field 1 will store values for all first names, field 2 for birth date, and so on:

records	field 1	field 2	field 3
record 1	John	29 Jun	...
record 2	May	10 Dec	...
record 3	Steve	24 Feb	...

There are two types of objects in Salesforce:

- Standard objects
- Custom objects

Standard objects

Standard objects are provided by default when you subscribe for Salesforce; this is dependent on the cloud type you subscribe to. Each object has its own uniqueness for specific functions, and the objects have built-in relationships to each other. Here are a few main standard objects when you subscribe to Sales and Service Cloud:

- **Account**: Account is used to store information about the businesses and organizations your company interacts with
- **Contact**: Contacts store information about the people that you work with-- prospects, customers, or suppliers
- **Opportunity**: Opportunity is used to store information about sales interactions with your customers; this is often known as the **Sales Cycle**

- **Lead**: Lead is to store information about people who might become customers or partners of your company
- **Case**: Case stores information about interactions with your customers related to the products or services you provide
- **Campaign**: Campaign stores information about your company's marketing activities and responses

Some other standard objects are Activity, Asset, Contract, Quote, Order, Products, and Price Book.

Each standard object comes with default fields based on the purpose of the object, for example, **Stage in Opportunity**, **Mobile Phone in Contact**, and so on. You can create your own fields in the Standard object; this is called as **custom field**. The maximum number of fields you can create depends on the Salesforce edition you subscribe to.

You can upgrade your Salesforce edition to a higher edition, such as Professional Edition to Enterprise Edition, by simply contacting your Account Executive and paying for the increased subscription fee. You will continue using the same organization with your existing database and customization. But if you plan to downgrade to a lower edition, it is actually not possible to downgrade. By the end of your contract, Salesforce will give you a brand new organization where you need to reconfigure and transfer all your data.

Custom objects

Custom objects are objects created within an organization to store data specific to that organization's business, and which cannot be stored using standard objects. Only users with admin access can create a custom object. Most AppExchange packages create and use custom objects, since they provide specific business processes. Just like standard objects, custom objects are used to store specific data in Salesforce.

Do not create custom objects to replace the functionality offered by standard objects. For example, if you create a custom Lead object, you will waste all the functionalities offered by Lead object, such as Lead Conversion.

A limited number of custom objects can be created depending on the Salesforce edition you subscribe to. If you have admin permission, you can create objects and fields in Salesforce with just Point and Click rather than complex SQL scripts as in the traditional database.

In a standard object, the standard fields available depend on the object, but each custom object comes with the following few standard fields, which is the same for all custom objects:

- ID
- Name
- Created By and Created Date
- Last Modified By and Last Modified Date
- Owner (if the object is not a child of other objects in Master-Detail Relationship)

Just as with Standard objects, you can create custom fields in a custom object.

> Use Standard object as it is designed for, for example, Salesforce CRM provides standard Account and Contact object, so do not create a custom field, such as a contact email address in Account.

Object relationships

You can relate an object to other objects in Salesforce. For example, relating a custom object Expense to custom object Project. With this relation, you'll know which expense record is used for which project. Project, in this example, will be considered as the parent object, and Expense as a child object. From the record-level perspective, one parent can have many children, while the child can only have one parent. To build this relationship from the child object, create a Lookup Relationship or Master-Detail Relationship field to the parent object.

There are three types of object relationships in Salesforce, which are as follows:

- Master-Detail Relationship
- Lookup Relationship
- Hierarchical Relationship

The following table compares the Master-Detail Relationship and Lookup Relationship:

Master-Detail Relationship	Lookup Relationship
You can define master-detail relationships between two custom objects, or between a custom object with a standard object (the standard object must be the parent).	You can define the relationship between any two objects, standard, or custom object.
When a record in the master object (parent) is deleted, all records in the detail object (child) related to the master record will be deleted.	You can configure the child object to control when the parent is being deleted, either to clear the parent record value in the child record, or to not allow deletion of the parent record.
All child records must have a related parent record.	The parent record may not be required, but you can configure to make the parent field required.
The ownership of a child record is determined by the related parent record; the child record does not have an owner.	Each child record has an owner.
A detail record inherits sharing and security from the master record.	There is no security sharing or inheritance between related parent and child records.
You can relate an existing custom object as a child object, but no records should exist in the child object.	To relate an object to another object, there is no validation on the existing number of records for the child object.
If you have a Roll-Up Summary field in the parent object, the create, edit, or delete actions in a child record will trigger edit action in the parent object. If you have validation rule in the parent object, it will trigger for the parent object as well.	You cannot create a Roll-Up Summary in Lookup Relationship using out-of-the-box Salesforce functionality.
Supports cross-object workflow; you can define to update a field in the parent record using the value from the child record.	Does not support cross-object workflow.
Ability to configure for a child record to allow re-parent to a new parent.	A child record can always re-parent to another parent record.
Ability to configure the sharing setting to allow to create, edit, or delete related Detail records based on permission on the parent record.	No sharing setting dependency between parent and child objects.

To create a Master-Detail Relationship for an existing object that contains records as a child object, you can initially set it as a Lookup Relationship, populate the parent field for all child records, and then change the relationship to Master-Detail Relationship.

Hierarchical Relationship is a special Lookup relationship available for the user object only. It lets users use a lookup field to associate one user with another, which does not directly or indirectly refer to itself. For example, you can create a custom Hierarchical Relationship field to store each user's reporting manager.

You can build a many-to-many object relationship using two Master-Detail Relationships in a single custom object; this is known as a **Junction object**.

Field types

Salesforce provides various data types to fit your business model. Some of them are built with business logic, for example, emails have to follow a valid e-mail format, and URLs have to follow a valid URL format; an invalid value will be auto rejected by the system. For each data type, you can determine additional options to specify including Required, Unique, Case sensitive, External ID, and Default Value.

Here is a list of the Salesforce data types:

- Auto Number
- Formula
- Roll-Up Summary if an object is the parent in Master-Detail Relationship
- Hierarchical relationship--only for a User object
- Lookup Relationship
- Master-Detail Relationship
- Checkbox
- Currency
- Date
- Date/Time
- Email
- Geolocation
- Number
- Percent

- Phone
- Picklist
- Picklist (Multi-Select)
- Text
- Text Area
- Text Area (Long)
- Text Area (Rich)
- Text (Encrypted)
- URL

Navigating to the Setup menu

Once you log into Salesforce, click on the gear icon in the top-right corner of the window, then click on the **Setup** link. This will open the Setup page in a new tab of the web browser.

In the left panel, there are many links for you to configure Salesforce. These links can be categorized into three main categories: **ADMINISTRATION**, **PLATFORM TOOLS**, and **SETTINGS**. Each category has many menus. For each menu, start with arrow >, click on the menu to open the submenu.

If you are not a system admin, you may see fewer menu options in the **Setup** page, or you may not even see the **Setup** page at all--it depends on the permission given to you.

If you know a setup name, but do not remember where it is located, or whether it is a part of a menu, you can type the setup name into the **Quick Find** textbox at the top of the panel; this will filter all setup menus quickly, as shown in the following screenshot:

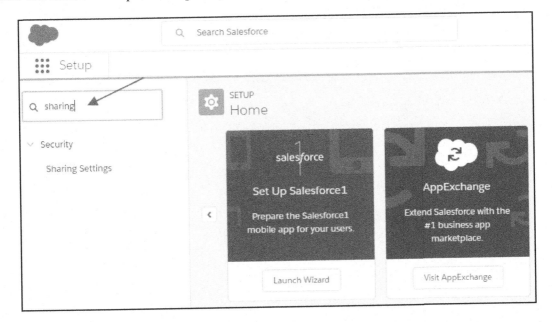

The center panel shows the last ten items most recently used in the Setup page (not records). Click on any link in that panel to open the related setup item. The top-right panel will give an admin shortcut to quickly create single or multiple users, custom object, custom tab, email template, and workflow process.

Navigating to reports and dashboards

The **Reports** and **Dashboards** tabs in Salesforce Lightning Experience are located under different tabs, as seen in this screenshot:

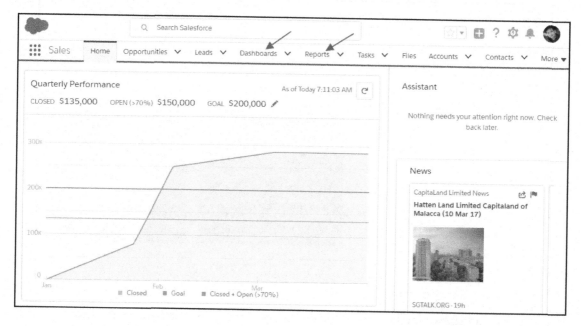

You may wonder, "Why do I not see those tabs when I am in Salesforce?". Here are two reasons why:

- Make sure your **Profile** or **Permission Set** for the **Reports** tab and **Dashboards** tab setting is **Default On** or **Default Off**, and not **Tab Hidden**. You need to check with your Salesforce system admin for this setting.
- Open **App Launcher** from the upper-left corner in the tab rows (under the logo); the icon for this is nine dots in a square. If you can find the Reports and Dashboards link here, it means that the app you opened does not have the Reports and Dashboards item added. You can access it from here, or ask your admin to add those items to the app as shown in the following screenshot:

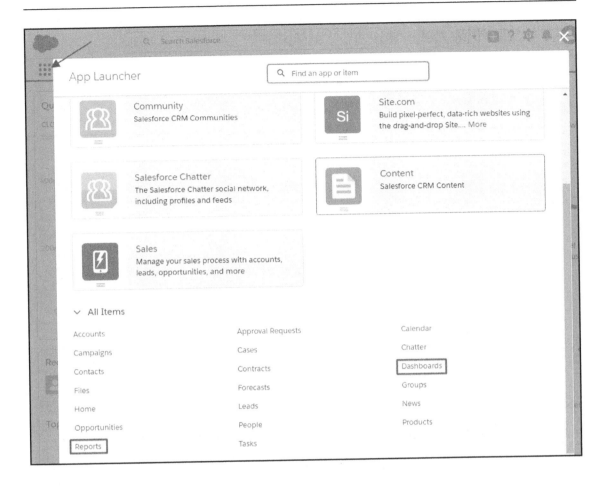

Reports / Dashboards tab and menu

When you click on the **Reports** tab, by default, you will see a list of reports recently opened. In the left panel, you will find a menu with the following items:

- **Created by Me**
- **Private Reports**
- **Public Reports**
- **All Reports**

The following folders are present in the **FOLDERS** subsection:

- **Created by Me**
- **Shared with Me**
- **All Folders**

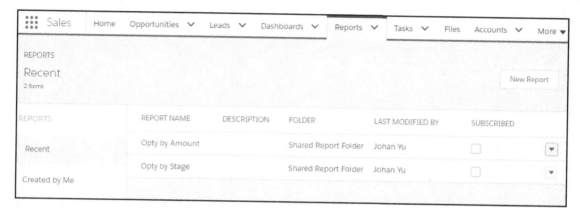

If you have the permission to create report, you will see the **New Report** button at the top-right corner of this page.

To run a report, just click on the report name, and it will open the report. The report generated is live data pulled from your organization.

In the main panel, there are few columns--**REPORT NAME, DESCRIPTION, FOLDER, LAST MODIFIED BY**, and **SUBSCRIBED**--and an arrow to perform a list of actions for the report. We will discuss most of these items in the next few chapters of this book.

The same is applicable for dashboard when you click on the **Dashboards** tab. You'll find the columns **DASHBOARD NAME, DESCRIPTION, FOLDER**, and **LAST MODIFIED BY** in the main panel.

Adding to favorites

Notice that there is an arrow next to most of the tabs. Clicking on the arrow will list all the recently opened records. The same is applicable to reports and dashboards--when you open a report or dashboard, it will be added to the Recent Records.

When your report or dashboard is open, you can bookmark that report or dashboard by clicking on **Add Favorite** (star icon), and the report or dashboard will be added to your personal favorites list, as seen in the following screenshot:

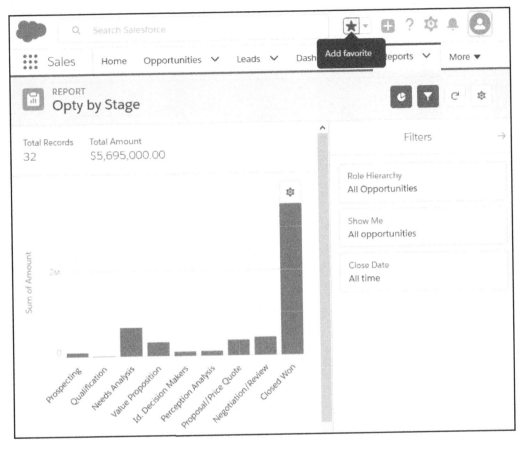

Now again click on the arrow next to the **Report** tab. You will see the report you just added as your favorite will be listed under **MY FAVORITES**.

Now check out the **MY FAVORITES** (star icon) button at the top of the page. On clicking the arrow next to the star icon, you will find the report or dashboard added earlier to your favorites. You can remove it from your favorite list by clicking on the **Edit Favorites** link:

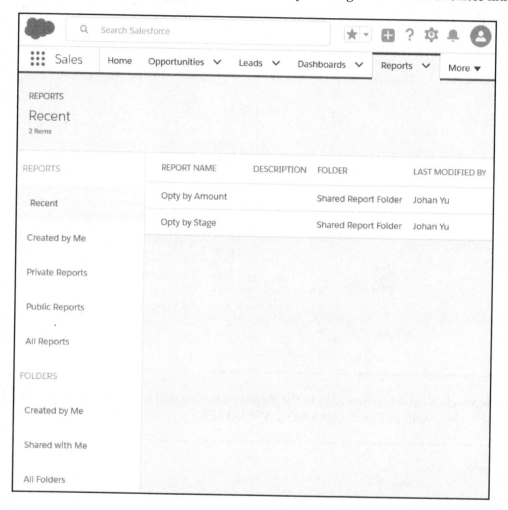

The same behavior is seen with Reports--you can also bookmark your favorite dashboards, and they will be added to the favorite icon. You click on the arrow next to the favorite icon to see it.

Summary

In this chapter, we started with a discussion on Salesforce architecture, the benefits of using the Salesforce technology, and the multiple products offered by Salesforce. Lightning Experience is the latest user interface, which offers many enhancements and more productivity over the older Salesforce Classic user interface. We discussed how to switch to Lightning Experience, and gave tips on rolling it out to your users if you are new to Lightning Experience.

We continued to discuss the Salesforce object model, how data is stored in Salesforce, the types of objects, and the difference between Standard and Custom objects. Topics like how to relate objects, the relationship between objects using Master-Detail Relationship and Lookup Relationship, and a comparison between both the relationship models were explained in depth. You also learned about the multiple field types for the objects.

Next, we explained how to navigate to the Setup menu, gave tips for **Quick Find** on the menu, and also mentioned about the recently open setup menu from the main panel. At the end of the chapter, we showed you where to find Reports and Dashboards in Salesforce, and gave you reasons if you can't find them. Then we shared how to navigate to the **Reports** and **Dashboards** tab, and to behind the arrow next to the tab. We ended with how to bookmark reports and dashboards using the Favorite icon in Lightning Experience, and how we can take advantage of that feature.

In the next chapter, we will cover the concept of Reports and Dashboards in Salesforce, how reports and dashboards are stored, backend data related to reporting, permissions related to reporting and dashboards, and the security built around them.

Concepts and Permissions in Reports and Dashboards

This chapter will explain the concept of reports and dashboards in Salesforce, and discuss the data source to generate reports and dashboards. We will continue with the mechanism on reports and dashboards stored in Salesforce with an explanation of the types of report and dashboard folders.

We will continue with permissions, which is a basic setting that controls what a user can do in Salesforce. The same is true for reports and dashboards; many permissions surface around reports and dashboards, such as the ability to create and modify reports, export reports, schedule reports, and so on.

By end of this chapter, you will have gained a strong understanding of data use for reports and dashboards, permissions around users, and granting permissions to a user with Profile and Permission Set.

Throughout the chapter, we will provide notes and tips to help you to understand important items. The topics covered in this chapter are as follows:

- Data for reports and dashboards
- Generating reports and dashboards
- Report and dashboard folder
- Report permissions
- Dashboard permissions

Data for reports and dashboards

First things first. You can only generate a report for data that exists in your Salesforce organization, unless you purchase Salesforce Connect to connect to an external database, which maps data stored outside into your Salesforce organization; the external data source could also be another Salesforce organization. Your report quality depends on the data quality, cleanness, and completeness. Therefore, system adoption is one of the most important keys to have great data and reports in Salesforce.

Once a report is created, you can store it privately, share with other users, subscribe to notifications when data in the report is changed and meets the conditions set, or schedule it for delivery to yourself and to other users.

In Salesforce, a report is the basic requirement to build a dashboard. Each component in a dashboard needs to have a report to serve as the data source. You can use the same report for multiple components in a dashboard, or across multiple dashboards.

You can use any field (with any field type) available in an object, or from multiple objects to create a report. You need to have read access to the object and the field, but it is not necessary to have permission to edit the data. If you need to learn more about object, field and field type, check out the *The Salesforce object model* section of `Chapter 1`, *Fundamentals of Salesforce Reports and Dashboards*. As you see now, objects and fields are foundations in creating reports.

Generating reports and dashboards

When you click on a report, Salesforce generates the report on the fly within seconds, and the data shown in the report is live data from your Salesforce organization. But what if I would like to see a report from yesterday's data or last week's data? No, you can generate report only for current data. If you would like to see historical data, you can set up **Reporting Snapshot** or **Field History**, but that's not the whole data snapshot on a certain date.

In the report, you can only see objects and fields that you have access to, assuming that the report is created by someone else. This means that for the same report, you may see fewer fields or columns than other users, because you do not have permission to those fields.

Similarly, for a data set, if the record is not visible to you in Salesforce, you will not see it in the report either. This is referred to as the object sharing setting and object permission.

However, dashboard is a different story. When you open a dashboard, it shows data as of the last dashboard refresh. If the dashboard was last refreshed by your colleague, you will see the data as of your colleague's last refresh, or you can refresh it manually. Salesforce offers the ability to auto refresh the dashboard, but within a limit.

The report and dashboard folder

Where are the reports and dashboards stored in Salesforce? They are stored in **Folders.** There is no limit on the number of reports and dashboards you can create and store. Folders created for reports can only be used to store reports, and the folders created for dashboards only to store dashboards. For simplicity in this book, let's call them the report folder and dashboard folder.

You can think of a folder here is similar to the folder in Windows Explorer, but without the drive and without a subfolder, and instead of storing files, it is used to store reports or dashboards depending on the folder type. As a folder manager, you can share the folder visibility to certain users, roles, roles and subordinates, or public groups.

Types of folders in Salesforce for reports and dashboards:

- A private folder
- Unfiled Public Folder (only for report)
- Public folder

A private folder

A private folder is a special folder available for each Salesforce user, and is also known as the **My Personal Custom Reports** folder for a report folder. For dashboards, it is called **My Personal Dashboards** (in Classic), or **Private Dashboards** (in Lightning Experience). In Lightning Experience, reports stored in this folder are called **Private Reports**.

All reports and dashboards in this folder are only visible to yourself; no one is supposed to be able to access, change, or delete the reports and dashboards in this folder. But if your admin has the same login access as you, she or he will be able to login and act as you with your reports and dashboards in the personal folder, here is the screenshot when you create a new dashboard:

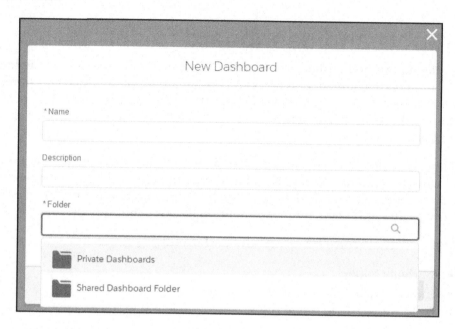

As you can see in the previous screenshot, this user has a choice to store the new dashboard into the **Private Dashboards** folder, or a public folder called **Shared Dashboard Folder**.

For the admin: Over time, the reports and dashboards fall out of use, or users become inactive and leave behind obsolete reports and dashboards in their private folders. Run an SOQL query, for example, **SELECT Id, Name, FolderName, OwnerId FROM Report USING SCOPE allPrivate WHERE LastRunDate < LAST_N_DAYS:365**

To get all private reports, do not run for more than one year. Then you can use Data Loader to mass-delete those reports if no longer needed.

Unfiled public folder

The **Unfiled Public Reports** folder in Classic, also known as the **Public Reports** folder in Lightning Experience, is another special report folder. Reports stored in this report folder are accessible by all users. If you also have permission to create and customize reports, then you will be able to store the reports into this folder.

Public folder

To create a public folder, you need to have the permission to create a report folder or a dashboard folder (we will discuss all permissions related to the folder in Chapter 3, *Implementing Security in Reports and Dashboards*). The public folder is the folder that you create for storing reports and dashboards; normally, this folder is shared by many users.

After you create a new report, you need to save the report to run it. You can store the report in a public folder to share with your colleagues for future usage or other purposes, for example, as the data source for a dashboard, or for e-mail delivery. Depending on the user permission and folder-level access, this will determine the folder's visibility and accessibility to a user--whether as read-only or with read-write accessibility. Remember, report accessibility is configured on the folder level, not in the report itself.

> When a folder is visible to a user, the user will be able to see and run all the reports stored in that folder. So the control is not by report, but by folder.

When you install an app from AppExchange, some apps will come with reports, and will be stored in their own folder. The folder will be created when you install the app.

Click on the **Reports** tab, then on **All Folders** to see all the report folders that you have access to. Let's compare users. The following screenshot is taken from an admin, which has access to all the folders:

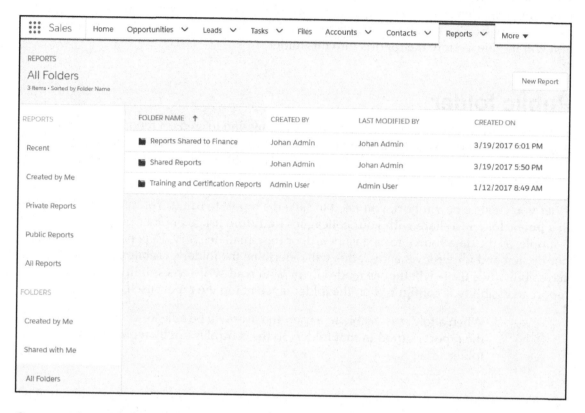

Compare this with the preceding screenshot with the following one taken from a Sales user. This Sales user can see only one folder instead of three folders, as in the preceding screenshot. The report folder manager can set folder accessibility for each user:

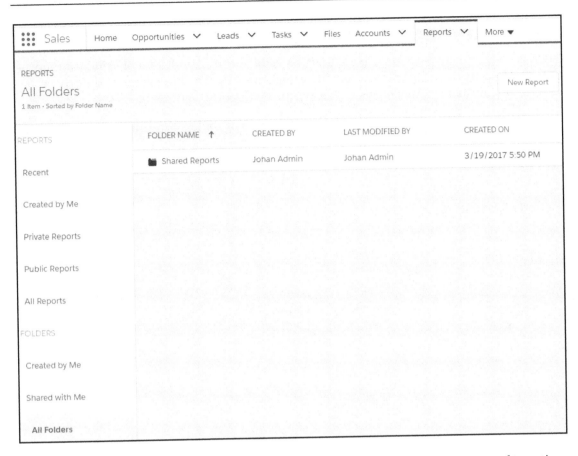

Each public folder can store either reports or dashboards, but not both. It is a good practice to have a good naming pattern for report names and folder names, for example, `NA Sales Reports` for a folder to store all reports related to Sales for North America, and `EMEA Sales Dashboards` folder for all dashboards related to EMEA sales. This will help you and other users to find the report easily, and keep things organized.

Standard reports and report folders

When you start using Salesforce, by default, Salesforce comes with a lot of standard reports for different purposes. They are stored and categorized by the object name and purpose, such as, Account and Contact Reports, Opportunity Reports, and so on.

As of the Summer '17 release, standard reports with their folders are only visible in Classic, but not yet in Lightning Experience.

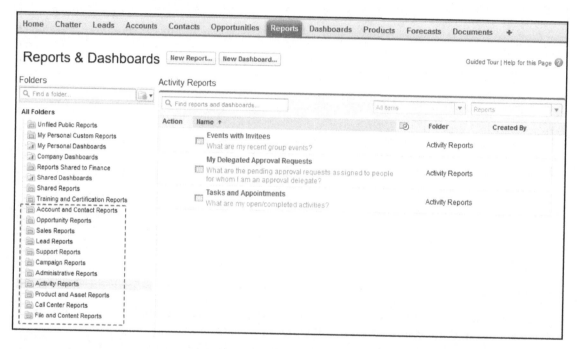

The preceding screenshot is taken from Classic (check the *Switch to Lightning Experience* section of `Chapter 1`, *Fundamentals of Salesforce Reports and Dashboards*, on how to toggle between Classic and Lightning Experience). Notice that in Classic, when you click on the **Reports** tab, you will see content from both reports and dashboards, and you can easily differentiate between the reports and dashboards folders by looking at the different icons before the folder name.

In Classic, you will be able to search within the tab, while in Lightning Experience, reports and dashboards are located in different tabs. No search box is available in the tab, but you can use Global Search to search for reports and dashboards.

Creating report and dashboard folders

Creating a report folder and dashboard folder in Salesforce is pretty simple. As long as you have the right permission, you should see the **New Folder** button in the **Reports** tab to create a report folder, and the **New Folder** button in the **Dashboards** tab to create a dashboard folder. You need to have the appropriate permissions to be able to create the report and dashboard folders. We'll discuss permissions in detail later in this chapter.

Let's have a quick hands-on exercise to create a report folder. Remember, each report needs to be stored in a folder, so it is good for you to understand the folder itself in more detail.

Hands-on exercise to create a report folder

Make sure you have appropriate permissions to create report folder. Let's create a report folder with the help of the following steps:

1. Navigate to the **Reports** tab.
2. Click on the **New Folder** button on the top-right corner of the window, as shown in the following screenshot:

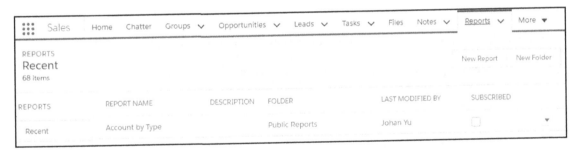

3. Enter My First Report Folder in **Name** as the report folder name.
4. Click on the **Save** button; a pop-up message will indicate whether the folder has been created successfully.

5. The folder we just created, `My First Report Folder`, will be shown in **All Folders**, and also in the **Created by Me** folder, as shown in the following screenshot:

REPORTS				
All Folders				New Report	New Folder
8 Items · Sorted by Folder Name				

REPORTS	FOLDER NAME ↑	CREATED BY	LAST MODIFIED BY	CREATED ON	
Recent	📁 Asia Sales	Johan Yu	Johan Yu	4/18/2017 6:43 AM	▼
Created by Me	📁 Best Practice Service Reports	Johan Yu	Johan Yu	5/21/2017 10:03 PM	▼
Private Reports	📁 Coba from Lex	Johan Yu	Johan Yu	6/6/2017 10:09 PM	▼
Public Reports	📁 Dashboard Reports - Adoption	Johan Yu	Johan Yu	5/21/2017 10:03 PM	▼
All Reports	📁 Lightning Folder	Johan Yu	Johan Yu	4/16/2017 4:13 PM	▼
FOLDERS	📁 My First Report Folder	Johan Yu	Johan Yu	6/6/2017 10:16 PM	▼
Created by Me	📁 My Report Folder	Johan Yu	Johan Yu	1/15/2015 7:11 AM	▼
Shared with Me	📁 Sales and Marketing Dashboard - I	Johan Yu	Johan Yu	5/21/2017 10:03 PM	▼
All Folders					

Looking at the preceding screenshot, let's walk through each menu under reports:

- **Recent reports:** This will show all the reports recently opened by you, so your colleagues will have different recently opened reports
- **Created by Me:** This contains all the reports you created no matter which folder the reports are stored in
- **Private Reports:** This is a secure folder to store reports for your personal usage; reports stored here are not accessible by other users and you cannot share the folder with other users
- **Public Reports:** This contains all reports which are visible to everyone

Since this folder is accessible by all users, and it can be edited or deleted by anyone, be careful not to store your private or important reports in this folder.

- **All Reports:** This will show all the reports that you have access to open

And here is the menu under **FOLDERS**:

- **Created by Me:** This will show all the report folders created by you
- **Shared with Me:** This is the list of report folders created by your colleagues, but shared with you
- **All Folders:** This will list all the report folders that you have access to including report folders created by your colleagues or installed as part of an app install from AppExchange

Report and dashboard folders sharing

The same with creating the report and dashboard folder, as of the Summer '17 release, sharing the public reports and dashboards folder can be done in Classic only.

Click on the **Reports** tab, hover your mouse over the folder you want to share, and click on the pin icon next to the folder name--you will see the **Share** option. If you just see **Pin to top** and **Share**, but not **Edit** and **Delete**, that means you are not the Manager for that folder. We'll walk through the folder access level in this chapter. Following is the screenshot to share report folder from Classic:

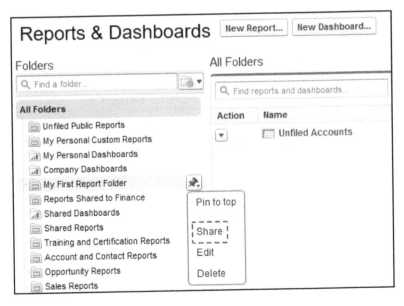

A user can share a folder with **Users**, **Roles**, **Roles and Subordinates**, or **Public Groups**, and with the level of access of **Viewer**, **Editor**, and **Manager**. Check the following screenshot for sharing reports with other users:

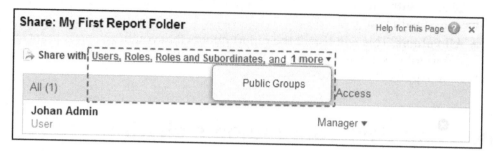

To share a report folder, a user must have the following:

- **Manager** access level on that report folder
- The Manage Reports in Public Folders permission

 When you create a folder, you will be automatically set as **Manager** for the folder.

There are three levels of access for report and dashboard folders, which are explained in the following table:

Viewer	Editor	Manager
• View a folder in the folder tree • View all contents • Run report, refresh dashboard	• Everything from **Viewer** access, and the following: • Edit all contents of a folder • Add contents to a folder • Delete contents from a folder	• Everything from **Editor** access, and the following: • Edit a folder name • Edit/delete/remove shares

Hands-on exercise for sharing report folders

Now, let us explain, step-by-step, how to share a report folder.

Use case: You would like to share the My First Report Folder folder with a user with the role as CEO with the level of access as **Viewer**, and to a Finance Manager, let's named it **Jack Fin** as folder Manager (you can use other usernames for this exercise). Assume the role CEO exists, and a user with the name Jack Fin has been created.

1. Navigate to the **Reports** tab.
2. Click on the report folder My First Report Folder created earlier, hover your mouse over the report folder name, and click on the pin icon, then on **Share**:

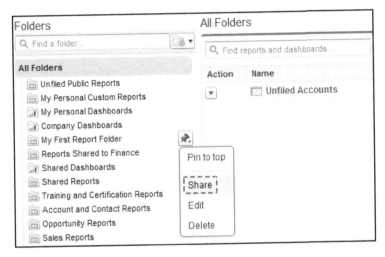

3. It will open a popup window; click on the **Roles** link, and then on the **Share** button next to CEO. Leave the access menu as **Viewer**, and click on the **Done** button to continue.

4. Next, click on the **Users** link, and look for Jack Fin. Click on the **Shared** button next to that user. The default access would be **Viewer;** click on the arrow next to it, and select **Manager.** Now click on the **Done** button to continue as shown in the following screenshot:

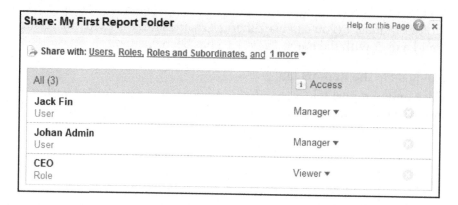

4. Click on the **Close** button to close the window.

In this hands-on exercise, you learned how to share a report folder with a user with Manager-level access, and with users in a role to view reports.

Report permissions

When we discussed the report and dashboard folders in the chapter earlier, you may have noticed that we talked about permissions to create report, to create report folder, and so on. Permission is the basic setting that controls the ability of a user to do things in Salesforce including reports and dashboards.

Before we start to create a report, we'll discuss a few permissions, which determine the ability of a user to run, create, edit, export, schedule, and subscribe reports in Salesforce.

Run reports

This is the basic permission needed to run a report. Without the **Run Reports permission,** you will not be able to run any report in Salesforce. When you try to click on the report, you will get an error message that says **You don't have permission to run reports. Check that you have the Run Reports user permission**, as shown in the following screenshot:

When all users in a profile need to run a report, the admin can simply enable this permission in Profile under the **General User Permissions** section. To assign this permission to users in different profiles, use **Permission Set** instead. Remember that Permission Set will only add permissions per user basis, not to remove permissions and is not related to the user Profile.

This permission also controls the ability of a user to access a dashboard. We will cover dashboards in detail in Chapter 9, *Building Dashboards in Lightning Experience*. If you cannot run a report, contact your admin to get this permission enabled.

Quick check if you have this permission enabled, click on the **Reports** tab, and then click on the **All Reports** menu. You should see the report generated in seconds, but if you see an error message as in the previous screenshot, this means you do not have permission to run the report. If you do not see the **Reports** tab at all, check out the *Navigating to reports and dashboards* section of Chapter 1, *Fundamentals of Salesforce Reports and Dashboards*.

Create and customize reports

The **Create and Customize Reports** permission controls the user's ability to create a new report, or modify an existing one. Without this permission, the user will not see the **New Report** button under the **Reports** tab. This permission requires the **Run Reports** permission, so, if the **Run Reports** permission is disabled for a user, automatically, the **Create and Customize Reports** is also disabled for the user. Similarly, when you enable the **Create and Customize Reports** permission, the **Run Reports** permission will be auto-enabled as well.

When you have this permission enabled, you should see the **New Report** button, otherwise, you will not be able to create and customize reports. Talk to your admin to get this enabled if you need to create or customize a report. The following screenshot shows the user has permission to create the report:

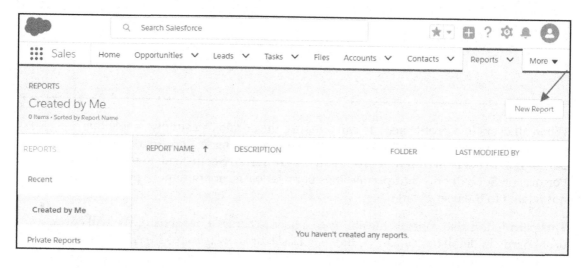

Export reports

The **Export Reports** permission manages a user's ability to export a report into Excel or CSV file format. Similar to the **Create and Customize Reports** permission, this permission also depends on the **Run Reports** permission. Disabling the **Run Reports** permission will auto disable this permission. But this permission does not depend on the **Create and Customize Reports** permission, which means that a user may be able to export a report even if she or he is not able to create or customize a report.

When you open a report, and you have this permission enabled, you will see the **Export** link under the arrow dropdown next to the **Edit** button. Consider the following screenshot:

In Classic, there is an option to export reports as printable view. The exported Excel file will retain the format, and the summary information with the report will be generated in Salesforce.

Subscribe to reports

The **Subscribe** to reports permission enables users to subscribe to reports for delivery to their email address without the need to open the report. When you subscribe to reports in Lightning Experience, you will receive refreshed report results by email on a schedule that you set--**Daily**, **Weekly**, or **Monthly**.

A user with this permission will see the **Subscribe** button after the report opens, as shown in the following screenshot. We will discuss subscribing to a report in detail in Chapter 8, *Working with Reports*:

There are two permissions related to this permission, which is as follows:

- **Subscribing to reports by adding recipients**: This permission will allow you to add other users to get the e-mail delivery. By default, you are included, but you can remove yourself when you add someone else.
- **Subscribing to reports by setting a running user**: This permission will allow you to specify the running user as someone else as long as that user has access to the report.

Dashboard permissions

After looking at report permissions in the last section, let's now look at dashboard permissions available in Salesforce. Permissions in dashboards determine the ability of a user to open, create, and edit dashboards in Salesforce.

Run reports permission

We have discussed the **Run Reports** permission in the *Report permissions* section, and we are not going to repeat that here, but we would like to emphasize that dashboards in Salesforce are based on reports. Each dashboard component in Salesforce is supported by a report as the backend data source.

To allow a user to open or view a dashboard in Salesforce, the user needs to have the permission to run reports, and the dashboard viewing user must have access to the reports used as the data source for the dashboard components. Without the **Run Reports** permission, the user will get an error message saying **You don't have permission to run reports. Check that you have the Run Reports user permission.** when opening a dashboard.

Run Reports is a basic permission needed by every user working with reports and dashboards in Salesforce, even to just run or open a report or dashboard.

Creating and customizing dashboards permission

The **Create and Customize Dashboards** permission controls the user's ability to create a new dashboard or modify an existing one. Without this permission, the user will not be able to see the **New Dashboard** button when they click on the **Dashboards** tab.

This permission requires the **Run Reports** permission too. If the **Run Reports** permission is disabled, enabling **Create and Customize Dashboards** is useless for the user.

Manage dynamic dashboards permission

The Manage dynamic dashboards permission allows users to create and edit dynamic dashboards. We will look into Dynamic Dashboards in more detail in Chapter 10, *Learning Advanced Dashboard Configuration*. But for now, you just need to understand that a dynamic dashboard allows login user to select other users as viewing user, based on the user permissions and role hierarchy.

When creating or editing a dashboard, a user with this permission will have options to set the dashboard running user as the logged-in user, or to allow a user who opens the dashboard to change the viewing user. The following screenshot shows enabling a dynamic dashboard:

The **View My Team's Dashboards permission**

The View my team's dashboards permission allows users to view dashboards owned by people under them in the role hierarchy.

When creating or editing a dashboard, the user with the **Manage Dynamic Dashboards** permission and **View My Team's Dashboards** permission has an option to set **Dashboard Running User**, and to enable **Let authorized users change running user.**

3
Implementing Security in Reports and Dashboards

This chapter will explain how you can secure reports and dashboards in Salesforce. As we discussed in the `Chapter 2`, *Concepts and Permissions in Reports and Dashboards*, each report and dashboard are stored in a folder, and the report and dashboard accessibilities are controlled by the folder that stores the report and dashboard--not by the report or dashboard itself.

We also discussed permissions related to reports and dashboards in the previous chapter. In this chapter, we will continue with permissions related to the reports and dashboards folder. There are many permissions available related to folders, for example, a user with certain permissions will be able to see all public folders, even if the username is not added in the folder. We'll go through all these scenarios.

By the end of this chapter, you will have gained a strong understanding of how to secure your reports and dashboards, and how to make sure that the reports and dashboards shared with your team are secure. As admin, you will become aware of the many types of permissions related to report and dashboard folders, and that these should not be enabled for each user.

The topics covered in this chapter are as follows:

- Private reports and dashboards
- Unfiled public reports
- Public reports and dashboards
- Report folder permissions
- Dashboard folder permissions
- Applying permissions

Securing private reports and dashboards

Private Reports are reports that are accessible to the report owner only (the user who creates the report) regardless of the user role or profile. The same also applies to **Private Dashboards**.

In Chapter 2, *Concepts and Permissions in Reports and Dashboards*, we explained that your admin may be able to access your private reports and dashboards. This is possible when the setting for **Administrators Can Log in as Any User** is enabled--the setting is located under the **Login Access Policies** setup. You can imagine this similar scenario with your office email, which can be accessed by the email server admin--they should not do this unless it is necessary and this activity is logged.

Users with the permission to create reports or create dashboards will be able to store the reports and dashboards that they create in their private folder. For reports, the folder is called **My Personal Custom Reports**, and for dashboards, it is called **Private Dashboards** (in Lightning) and **My Personal Dashboards** (in Classic). Consider the following screenshot:

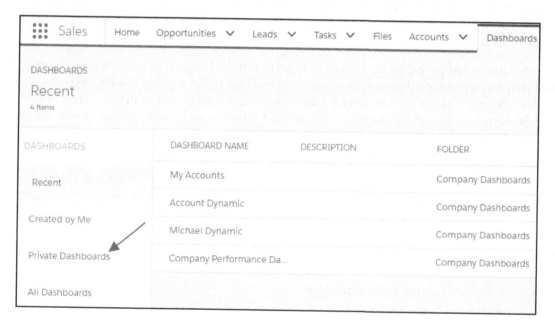

To secure your personal reports, which means that no one should able to view, change, or delete the reports, store the report in the **My Personal Custom Reports** folder. The report will be not accessible by other users, even if they have the URL. The same can be done for dashboards--store them in the **Private Dashboards** folder for private access. Consider the following screenshot:

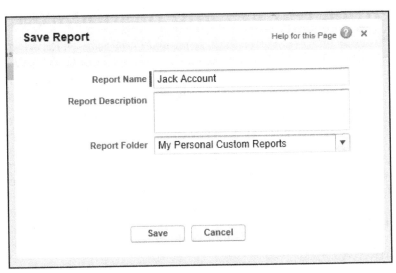

But even if it is a private report, the report will still honor data visibility; you will see only that data in the report which only you can see. Similarly, when you create or edit a report, you can add only those objects and fields into the report which you have permission for. Object and field visibility in a report is also controlled by report type, and we will discuss report type in chapter 5, *Understanding Report Types*.

In short, to secure your private reports and dashboards, store them in your personal folders, that's all. Since those reports and dashboards will not be accessible to anyone, you will not be able to share them with other users.

Using Unfiled Public Reports

In Chapter 2, *Concepts and Permissions in Reports and Dashboards*, we discussed **Unfiled Public Reports** briefly. This folder is accessible by any user, so any user with **Run Report** permissions will be able to run the reports stored in this folder, and to copy (save as) the report from this folder to other folders (including to the user's private folder). There is nothing that can be done to secure this folder.

But this does not mean you can delete or modify any reports stored in this folder. You will be only able to delete or modify reports that you create and store in this folder unless you have specific permissions--we will discuss this further in this chapter.

Using public reports and dashboards

We discussed Public Folder in `Chapter 2`, *Concepts and Permissions in Reports and Dashboards*, all reports and dashboards stored in public folder is known as public report and public dashboard. Public report is one of the easiest ways to make sure that your team sees its data as defined, for example, the report **My Team's Pipeline Next Quarter** will show all the opportunities under your team (yourself and your subordinates, including the subordinates of your subordinates--imagine this as multilevel hierarchy) that need to be closed by the next quarter. Your organization may have its own pipeline stages, and maybe, a different quarter period. With a shared team report, all sales managers will see the correct pipeline for their team, while a sales representative (individual contributor) will see the pipeline for himself, with defined stages and period.

Let's take a look at the following screenshots. Michael is a sales manager, and Jack is a sales representative who reports to Michael. When Michael opens the report, he will see the following report:

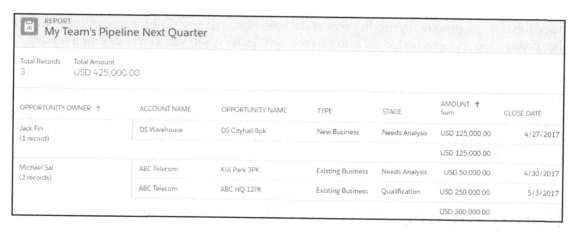

Because Jack is Michael's subordinate under the role hierarchy, Jack's pipeline will show in Michael's report.

Ideally, each user in Salesforce has a role defined by the admin. The role determines data visibility of a user in Salesforce. A role may have multiple direct roles below that role, but only one direct role above. This relationship forms the role hierarchy, which pretty much resembles the company's organization chart. A record owned by a user will be visible to users with role hierarchy above the record owner.

When Jack opens the same report, since he doesn't have any subordinate, he sees only his own pipeline, as shown in the following screenshot:

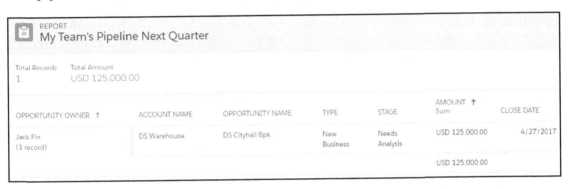

The same type of report can be used for the whole organization. The report will respect the role hierarchy defined for all users, from CEO down to the sales representative role. To create this kind of report, technically you just need to filter with criteria to show **My team's opportunities**, as shown in the following screenshot:

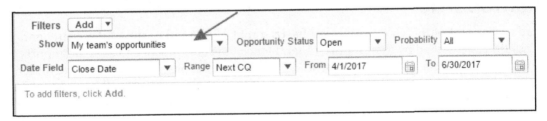

If the report has to serve all the users in the company, make sure it is stored in a folder accessible by all users, such as report of global sales.

 To share a folder with all users within the company, you can share it with a group called **All Internal Users.** This group is auto-generated by the system, and has all active users added as members.

Why do we need to store this report in **Global Sales Reports** instead of the **Unfiled Public Reports** folder discussed earlier? Housekeeping and best practice. It is easier to find a report from a specifically named folder rather than putting them all together into **Unfiled Public Reports**. Over time, the Unfiled Public Reports folder will become very messy with all reports added if not properly managed and cleaned.

The team report can also be used for individual consumption. For example, the **My Closed Opportunity This Fiscal Year** report will show all the closed opportunities owned by the user who runs the report--this should show all the won and lost opportunities owned by you within the company fiscal year. When the report is run, each user will see different opportunities based on ownership. Management can define the keys matrix for the report, which each team member should take care of, such as **Amount**, **Close Date**, **Probability**, and so on. To create this kind of report is even simpler--you just need to filter with the criteria to show **My opportunities**. Consider the following screenshot:

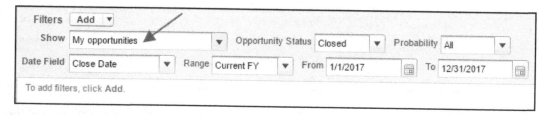

Sharing and securing public reports and dashboards

In an earlier part of this chapter, we emphasized that report and dashboard security and accessibility is defined by their report folder. Hence, it is best practice to store all reports and dashboards for a team in the same folder. If you are the one who manages the folder, you need to create report folder permissions, or get your admin to create the report folder for you, and assign Manager-level access to the report folder. This also applies for dashboard as well.

The one who creates the report folder will automatically have Manager-level access for that folder.

In the previous chapter, we discussed how to manage folder sharing. You need to have Manager-level access to that folder to manage the folder. In short, the folder Manager has the additional following permissions:

- Managing report or dashboard accessibility through sharing
- Changing the report or dashboard folder name
- Deleting a report or dashboard folder

Let's have a sample for sharing a report folder, which is accessible to the whole sales team in APAC. Let's name it APAC Shared Reports; the manager can share the folder to Roles and Subordinates of **APAC Sales Director**. Consider the following screenshot:

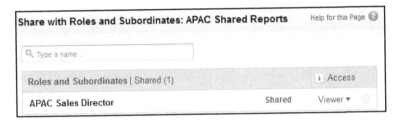

As of the Summer '17 release, you need to switch back to Classic to manage report folder sharing; this is not available yet in Lightning.

Report folder permissions

We discussed many permissions related to reports in the previous chapter. Permissions related to a report determine a user's abilities to work with a report, such as run a report, create a report, export a report, and so on. But it does not determine the user's ability to work with report and dashboard folders, folder control report, and dashboard accessibility and security.

In this section, we'll explain each permission related to a report folder, starting with permission to create a report folder, view a report in a public report, manage a report in a public report, and so on.

The Create Report Folders permission

The **Create Report Folders** permission gives users the ability to create a new report folder. The **Create and Customize Reports** permission is required to be enabled for this permission.

When this permission is enabled, once you are in the **Reports** tab, you will see the **New Folder** button; to create a report folder, click on the button, and provide the folder name under the **Create Folder** window, as shown in the following screenshot:

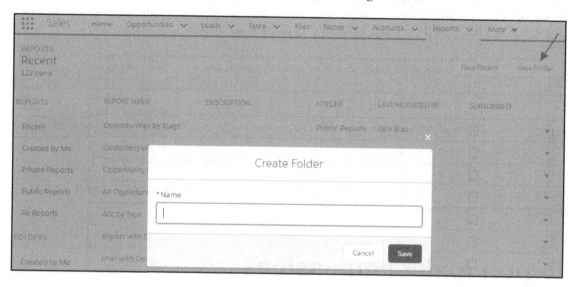

The View Reports in Public Folders permission

The **View Reports in Public Folders** permission gives the user visibility and access to all public report folders, although the user is not listed in the sharing access for that particular report folder. When you check through the Share menu in the report folder, the username with this permission will be not listed there.

This permission is limited only to view a report, not to create a new report and store to that folder, or to customize the existing report in that folder. This permission should not be given to the standard user.

The Edit My Reports permission

The **Edit My Reports** permission requires **Create and Customize Report** permission too. This permission allows the user to edit, move, save, and delete a report created by that user (not created by other users) in shared folders.

When the user has access to a report folder, the user is able to store a new report to a report folder; even user accessibility to the report folder is only as **Viewer**. The user will also able to edit and delete reports created by that user in the public report folder, with the user access is Viewer.

Without this permission, if user access to the report folder is **Viewer**, the user will not be able to overwrite a report stored in the public folder even if the report is created by that user. This scenario will be only possible when the report is moved by someone from a folder who has **Editor** access to other folders where the user has Viewer access only.

As with the **View Reports in Public Folders** permission, this permission should not be given to everyone. It allows the user to store reports to any public report folder where the user has access, even only as **Viewer**.

The Manage Reports in Public Folders permission

The **Manage Reports in Public Folders** permission requires the following permissions: **View Reports in Public Folders**, **Edit My Reports**, and **Create Report Folders**. With this permission, users will be able to access and edit all reports in the public reports folder.

On top of that, this permission also allows users to share, edit, and delete any public report folder, so this is a very powerful permission.

Be very careful to give this permission only to those users who absolutely need it. Make sure users with this permission will not mess up important reports created by other users.

The Manage All Private Reports and Dashboards permission

This permission does not relate to user ability to access reports from the Salesforce Lightning (including Classic) user interface. The purpose of this permission is to report cleaning, which includes private reports.

Over time, reports and dashboards fall out of use, or users become inactive and leave behind obsolete reports and dashboards in their private folders. With this permission, a user is able to query and delete reports and dashboards saved in other users' private folders.

We will not discuss query in this book, but as a reference, use the WHERE keyword after USING SCOPE allPrivate, and specify OwnerId after the WHERE keyword, for example:

```
SELECT Id FROM Report USING SCOPE allPrivate WHERE OwnerId =
'00541000001cTYgAAM'
```

There are many options to execute **Salesforce Object Query Language (SOQL)**, from using Developer Console, Data Loader to a famous free tool called **Workbench**. You can open Workbench from http://workbench.de veloperforce.com/login.php

Dashboard folder permissions

Now that we've seen permissions related to the report folder in the preceding section, let's continue with permissions related to the dashboard folder. They are pretty similar-- permissions in the dashboard folder determine the ability of a user to view, create, and edit dashboards in Salesforce.

The Create Dashboard Folders permission

The **Create Dashboard Folders** permission gives users the ability to create a new dashboard folder. The **Create and Customize Dashboards** permission is required to be enabled for this permission.

When this permission is enabled, once you are in the **Dashboards** tab, click on the **New Folder** button; you will just need to provide the folder name in the **Create Folder** window. Consider the following screenshot:

The Edit My Dashboards permission

We mentioned the **Edit My Reports** permission in an earlier section. **Edit My Dashboards** is a similar kind of permission, but for dashboards. It allows users to edit, move, save, and delete dashboards created by them in public dashboard folders.

When a user has access to the folder, the user is able to save a dashboard to that folder. The user access to that folder is only as **Viewer**. The user is also able to edit and delete reports created by themselves in a public dashboard folder where the user has **Viewer** access.

This permission should not be given to standard users, as it will allow the user to overwrite dashboards created by other users; access is given to that dashboard folder which has access only as **Viewer**.

The View Dashboards in Public Folders permission

The **View Dashboards in Public Folders** permission gives the user visibility and access to all dashboards stored in the public dashboard folders even if the user is not listed in the sharing access for that particular dashboard folder.

Similar to the **Edit My Dashboards** permission, this permission is also not supposed to be given to a normal end user.

The Manage Dashboards in Public Folders permission

The **Manage Dashboards in Public Folders** permission requires permissions to **Create Dashboard Folders**, **View Dashboards in Public Folders**, and **Edit My Dashboards**. With this permission, users are able to access and edit all dashboards stored in public dashboard folders.

On top of that, this permission also allows users to share, edit, and delete any public dashboard folder. So, this is a very powerful permission.

 Be careful to give this permission only to users who absolutely need it. Make sure users with this permission will not mess up dashboards created by other users.

Applying permission

Now you've understood that the ability to run a report, create a report, export a report, create a dashboard, and so on is controlled by permissions--only users granted with these permissions are able to perform such activities, as we discussed in the previous sections.

Securing a report or dashboard means to make sure the report or dashboard is accessible only to users that should have access; some users may just need to be able to run a report, but not to modify it. This is controlled in the folder that stores the report or dashboard instead of the report or dashboard itself. Managers of the folder are able to configure and share the folder with other users, and determine their access level.

Earlier in this chapter, we also mentioned that there are many types of permissions related to report and dashboard folders. With additional permission, a user will be able to access all reports (except private reports and private dashboards), even if the user is not added to the group accessibility. As admin, you should make sure just to grant permissions to users that need it.

Here is the difference assigning permissions through **Profile** and **Permission Set**:

- **Profile**: All users within the profile will get the permission enabled for the profile. This is a good option when you need to grant a permission to all users in the same profile, such as permission to run a report.
- **Permission Set**: The admin can create a permission set with one permission only, or with multiple permissions. This is a more flexible option when you need to grant certain permissions to users across profiles, such as permission to create report folders--you may not want everyone to be able to create folders, which could make your report folders messy if not controlled.

Hands-on exercise for adding permission in a Profile

In this exercise, we are going to grant **Create and Customize Reports** permission to a custom **Profile** called **Sales Ops.** Assume that the profile has been created earlier.

1. Click on the **Setup** gear icon in the top-left menu, as shown in the following screenshot:

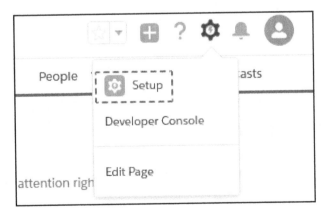

2. Click on **Users** from the left menu, then on the **Profiles** submenu.

3. Find the profile name--in this exercise, we will use the Sales Ops profile (it may be different in yours)--then click on the Edit link before the profile name.

4. Scroll down, and look for **Create and Customize Reports** permission. It is available under the **Administrative Permissions** section. Select the checkbox to grant permission. Consider the following screenshot:

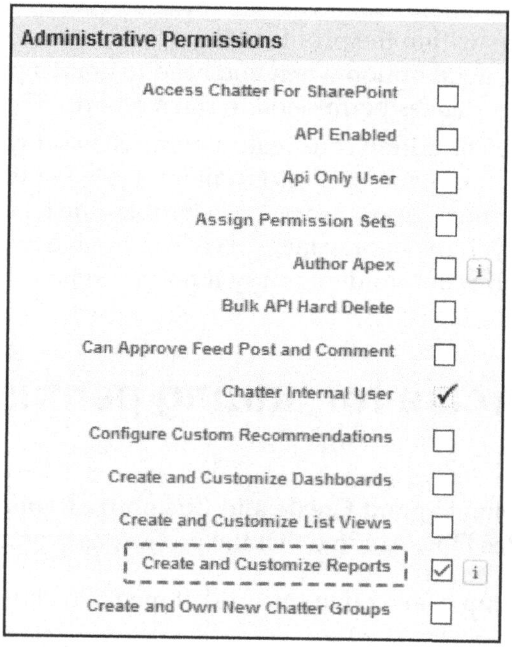

5. Click on the **Save** button and it is done.

All users within that profile will now be able to run the report.

Hands-on exercise utilizing permission with Permission Sets

Next, we are going to create a new permission set called **Regional Admin**. Users with this permission set will be able to create report folders and dashboard folders. Follow these steps for this exercise:

1. Click on the **Setup** gear icon from the top-left menu.

2. Click on **Users** from the left menu, then on the **Permission Sets** submenu.

3. Click on the **New** button under the **Permission Sets** window to continue.
4. For **Label**, enter `Regional Admin`. **API Name** will be auto filled when you fill the **Label** text box. It is always best practice to enter **Description;** for this exercise, type in `Additional permissions for regional admin users`.
5. You can leave **License** as **--None--**, and click on the **Save** button. Consider the following screenshot:

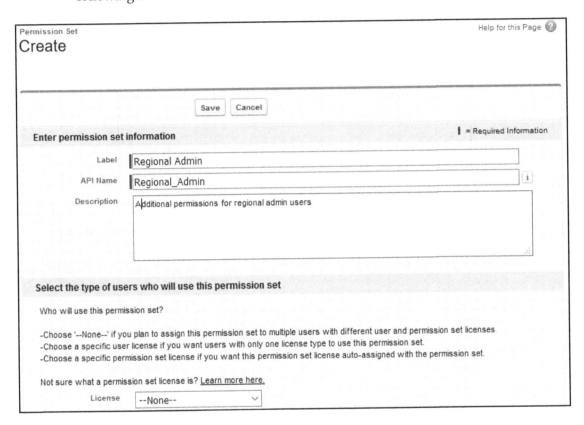

6. In the next screen, type `create report` in the text box, and the system will search for the permission that contains the characters typed into the search box, as shown in the following screenshot:

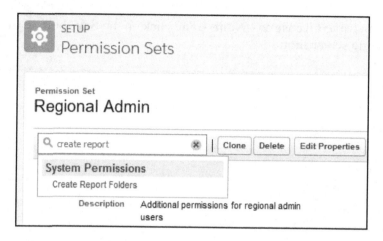

7. Click on **Create Report Folders**; it will open the permission, then scroll up or down to click on the **Edit** button.

8. Find the permission again; check the textbox next to it, as shown in the following screenshot:

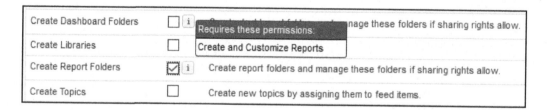

9. You may notice there is an info icon, which tells you that the permission requires another permission--in this case, the **Create Report Folders** permission is required for the **Create and Customize Reports** permission. Because of this, the **Create and Customize Reports** permission will be auto-enabled for the permission set.

10. Click on the **Save** button to continue.

11. Click on the **Manage Assignments** button to check any users assigned for this permission. If you would like to add users for this permission, click on the **Add Assignments** button.

12. Find all users who need to have this permission set; click on the checkbox next to the users, then click on the **Assign** button, as shown in the following screenshot:

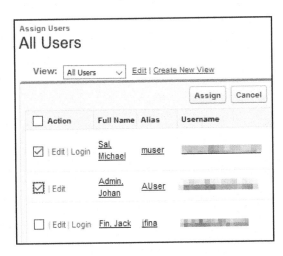

13. Users added to the permission set will be displayed, click on the **Done** button to end.

Summary

In this chapter, we started with securing private reports and dashboards for personal usage. Then, we continued to discuss the **Unfiled Public Report** folder, where users with permission to create reports are able to store the reports created in this folder. One of the purposes of this folder is to store the report temporarily before the real folder is created, but please note that reports stored here will be accessible by everyone in your organization.

Next, we continued with sharing and securing public reports and dashboards. All permissions related to the report folders and dashboard folders were discussed as well.

Before ending the chapter, we provided hands-on exercises to grant permissions through **Profile**, which is for all users with the profile, and to grant permissions via **Permission Sets**, where we have the flexibility to grant permission across user profiles.

4
Creating and Managing Reports

You learned about the concept of the Salesforce report in Chapter 2, *Concepts and Permissions in Reports and Dashboards*. We learned how to generate reports from the data source, how data will be shown when a report is generated in Salesforce, how reports are stored in Salesforce, how to share reports with your team or everyone in your organization, and how to acquire the permissions required to work with report. In Chapter 3, *Implementing Security in Reports and Dashboards*, we learned about how to secure our reports and dashboards.

In this chapter, we will hands-on create reports, discuss more technical details when working with reports, explore what kinds of report you can build in Salesforce, and discover how easy it is to create a new report and maintain existing reports. We will start with multiple types of report format available in Salesforce, why a report format is so important in relation to reports and the benefits and limitations of each format; then we will continue with adding filters to reports.

By the end of this chapter, you will gain knowledge on how to select the correct report format based on the requirements and also learn how to customize the reports using report filters.

Throughout this chapter, we will provide notes and tips to help you to understand important items. The following topics will be covered in this chapter in depth:

- Selecting the report format
- Adding report filters

Selecting the report format

Why is the report format important in creating a report? Each Salesforce report is constructed with a report format, and the report format will determine the report layout, options, and settings for the report. It also determines whether the report can be used as the data source in a dashboard.

There are a few report formats available in Salesforce, from the simple tabular report to the complex matrix and joined report. Each report format has different usages and purposes.

Types of report format

When you create a new report, **Tabular** is the default report format selected. You will able to modify the report format anytime, even after you save the report, but you may lose some configured items, depending on the original and target report format.

There are four report formats available in Salesforce:

- **Tabular**
- **Summary**
- **Matrix**
- **Joined**

Let's try to understand each of them individually.

The Tabular report format

The **Tabular** report is the default report format when you create a new report; this format is considered the simplest; it presents data in a manner similar to that of a spreadsheet. Data will be presented in the row and column format; each row presents one record and each column presents one field, and a column can also be a bucket field or a custom summary formula. The availability of fields for a report depends on the report type used.

We will discuss report types thoroughly in Chapter 5, *Understanding Report Types*, while bucket field and custom summary formulas will be discussed in Chapter 6, *Advanced Report Configuration*. For now, the report type will determine the fields available to use in a report; it may have all or some fields from one object or from a few related objects.

Although **Tabular** is the simplest format, it offers many abilities for you to sort data by columns, adding filters, summarizing fields, adding a bucket field, record count, exporting reports, subscribe report, and so on. All of these features are also true for **Summary** and **Matrix** reports. The focus on a **Tabular** report is on letting you see the details of each record that meets your filter criteria, similar to a spreadsheet.

Let's look at the limitations of the **Tabular** format:

- No grouping
- No chart
- Not used as the data source for a dashboard unless the **Row Limit** filter is configured

Other limitations related to the **Tabular** format are as follows:

- The report builder preview shows a maximum of 50 rows.
- Reports display a maximum of 2,000 rows. To view all the rows, export the report to Excel.

The **Tabular** report format has the best performance figures when generating reports. Here is a sample of a **Tabular** report:

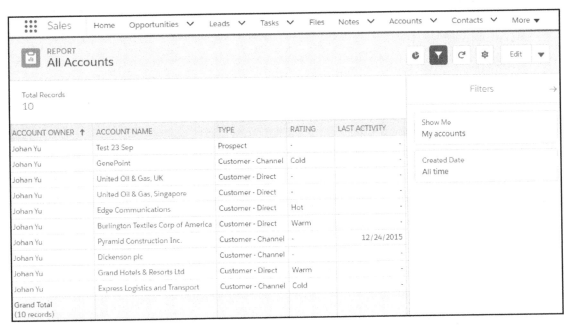

Hands-on exercise for creating a Tabular report

Let's consider a use case. We are tasked with showing the first five accounts, sorted by the number of employees in descending order, and filtering with account Type contains Customer. In this exercise, we assume that you have more than five accounts with Type contains Customer text exists, and the number of employees is populated:

1. Navigate to the **Reports** tab and click on **New Report..** button.
2. Select the **Accounts** Report Type and click on the plus sign under the **Accounts & Contacts** category.
3. Click on the **Create** button to continue.

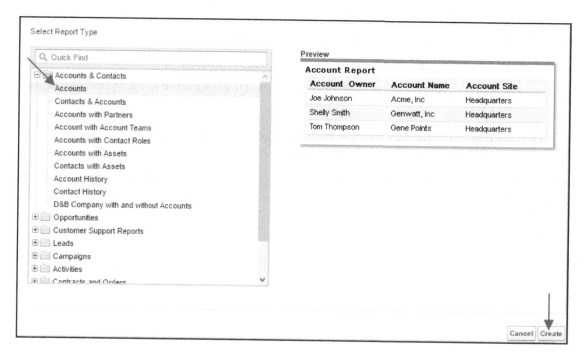

4. Now we are in the **Report Builder**, with the preview showing a limited number of records.

5. Change the **Show** field to **All accounts.** Change the **Date Field Range** to **All Time**.

6. Add the **Employees** field to the report area and remove the unnecessary fields, such as **Last Activity**, **Last Modified Date**, **Rating**, and **Billing State/Province**.

You can find a field quickly by typing the field name in the **Quick Find** textbox in the left-hand side panel; the fields shown below the textbox will be auto-filtered as you type.

To add a field to the report, double-click on the field; if the field has not been added in the report earlier, it will be added into the last column. Another option is to drag and drop the field into the report area; note the green check and red block icon when you drag the field.

To remove a field from the report, drag the field header and drop it into the field area in the left-hand side panel; or hover the mouse over the field header in the report, click on the arrow icon, and then click on **Remove Column**.

7. Click on the **Add** button in **Filters** and continue with the following actions:

- Select **Type** from the list of available fields (you also can manually type the field name and the select the field).
- Select **contains** from the list of operators.

- Click on the magnifying glass and select **Customer** from the pop-up value available. In my case, I have **Customer - Direct** and **Customer - Channel** but without just Customer, so I manually type Customer. Since our operator here is **contains**, this will cover both **Customer - Direct** and **Customer - Channel**.
- Click on the **OK** button to confirm.
- Click on the small arrow next to the **Add** button and then select **Row Limit** to 5, **Sorted By Employees** with **Descending** order and click on the **OK** button to apply.

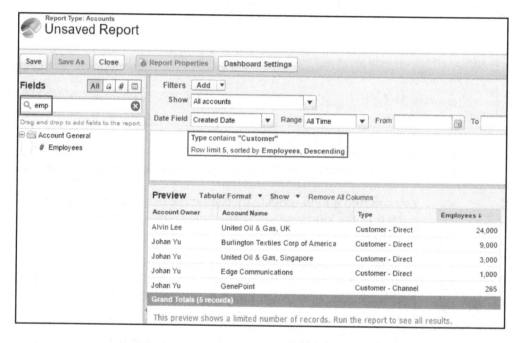

- Click on the **Save** button; this will open a pop-up window to save the report.

- Enter **Report Name** as `Top 5 Customers by No of Employee`. **Report Unique Name** will be auto-filled.

It is always a good practice to enter some **Description** for future reference.

- Select **My Personal Custom Reports** in the options for **Report Folder** so no one can access it.
- Click on the **Save** button again to save the report.
- Click on the **Run Report** button, and you should see the report generated immediately.

The following screenshot shows the report generated; you may see different data, but it should have five records in the result or fewer or no record if your Salesforce organization does not have the customer type for account:

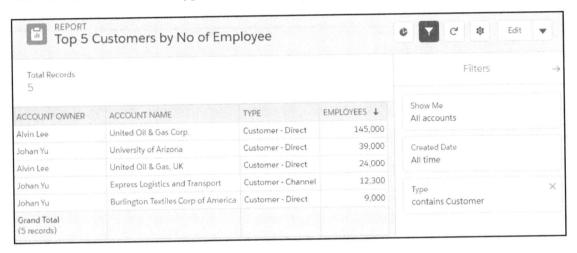

The Summary report format

The main difference between a **Summary** report and a **Tabular** report is the **Summary** report's ability to group using any field available (included bucket field) for the report. If there are no fields defined for grouping in the **Summary** report, the report will run as a **Tabular** report.

A **Summary** report is considered more advanced than a **Tabular** report; in addition to the features stated in a **Tabular** format, the **Summary** report offers additional abilities, such as the following:

- In order to group reports based on the values, you can group reports with up to three levels of grouping. You also can summarize data for numeric fields and display record counts for each group.

- Add a chart to the report.
- Use the report as the data source for the dashboard; for a tabular report, only the one with **Row Limit** is configured.
- Sort by different fields for grouping.
- Explore the ability to hide individual record details to make it easier to see summarized business data.

Compared to **Tabular** report, you cannot add **Row Limit** in the **Summary** format report.

Here is a sample of a **Summary** report:

REPORT
Summary Customers

Total Records
14

TYPE ↑	ACCOUNT OWNER ↑	LAST MODIFIED DATE ↑	ACCOUNT NAME	EMPLOYEES ↑
Prospect (3 records)	Alvin Lee (1 record)	CY2017 (1 record)	Element Industry Ltd	500
	Johan Yu (2 records)	CY2017 (2 records)	Super Force Inc	800
			PMA Manufacturing	1,500
Customer - Direct (7 records)	Johan Yu (7 records)	CY2014 (7 records)	Edge Communications	1,000
			United Oil & Gas, Singapore	3,000
			Grand Hotels & Resorts Ltd	5,600
			Burlington Textiles Corp of America	9,000
			United Oil & Gas, UK	24,000
			University of Arizona	39,000
			United Oil & Gas Corp.	145,000
Customer - Channel (4 records)	Johan Yu (4 records)	CY2014 (3 records)	Dickenson plc	120
			GenePoint	265
			Express Logistics and Transport	12,300
		CY2016 (1 record)	Pyramid Construction Inc.	2,680
GRAND TOTAL (14 RECORDS)				

Hands-on exercise for creating a Summary report

Let's consider a use case: Show all accounts group by Account creation by **Calendar Year** and by **Account Owner**, follow these steps for this hands-on exercise:

1. Navigate to the **Reports** tab and click on the **New Report** button.
2. Select the **Accounts** Report Type and click on the plus sign under the **Accounts & Contacts** category.
3. Click on the **Create** button to continue.
4. Change **Show** to **All accounts**.
5. Change the **Date Field Range** to **All Time**.
6. Change the report format from **Tabular** to **Summary**:

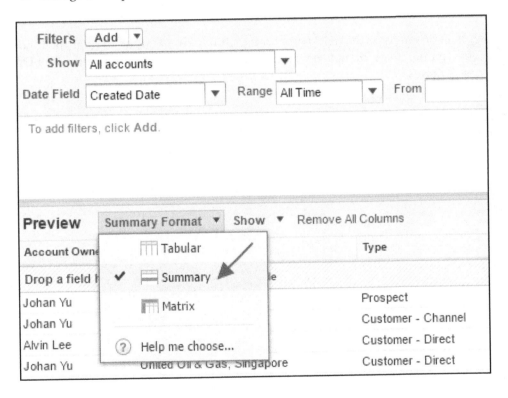

7. Click on the **Add** button in **Filters** and continue with the following actions:

- Select **Type** from the list of available fields; you can also manually type the field name and then select the field.
- Select **contains** from the list of operators.
- Click on the magnifying glass and select **Customer** from the pop-up value available. In my case, I have **Customer - Direct** and **Customer - Channel** but not Customer, so I manually type Customer. As our operator here is contains, this will cover both **Customer - Direct** and **Customer - Channel.**
- Click on the **OK** button.

8. Drag **Created Date** into the drop zone in the report.

You can type the field name in the **Quick Find** textbox to filter the field name. If you do not see the grouping zone, click on **Show** and select **Drop Zones**.

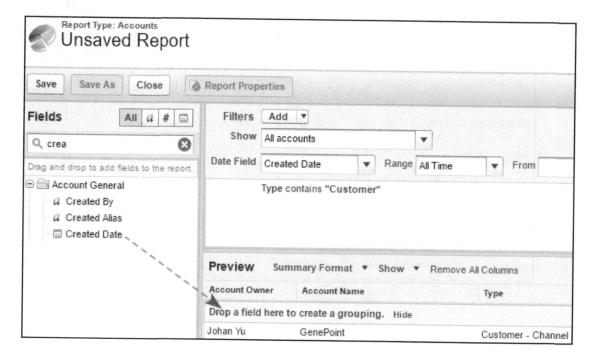

9. Once the field is added to the grouping, click on the arrow on the left-hand side of **Created Date** in the drop zone and navigate to **Group Dates By** | **Calendar Year**. **Group Dates By** is only available when the field you would like to group is Date and Date Time fields. Consider the following screenshot:

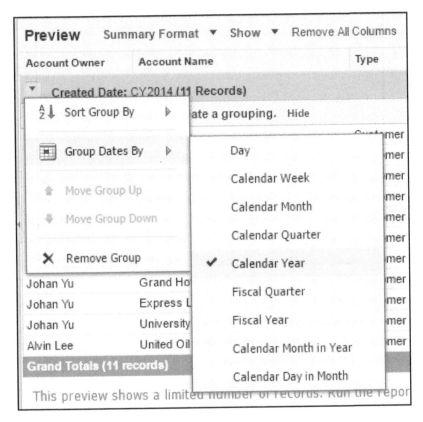

10. Drag **Account Owner** into the drop zone below **Created Date**. By default, **Details** in **Show** is selected; let's hide the detail.
11. Click on the **Show** menu and uncheck **Details:**
12. Click on the **Save** button; this will open a pop-up window to save the report:
    - Enter **Report Name** as **All Account by creation Year and owner**
    - **Report Unique Name** will be auto-filled
    - It is always a good practice to enter a **Description** for future reference
    - Select **My Personal Custom Reports** in **Report Folder**, so no one can access it
    - Click on the **Save** button to save the report

13. Click on **Run Report**, and you should see a report similar to what is shown in the following screenshot:

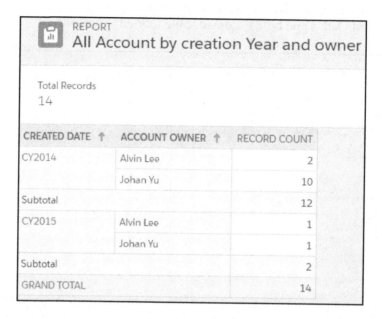

14. By default, **Summary** report will sort by the first group ascending and then the second group ascending. In our exercise, it is **Created Date** and **Account Owner**. You can change the sort order by editing the report in report builder, clicking on the arrow next to the field in the drop zone, and selecting **Sort Group By** as shown in the following screenshot:

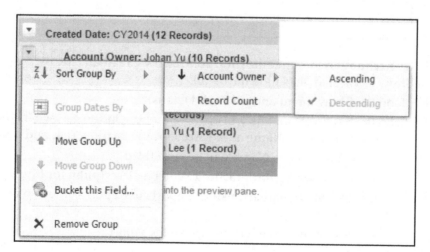

15. To show data details from an open report, click on the gear icon and check **Details** in the Options window; remember that, in Step 11 of this exercise, we had unchecked **Show Details**. The report will be regenerated with details for each record, but the report grouping and sort will stay:

REPORT
All Account by creation Year and owner

Total Records
14

CREATED DATE ↑	ACCOUNT OWNER ↓	ACCOUNT NAME	TYPE	LAST MODIFIED DATE
CY2014 (12 records)	Johan Yu (10 records)	GenePoint	Customer - Channel	5/24/2014
		United Oil & Gas, Singapore	Customer - Direct	5/24/2014
		Edge Communications	Customer - Direct	5/24/2014
		Burlington Textiles Corp of America	Customer - Direct	5/24/2014
		Pyramid Construction Inc.	Customer - Channel	8/21/2016
		Dickenson plc	Customer - Channel	5/24/2014
		Grand Hotels & Resorts Ltd	Customer - Direct	5/24/2014
		Express Logistics and Transport	Customer - Channel	5/24/2014
		University of Arizona	Customer - Direct	5/24/2014
		Super Force Inc	Customer - Direct	4/15/2017
	Alvin Lee (2 records)	United Oil & Gas, UK	Customer - Direct	4/14/2017
		United Oil & Gas Corp.	Customer - Direct	4/14/2017
CY2015 (2 records)	Johan Yu (1 record)	King Inc	Customer - Direct	4/15/2017
	Alvin Lee (1 record)	Accurate Glass	Customer - Channel	4/15/2017
GRAND TOTAL (14 RECORDS)				

16. Click on **Save** from the drop-down arrow to save all changes in the report. With this, you can save the report without the need to edit it from report builder:

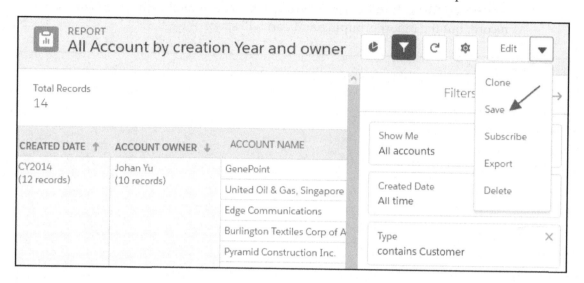

The Matrix report format

The **Matrix** report is pretty similar to the **Summary** report, but with the additional capability to group by both rows and columns. You also can have up to two levels of grouping for both rows and columns.

Similar to the **Tabular** and **Summary** report format, you can add summarizable fields in **Matrix** reports. By default, the record count is added into the report matrix. When you add the summary field in the **Matrix** report, the field and summary will be shown in the matrix, not at the bottom of the column as in the **Summary** or **Tabular** report format. Once you add a summary field to the **Matrix** report, you can remove the default record count from the matrix if you don't need it.

This report's format is good when you have large amounts of data to summarize and need to compare records with different values in the same field with the **Matrix** report. The **Matrix** report, without at least one row and one column grouping, will be shown as a **Summary** report when you run the report.

You can change from the **Tabular** or **Summary** report to the **Matrix** report when you change a report from **Summary** to **Matrix** format:

- First-level grouping will automatically become first-level row grouping
- Second-level grouping will automatically become first-level column grouping
- Third-level grouping will automatically become second-level row grouping

In the following example, we use the same summary format report created earlier in **All Account by creation Year and owner**; the report shows the same data and criteria used--just in a different format. Note that the record count is added by default when you create a **Matrix** report. The following screenshot shows us a **Matrix** report converted from **Summary** format report:

REPORT
Account by creation Year and owner mtrx

Total Records
14

ACCOUNT OWNER	JOHAN YU	ALVIN LEE	Total				
CREATED DATE	COUNT	COUNT	COUNT	ACCOUNT NAME	TYPE	LAST MODIFIED DATE	EMPLOYEES
CY2014	1			GenePoint	Customer - Channel	5/24/2014	265
	1			United Oil & Gas, Singapore	Customer - Direct	5/24/2014	3,000
	1			Burlington Textiles Corp of America	Customer - Direct	5/24/2014	9,000
	1			Dickenson plc	Customer - Channel	5/24/2014	120
	1			Express Logistics and Transport	Customer - Channel	5/24/2014	12,300
	1			University of Arizona	Customer - Direct	5/24/2014	39,000
	1			Super Force Inc	Customer - Direct	4/15/2017	800
	1			Grand Hotels & Resorts Ltd	Customer - Direct	5/24/2014	5,600
	1			Pyramid Construction Inc.	Customer - Channel	8/21/2016	2,680
	1			Edge Communications	Customer - Direct	5/24/2014	1,000
		1		United Oil & Gas, UK	Customer - Direct	4/14/2017	24,000
		1		United Oil & Gas Corp.	Customer - Direct	4/14/2017	145,000
Subtotal	10	2	12				
CY2015	1			King Inc	Customer - Direct	4/15/2017	-
		1		Accurate Glass	Customer - Channel	4/15/2017	-
Subtotal	1	1	2				
Total	11	3	14				

Hands-on exercise for creating a Matrix report

Let's consider a use case: showing the record count for all accounts in a **Matrix** format, row grouping by Account creation for **Calendar Year**, and column grouping by **Account Owner**:

1. Instead of creating it from scratch, let's modify the existing **Summary** report `All Account by creation Year and owner` and convert it into a **Matrix** report.

2. Open the **All Account by creation Year and owner** report and click on **Edit** button or navigate to **Reports** tab, look for the report, click on the arrow in the last column, and then click on **Edit** to open report builder.

3. Change the report format from **Summary** to **Matrix**.

4. The first group of the summary report will automatically become row grouping, while the second group will become column grouping; in our exercise, **Created Date** will be a row grouping and **Account Owner** will be a column grouping.

   Let's take a look at the following screenshot and notice that the first-level and second-level grouping of the Summary report has been transformed:

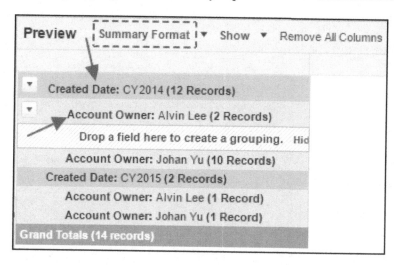

When the report format changes from **Summary** to **Matrix** report:

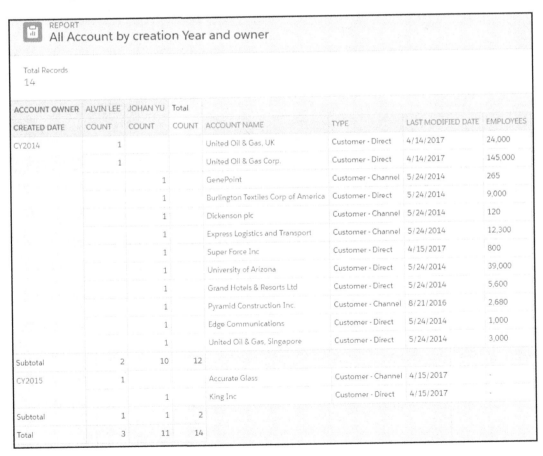

Preview	[Matrix Format] ▼	Show ▼	Remove All Columns			
		→ Account Owner		Alvin Lee	Johan Yu	**Grand Total**
		Drop a field here to create a column grouping.				
Created Date	Drop a field here to create a row grouping.	Drop summarizable fields into the matrix.				
CY2014		Record Count		2	10	12
CY2015		Record Count		1	1	2
	Grand Total	**Record Count**		**3**	**11**	**14**

5. Since this report was originally saved as a Summary report, you can just click on the Run Report button to see the report result in a Matrix format. In Lightning Experience, a report needs to be saved before you are able to run it:

REPORT
All Account by creation Year and owner

Total Records
14

ACCOUNT OWNER	ALVIN LEE	JOHAN YU	Total					
CREATED DATE	COUNT	COUNT	COUNT	ACCOUNT NAME	TYPE	LAST MODIFIED DATE	EMPLOYEES
CY2014	1			United Oil & Gas, UK	Customer - Direct	4/14/2017	24,000
	1			United Oil & Gas Corp.	Customer - Direct	4/14/2017	145,000
		1		GenePoint	Customer - Channel	5/24/2014	265
		1		Burlington Textiles Corp of America	Customer - Direct	5/24/2014	9,000
		1		Dickenson plc	Customer - Channel	5/24/2014	120
		1		Express Logistics and Transport	Customer - Channel	5/24/2014	12,300
		1		Super Force Inc	Customer - Direct	4/15/2017	800
		1		University of Arizona	Customer - Direct	5/24/2014	39,000
		1		Grand Hotels & Resorts Ltd	Customer - Direct	5/24/2014	5,600
		1		Pyramid Construction Inc.	Customer - Channel	8/21/2016	2,680
		1		Edge Communications	Customer - Direct	5/24/2014	1,000
		1		United Oil & Gas, Singapore	Customer - Direct	5/24/2014	3,000
Subtotal	2	10	12				
CY2015	1			Accurate Glass	Customer - Channel	4/15/2017	-
		1		King Inc	Customer - Direct	4/15/2017	-
Subtotal	1	1	2				
Total	3	11	14				

6. If you just need to see the report summary without any detail, click on the gear icon next to the refresh icon (not the topmost gear icon with lightning inside the gear) and then uncheck the **Details** checkbox. Often, we need to do this when we present the report and want to focus on the summary only, without the need to see the details, as shown in the following screenshot:

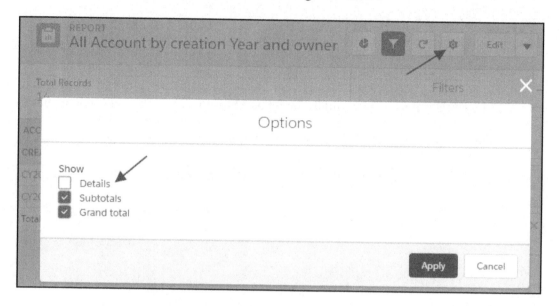

7. Here is the report result which just shows the summary based on **Created Date** and **Account Owner** in a **Matrix** format:

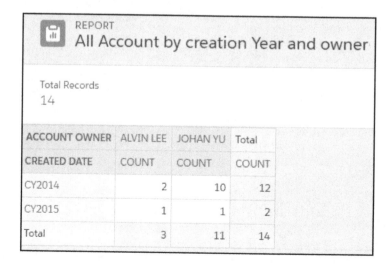

8. If you click on **Save** from here, this will overwrite your **Summary** report created earlier. So instead of clicking on Save, click on **Clone** to save the report as a new report, enter the new report name, select the folder, and then click on the **Create** button in the pop-up window to confirm.

9. Alternatively, when you are in report builder in step 5, instead of clicking on the **Run Report** button to run the report, click on the **Save As** button to store the report as a new report.

Hands-on exercise for adding a Summary field to Matrix reports

Let's consider a use case: showing all opportunities with the total amount in a **Matrix** format, row grouping by **Opportunity Stage**, and column grouping by **Opportunity Owner**:

1. Navigate to the **Reports** tab and click on the **New Report** button.
2. Select the **Opportunities** Report Type and click on the plus sign under the **Opportunities** category.
3. Click on the **Create** button to continue.
4. Change **Show** to **All opportunities**.
5. Change the **Date Field** range to **All Time**.
6. Note that the **Opportunity Status** and **Probability** filters are next to **Show**; these specific filters are there only when we use the **Opportunity** Report Type. For this exercise, just leave the default value **Any** for **Opportunity Status** and **All** for **Probability**.
7. Change the report format from **Tabular** to **Matrix**.

8. Remove all fields by dragging and dropping them out to the **Fields** area except for **Opportunity Name**, **Amount**, **Stage**, and **Opportunity Owner** fields. Now you should see something similar to what is shown in the following screenshot:

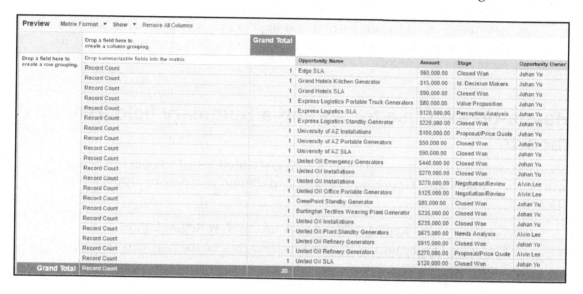

9. To sum the amount, hover your mouse over the **Amount** header, click on the arrow icon in **Summarize this Field...**, select **Sum**, and click on the **Apply** button as shown in the following screenshots:

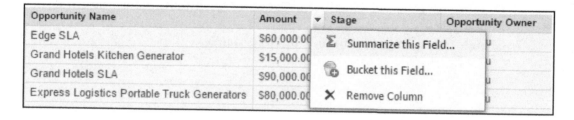

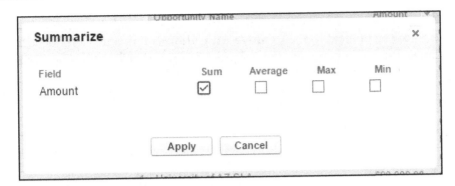

If the field you would like to summarize is not added to the report yet, you can drag the summarizable fields (such as the currency, number, and percentage) directly into the matrix, and the system will prompt you to summarize by Sum, Average, Max, or Min.

You can change the field order added to the matrix by dragging and dropping the summarized field. To remove the summarized field from the matrix, you can just simply drag it out to the field area in the left-hand side panel.

10. Now you should see the amount and its value in a matrix; refer to the screenshot in Step 11.

11. Drag **Stage** as the row grouping and **Opportunity Owner** as the column grouping as shown in the following screenshot:

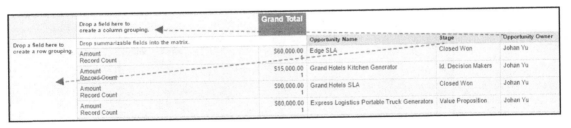

12. Note that you can drag another field as a level 2 grouping for both the row and column grouping.

13. As we just want to focus on the summary value, let's hide the report detail by clicking on **Show** next to the **Remove All Columns** link and then unchecking **Detail**.

14. Next, let's also remove the record count as we just need the amount value. Click on **Show** again next to the **Remove All Columns** link and then uncheck **Record Count**. Remember that we can only remove the record count when a field has been added as the summarized field in the matrix.

15. Click on the **Save** button; this will open a pop-up window to save the report:
    - Enter **Report Name** as Opportunity by Stage and Owner
    - **Report Unique Name** will be auto-filled
    - It is always a good practice to enter some **Description** for future reference
    - Select **My Personal Custom Reports** in **Report Folder**, so no one can access it
    - Click on the **Save** button to save the report

16. Click on **Run Report**, and you should see a report similar to the following report:

REPORT
Opportunity by Stage and Owner

Total Amount
$5,911,000.00

OPPORTUNITY OWNER	ALVIN LEE	JOHAN YU	Total
STAGE	AMOUNT Sum	AMOUNT Sum	AMOUNT Sum
Prospecting	$0.00	$80,000.00	$80,000.00
Qualification	$0.00	$115,000.00	$115,000.00
Needs Analysis	$675,000.00	$0.00	$675,000.00
Value Proposition	$0.00	$330,000.00	$330,000.00
Id. Decision Makers	$0.00	$110,000.00	$110,000.00
Perception Analysis	$0.00	$120,000.00	$120,000.00
Proposal/Price Quote	$270,000.00	$100,000.00	$370,000.00
Negotiation/Review	$395,000.00	$0.00	$395,000.00
Closed Won	$0.00	$3,716,000.00	$3,716,000.00
Total	$1,340,000.00	$4,571,000.00	$5,911,000.00

The Joined report format

As of the Summer '17 release, the **Joined** report is not available yet in Lightning Experience; it is only available in Classic.

Joined reports let you create a report with different types of information in one report. You can get the data from multiple report types and group it with common fields. Each report in a **Joined** report is displayed in its own report block. The report is presented in multiple blocks, where each block may have the same or a different report type.

You can group the report using common fields; the list of common fields will be shown on top of the **Fields** panel once you have more than one report type in the report. Common fields are marked with a black square icon in the joined report.

Similar to the **Matrix** and **Summary** report, you can add summarizable fields into the report's block, and you also can hide report details to show the report in the summary.

The filter criteria in a report's blocks are not related to other report blocks, and you cannot relate them. So make it a point to verify that each of them has the right filter. In terms of performance, the more blocks you have, the more time is needed to run a joined report. Following screenshot shows a **Joined** report with 2 report blocks, which is opportunities and cases:

	OPPORTUNITIES Won Opportunities		CASES All Cases
	Record Count	Amount	Record Count
Account Name: ABC Song	1	USD 800.00	
Account Name: Acc General	1	USD 35,000.00	1
Account Name: Acme Corp	2	USD 19,002.00	3
Account Name: Ahui Jack	1	USD 71,000.00	
Account Name: Ahui Maria			2
Account Name: Ahui Song	1	USD 40.00	1
Account Name: Big Corp	1	USD 750.00	2
Account Name: Firing Air	1	USD 11,000.00	1
Account Name: Gajah	1	USD 5,000.00	
Account Name: Global Data	1	USD 500,000.00	3
Account Name: Kisaran Corp	2	USD 205,500.00	1
Account Name: New Water Ltd	1	USD 250.00	
Account Name: Star Mart	2	USD 100,180.00	1
Account Name: XYZ Corp			1
Grand Totals	15	USD 948,522.00	16

Hands-on exercise for creating a Joined report

Let's consider a use case: showing all won opportunities and cases related to the accounts in one report for the last year. Remember that, as of the Summer '17 release, the **Joined** report is available only in Classic, so you need to do the following in the Classic user interface only:

1. Navigate to the **Reports** tab and click on the **New Report...** button.
2. Select the **Opportunities** report type; it is under the **Opportunities** category.
3. Click on the **Create** button to continue.
4. Change the **Show** field to **All opportunities**.
5. Change **Date Field** to **Close Date** and **Range** to **Previous CY**.
6. Click on the **Remove All Columns** link, click on **OK** to confirm, and then add these fields to the report: **Opportunity Name**, **Account Name**, and **Amount**.
7. Click on the **Add** button to add the filter criteria where **Won** equals **True**.
8. Hover your mouse over **Amount**, click on the arrow, select **Summarize the Field...**, select the **Sum** checkbox, and then select the **Apply** button. Change the report format to **Joined**.
9. Once the report format has changed to Joined, the **Add Report Type** button will become available and the **Opportunity block** will be added to the report.
10. Click on the block labelled **Opportunities block 1** and change it to `Won Opportunities Last Year`:

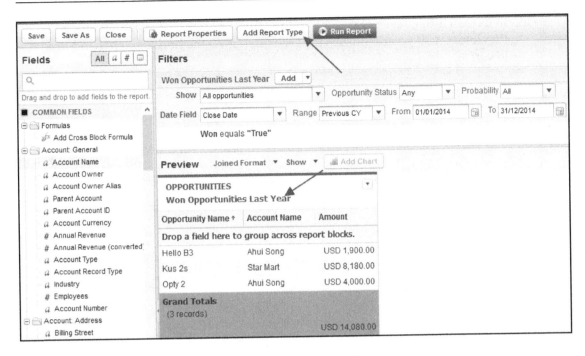

11. Click on the **Add Report Type** button to continue.

12. Select the **Cases** Report Type under the **Customer Support Reports** category and click on the **OK** button to continue.

13. Remove all fields in the case block one by one, except for **Subject** and **Account Name**.

14. Click on the block label **Cases block 2** and change it to `All Cases Last Year`.

15. In the case filter, leave **Date Field** set to **Opened Date**, but change **Range** to **Previous CY**. If you do not see the case filter, grab the horizontal bar and drag it lower:

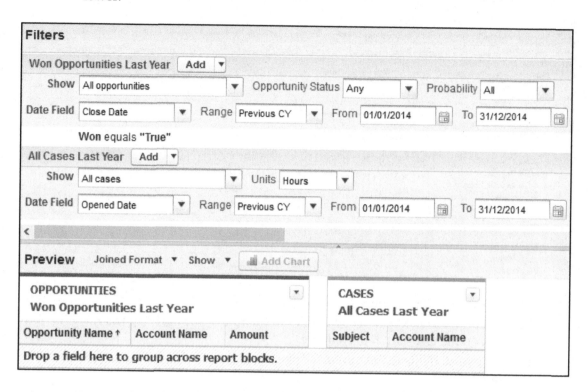

16. From **COMMON FIELDS** on the left-hand side, drag **Account Name** into the drop zone; **Account Name** will be automatically removed from both blocks. Consider the following screenshot:

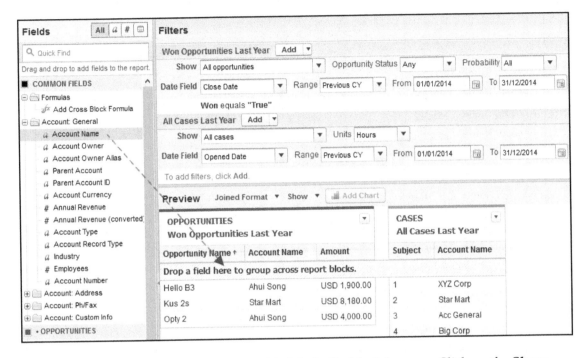

17. By default, **Details** will be enabled; let's disable it for now. Click on the **Show** menu and uncheck **Details**.

18. Click on the **Run Report** button, and you should have a joined report similar to what is shown in the following screenshot:

	OPPORTUNITIES Won Opportunities Last Year		CASES All Cases Last Year
	Record Count	Amount	Record Count
Account Name: Acc General			1
Account Name: Ahui Song	2	USD 5,900.00	1
Account Name: Big Corp	1	USD 85,200.00	1
Account Name: Firing Air			1
Account Name: Global Data	1	USD 15,000.00	2
Account Name: Kisaran Corp			1
Account Name: Star Mart	1	USD 8,180.00	1
Account Name: XYZ Corp			1
Grand Totals	5	USD 114,280.00	9

19. Click on the **Show Details** button to show opportunity and case details when needed.
20. Click on the **Save As** button:
    - **Report Name** is Last Year Won Opportunities with Cases
    - **Report Description** is All Accounts for Last Year closed Won opportunities and Cases
    - **Report Folder** is **My Personal Custom Reports**

21. And we're done.

This report will show all won opportunities count with the sum of amounts and cases for last year grouped by **Account Name**.

Note the following about **Joined** reports:

- To use a **Joined** report as a data source in a dashboard, add a chart to the report and select **Use charts as defined in source report** in the dashboard settings
- the report type can be added once to the report, but you can use the same report type for multiple blocks
- To add a new block using the same report type, drag the field to the report area further right from the last block

Working with report filters

A report is one of the most powerful features of the Salesforce platform; depending on your permissions, you can build your own reports within minutes and manage them without help from Salesforce administrator or Salesforce developer.

We have discussed many things related to the report in previous chapters, including the permissions to create a report, permissions related to the report folder, and the report format that presents the report layout.

Another important item related to reporting is **report filters**. Report filters allow you to define which data conditions you want to use in order to include records in a report based on some criteria. The filter criteria in the report are almost similar to the filter criteria we found in other Salesforce features, such as List Views, Workflow Rules, and other areas in Salesforce, but the filter criteria in the report are even more powerful.

For each filter criterion, you need to set the field, operator, and value. You can have multiple filters for a report. The default relationship for each filter is the one using AND, but you can customize it using filter logic.

When you are in the report builder, if you click on the **Add** button for Filters, it will automatically add a new filter, but note that there is a small arrow button next to **Add**; if you click on this arrow, a few options available for the report filter are as follows:

- **Field Filter**: This is the same action as clicking on the **Add** button
- **Filter Logic**
- **Cross Filter**
- **Row Limit**: Only for the **Tabular** report format

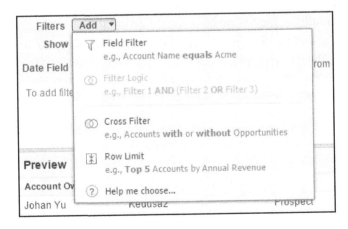

Field filter

Simply click on the **Add** button in the report builder to add a field as a filter, or you also can drag fields from the **Fields** panel to the **Filters** panel to add a report filter.

Once the field is added to the **Filters** pane, select the operator and then enter the value.

> If you would like to add multiple values to a filter value, simply use a comma to separate the values.

For each filter, you can enter special values based on the field type for that particular filter. Some items you need to know related to the report filter are as follows:

- The filter value is case-insensitive.
- When you filter the **Date** field, you can enter special date values, such as TODAY, NEXT WEEK, LASTWEEK, LAST <x> DAYS, LAST <x> YEARS, and so on. For complete Date Formats and Date Literals, refer to this Salesforce link https://developer.salesforce.com/docs/atlas.en-us.soql_sosl.meta/soql_sosl/sforce_api_calls_soql_select_dateformats.htm.
- For filtering values with a comma, put quotation marks around the text, for example, Johan, LLC; otherwise, it will filter as Johan or LLC.
- If you implement Multi-Currency, you can add the currency code in the filter criteria, such as USD 2500, SGD 8000, JPY 10000.
- For the picklist field, you can use the magnifying glass to select one or more choices to be included in the filter, or you can also manually type it in. But when you edit the filter again, the existing selected values will not be selected when you use the magnifying glass; if the existing values are no longer valid, delete them manually in the textbox.
- For multi-select picklist fields, type in the values and use a semicolon between values to specify the exact match.
- You can lock filters added by ticking the **Locked** checkbox, so other users will not able to change or remove them when they run the report.

> If you do not have access to a field defined as a filter, it will be removed from the filter criteria and will display results based on the remaining filters.

The Filter Logic

If you have more than one filter in a report, adding filter logic will let you specify conditions for your filters using logical operators between the filters. When you add filters to a report, by default, all filters are related as AND logic, for example:

- Type contains Customer
- Country equals United States
- Employees greater than 1000

This is how it would look when you configure it into Salesforce:

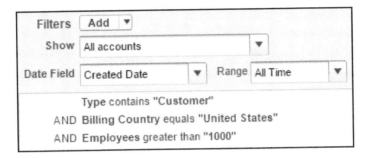

If you notice, **AND** will be added to a new filter line by default. With filter logic, you can specify whether to use the **AND, OR,** or **NOT** operator.

With the preceding filter criteria, the report will generate all accounts with **Type contains "Customer", Billing Country equals to "United States"**, and **Employees more than "1000"** people. But how about if we would like to get all accounts with **Type contains "Customer"** and **Billing Country equals to "United States"** or **Employees more than "1000"** people, where the last filter (Employee) does not depend on Type and Country.

Without filter logic, we need to create two separate reports and combine them manually, one report with the filter **Type contains "Customer" AND Billing Country equals "United States"** and another report with the filter **Employees greater than "1000"**.

With the logic filter, we can combine it into one report by adding **OR** to the filter logic; we can then modify the filter easily to meet the requirement "(Type contains Customer **AND** Country equals United States) **OR** Employee greater than 1000". Use open and close parentheses to let the system understand which filters should come first while also helping us as users to understand the filter logic easily. This is shown in the following screenshot:

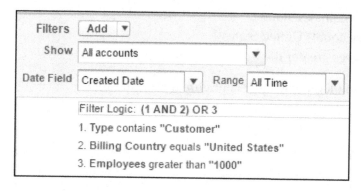

Within seconds, our report will produce data as required. See how easy and powerful using filter logic is!

Hands-on exercise for using the Filter Logic

Let's consider a use case: showing all accounts with **Type contains Customer** and Country in United States or United Kingdom and include Account with Employee more than 1000 people, regardless of the Account Type and Country:

1. Navigate to the **Reports** tab and click on the **New Report** button.
2. Select **Accounts** Report Type and click on the plus sign under the **Accounts & Contacts** category.
3. Click on the **Create** button to continue.
4. Change **Show** to **All accounts**.
5. Change the **Date Field Range** to **All Time**.
6. Click on the Add button, select **Type** contains **Customer - Direct, Customer - Channel**, and tick **Locked** checkbox.
7. Click on the **OK** button to confirm the filter.
8. Type country in the **Quick Find** textbox in the left-hand side panel and drag **Billing Country** into the filter area, enter the value **United States, United Kingdom**, and tick the **Locked** checkbox.

9. Click on the **OK** button to confirm the filter:

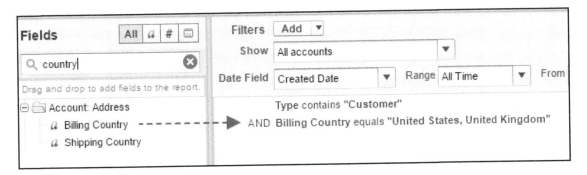

10. Type `employees` in **Fields** textbox on the left, drag it into the filter area, and tick the **Locked** checkbox.
11. Change the operator to **greater than** and enter value `1000`.
12. Click on the **OK** button to confirm the filter:

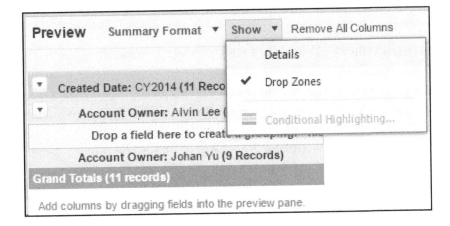

13. In **Filters**, click on the arrow after navigating to the **Add** button | **Filter Logic**. Refer the following screenshot:

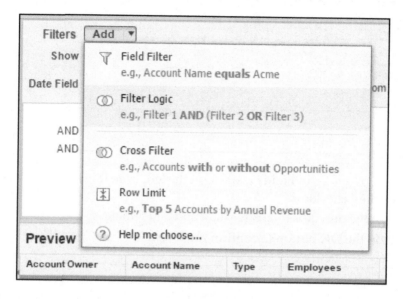

14. The default filter logic value is **1 AND 2 AND 3**; manually change it to (1 AND 2) OR 3.

15. Click on the **OK** button to confirm the filter logic.

16. Click on the **Save** button and do the following:
    - **Report Name** is Account with Filter Logic
    - **Report Description** is All Accounts with No of Employee more than 1000, or Customer in US or UK
    - **Report Folder** is **My Personal Custom Reports**

17. Click on the **Run Report** button to generate the report.

You can enhance the preceding filter logic as required; ensure that it has the right pairs of parentheses with the correct values and operators. Another thing we learned from this exercise is that we use a comma in filter values; simply add a comma in the filter value if you have more than one value, such as **Billing Country equals United States, United Kingdom**.

Here is the final result of the report for the use case requirement because we lock all the filters; note that the user cannot change or remove the filters when they run the report. But if you have permission to edit the report, click on the **Edit** button to modify the filters added, delete existing filters, or add more filters:

ACCOUNT OWNER	ACCOUNT NAME	TYPE	EMPLOYEES	BILLING COUNTRY	
Johan Yu	PMA Manufacturing	Prospect	1,500	-	**Show Me** All accounts
Alvin Lee	United Oil & Gas, UK	Customer - Direct	24,000	-	
Johan Yu	United Oil & Gas, Singapore	Customer - Direct	3,000	-	**Created Date** All time
Johan Yu	Burlington Textiles Corp of America	Customer - Direct	9,000	USA	
Johan Yu	Pyramid Construction Inc.	Customer - Channel	2,680	France	🔒 Locked Filters
Johan Yu	Grand Hotels & Resorts Ltd	Customer - Direct	5,600	-	(1 AND 2) OR 3
Johan Yu	Express Logistics and Transport	Customer - Channel	12,300	-	
Johan Yu	University of Arizona	Customer - Direct	39,000	-	1. Type contains Customer
Alvin Lee	United Oil & Gas Corp.	Customer - Direct	145,000	-	2. Billing Country equals United States, United Kingdom
Johan Yu	Super Force Inc	Customer - Direct	800	United States	
Alvin Lee	Accurate Glass	Customer - Channel	-	United States	3. Employees greater than "1,000"
Johan Yu	Quality Materials	Customer - Channel	-	United Kingdom	
Grand Total (12 records)					

The Cross Filter

With **Cross Filter**, you can create a report for an object and dependencies to other objects and their fields. You can use the **WITH** keyword, such as **All Account WITH Opportunity**. Furthermore, you can also use the **WITHOUT** keyword for an exception report, such as **Account WITHOUT Closed Won Opportunity this year**. This report is important for the sales manager and the management team to evaluate dormant customers.

 This filter will not be available in a **Joined** format or any report where the report type does not allow optional related objects

Hands-on exercise for using the Cross Filter

Without any further explanations, let's walk through how to create a **Cross Filter** in a report.

Let' consider a use case: **Show all accounts** with **Type** as **Customer** and have **Opportunities**:

1. Navigate to the **Reports** tab and click on the **New Report** button.
2. Select the **Accounts** Report Type and click on the plus sign under the **Accounts & Contacts** category.
3. Click on the **Create** button to continue.
4. Change **Show** to **All accounts**.
5. Change the **Date Field Range** to **All Time**.
6. Click on the **Add** button and select **Type contains Customer - Direct, Customer - Channel**.
7. Click on the **OK** button to confirm the filter.
8. In Filters, click on the arrow after navigating to the **Add** button | **Cross Filter**.
9. Select **Accounts with Opportunities**. This is shown in the following screenshot:

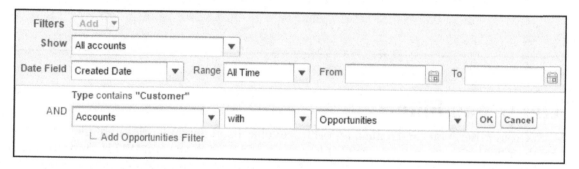

10. Click on the **OK** button to confirm the filter.
11. Click on the Save button:
    - **Report Name** is Customer with Opportunities
    - **Report Description** is All Customer with Opportunities
    - **Report Folder** as **My Personal Custom Reports**

12. Click on the **Run Report** button to generate the report.

This is how the report with the **Cross Filter** applied will look like:

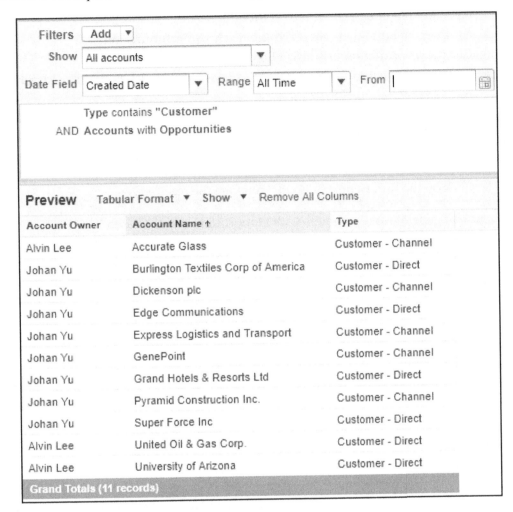

Hands-on exercise for creating more scenarios using the Cross Filter (1)

The preceding report will generate all Customers with Opportunities, but management would like to limit these to accounts with the following:

- Won Opportunity
- Opportunity Close Date within last 1 year

Let's use the same report and customize it:

1. Open the report and click on the **Edit** button.
2. Click on the **Edit** link in the **Accounts with Opportunities** filter.
3. Click on the **Add Opportunities Filter** link.
4. Select **Won equals True**; since this is a picklist field, you can use the magnifying glass icon to select the value.
5. Click on the **Add Opportunities Filter** link again.
6. Enter **Close Date greater or equal** LAST 365 DAYS; using a Relative Date value is a good idea to make the report dynamic rather than having a hardcoded value.
7. Click on the **OK** button to confirm the filters.
8. Click on the **Run Report** button to generate the report.

This report will generate all Customers with Opportunity where Closed Won Date is within the last 1 year from today:

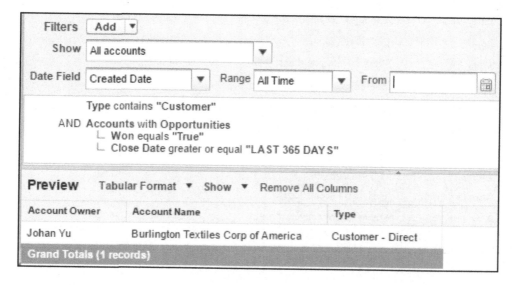

Hands-on exercise for creating more scenarios using the Cross Filter (2)

Let's look at a few more scenarios using the **Cross Filter** with the same report as the preceding one. Here is the use case: the management would like to get a list of Customers without Won opportunities, including Customers without Opportunities.

First, let's look at the following two reports:

1. Report with following filters **Account with Opportunities: Won equals True**:

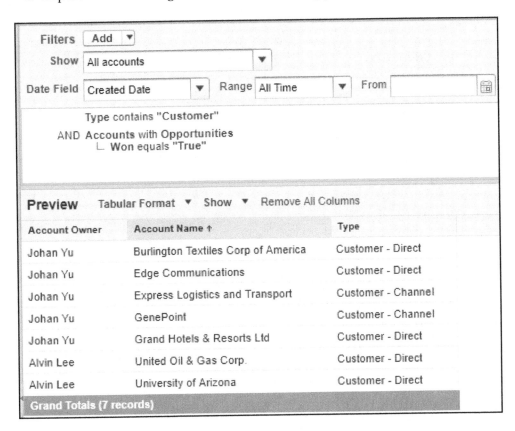

2. Report with following filters **Account with Opportunities: Won equals False**:

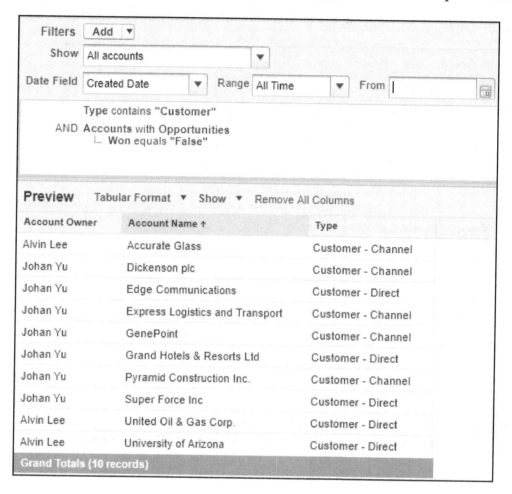

A few accounts from the preceding screenshots, **Edge Communications**, **Express Logistics and Transport**, **GenePoint**, **Grand Hotels & Resorts Ltd**, **United Oil & Gas Corp.**, and **University of Arizona** show in both reports. This is because these accounts have opportunities with **Stage Closed Won** and also opportunities that are either still **Open** or **Closed Lost**. Remember that one account may have multiple opportunities.

For this use case, using a cross filter is not be the right approach. The solution is to use a **Roll-up Summary** field in account and add it to the filter logic.

Creating the Summary field

Let's walk through the steps:

1. From **Setup**, open **Object Manager** and click on **Account**.
2. On the left sidebar, click **Fields & Relationships**.
3. Click **New**.
4. Choose the **Roll-Up Summary** field type, and click **Next**.
5. For **Field Label**, enter Sum of Opportunities and click **Next**.
6. The Summarized Object is the detail object that you want to summarize. Choose **Opportunity**.
7. Choose the **Count** summary type and choose Filter Criteria = **Won** equals **True**.
8. Click **Next**, **Next**, and **Save**:

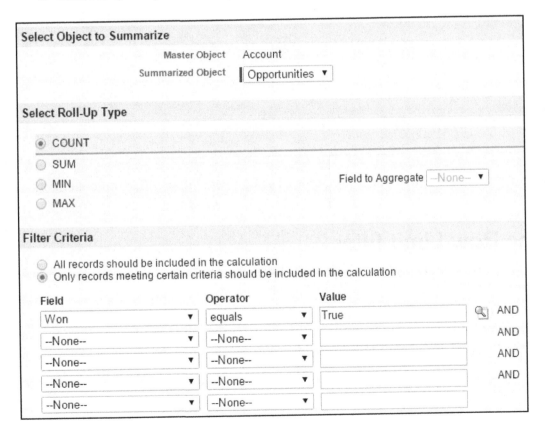

9. Create an Account report and use the `No of Won Opportunity` field as the report filter; let's name it **Customer with No Won Opportunities**:

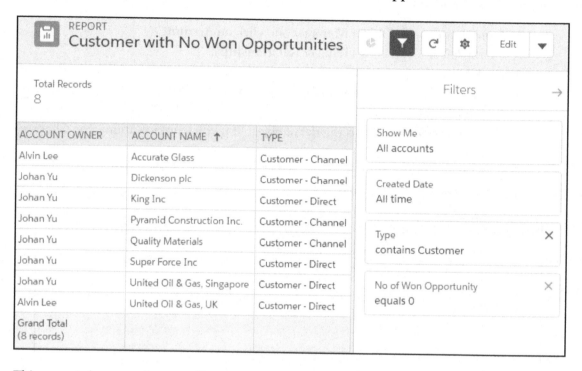

This report shows us that not all scenarios fit using **Cross Filter** with additional filters.

The Row Limit filter

The **Row Limit** filter is only available for **Tabular** reports. When you are using **Summary**, **Matrix**, or **Joined** format reports, it will be not available.

Once you add a row limit in a **Tabular** report, you can configure **Dashboard Settings**. From Dashboard Settings, choose a name and value to use in dashboard tables and charts. The tables show both the name and value, while charts are grouped by name.

The **Tabular** report with **Dashboard Settings** configured can be used as the data source in the Dashboard component.

Hands-on exercise for adding Row Limit and the Dashboard Settings button

Let's consider a use case: creating a report that shows the top five Accounts with the most number of Employees and configuring the report as the data source for the dashboard:

1. Navigate to the **Reports** tab and click on the **New Report** button.
2. Select the **Accounts** Report Type and click on the plus sign under the **Accounts & Contacts** category.
3. Click on the **Create** button to continue.
4. Change **Show** to **All accounts**.
5. Change the **Date Field** range to **All Time**.
6. Remove unwanted default fields from the report and leave only **Account Owner** and **Account Name**.
7. Add the **Employees** field by dragging and dropping it into the report area.
8. In **Filters**, click on the arrow next to the **Add** button | **Row Limit**.
9. Change **Row Limit** to **5**, **Sorted By Employees - Descending**. Consider the following screenshot:

10. Click on the **OK** button. You will notice the **Dashboard Settings** button appear at the top row buttons.
11. Click on the **Dashboard Settings** button.
12. Select **Account Name** for **Name** and **Employees** for **Value** and click on the **OK** button. Once the **Dashboard Settings** button is configured, this report will be able to use it as the data source in the dashboard component. We'll discuss dashboards in Chapter 8, *Working with Reports*.

13. Click on the **Save** button:
     - **Report Name** is **Top 5 Accounts by Employee**
     - **Report Description** is **Top 5 Accounts with most number of employees**
     - **Report Folder** is **Unfiled Public Reports**; this will make the report visible for all other users

14. Click on the **Run Report** button to generate the report:

REPORT Top 5 Accounts by Employee		
Total Records 5		
ACCOUNT OWNER	ACCOUNT NAME	EMPLOYEES ↓
Alvin Lee	United Oil & Gas Corp.	145,000
Johan Yu	University of Arizona	39,000
Alvin Lee	United Oil & Gas, UK	24,000
Johan Yu	Express Logistics and Transport	12,300
Johan Yu	Burlington Textiles Corp of America	9,000
Grand Total (5 records)		

Filtering by Role Hierarchy

For the opportunity report, we have an additional report to filter the report by **Role Hierarchy**. This filter will be visible when you run the report, not when you configure the report in the report builder.

Once you apply the filter, the data will be filtered to show only opportunities owned by users in that role, including all users under **Users** in that role hierarchy.

But if you would like to filter the opportunities owned by a specific user, narrow your **Role Hierarchy** filter by selecting the role and then select a user. Check the following screenshot for filtering opportunity report with **Role Hierarchy**:

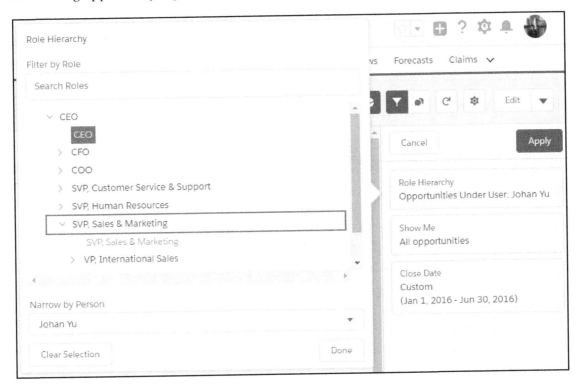

Filtering by Relative Date

If you need the report to always filter with a specific time frame, such as last month, this month, last quarter, and so on, instead of putting in a fixed date, you can select a relative date option. With relative date, when you create a report called **Last Month Opportunities Won**, you do not need to adjust the close date manually every month.

First of all, when you configure the report, you need to add the **Date Field** to the filter drop zone, not the one in the **Date Field** filter, see the following screenshot for adding filter on drop zone filter:

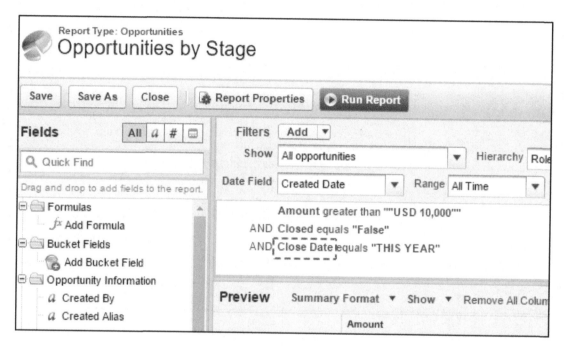

When a user runs the report, they also can modify this at runtime:

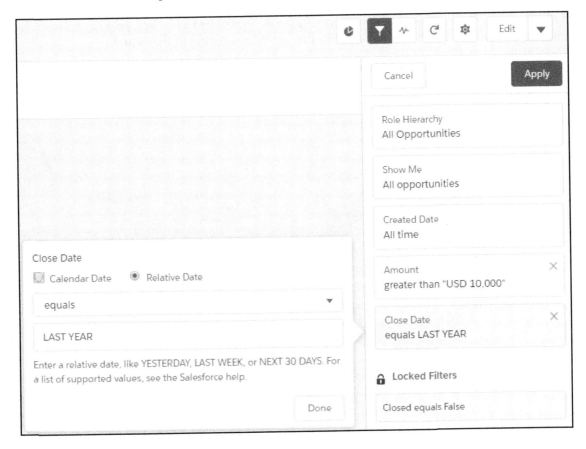

Filtering by clicking on a chart

When a report is added with a chart, did you know that, when you click on a segment in the chart, the report will be auto-filtered with the segment selected in the chart?

Let's say I have an opportunity report called **Opportunities by Stage** with the chart added. Following screenshot shows report with chart added:

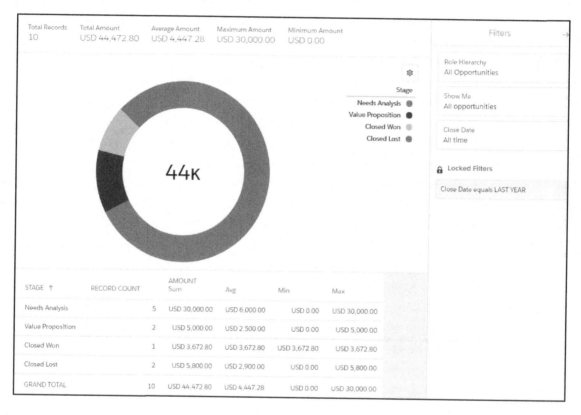

What I would like is to drill down only for opportunities with **Stage = Needs Analysis.**
Since we have the chart here, I can just click on the blue segment in the chart, and the report
will be automatically filtered with **Stage = Needs Analysis**:

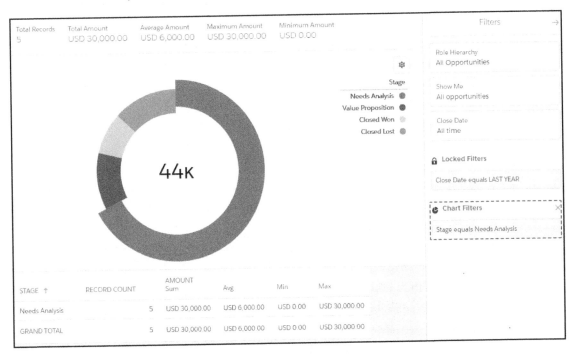

To clear the chart filter, just click on the cross icon in **Chart Filters** in the **Filters** panel.
However, when you save the report with chart filters, the filters will be not included.

The Lock Filter

When adding filters to a report in the report builder, there is a **Locked** checkbox before the **OK** button. This determines the ability of the user who runs the report to edit or delete filters while viewing a report. Consider the following screenshot:

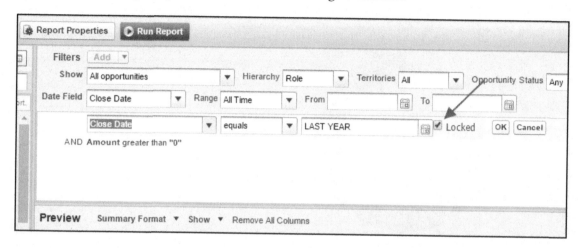

When filters are locked, they will be shown under the **Locked Filters** area, and the user who runs the report will be not able to edit or delete it. Consider the following screenshot:

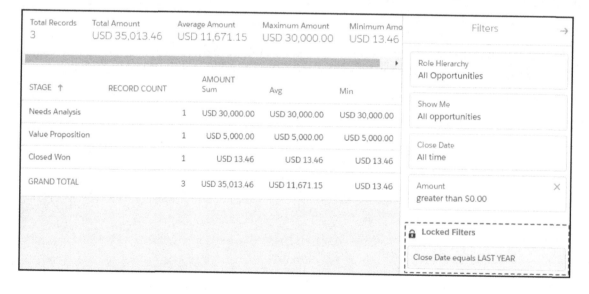

Summary

In this chapter, we became more familiar with components when working with reports on the Salesforce platform. We explored the different types of report formats and looked at the uniqueness of each type of format. We saw how easy it is to add filters to a report. To customize the reports further, we can include **Filter Logic**, **Cross Filter**, and **Row Limit** for a **Tabular** report.

Although we kept made many passing references to dashboards many times in this chapter, we did not discuss them in detail. Dashboards will be discussed in depth in Chapter 9, *Building Dashboards in Lightning Experience* onward. This chapter is completely focussed on reporting only.

In the next chapter, we will discuss report types in detail, look at why the report type is so important, and also look at how to create a report, as you have read about report types so many times in this chapter.

5

Understanding Report Types

You learned about creating and managing reports in Chapter 4, *Creating and Managing Reports*. In that chapter, we discussed how important it is to select the correct report format that determines report layout, and we also discussed how to add report filters, **Filter logic**, **Cross Filter**, and **Row Limit** to get the report result required.

You read about report type many times in previous chapters. In this chapter, we will discuss report types in depth, starting with the report type category, standard report type, custom report type, and end with a few hands-on exercises to create custom report types, extend custom report types, and apply them by creating new reports. In this chapter, we will also share the benefits and limitations when using custom report types.

By the end of this chapter, you will gain knowledge on what a report type is, what you need to know about report types when creating a new report, how to create a custom report type, and how to benefit from custom report type. The report type setup user interface is the same for both Lightning and Classic, so all screenshots in this chapter are applicable to both user interfaces.

Throughout this chapter, we will provide notes and tips to help you understand important items. The following topics will be covered:

- Report Type introduction
- Report Type category
- Standard report type
- Custom report type

Report Type introduction

As mentioned in earlier chapters, each report needs to be built on a report type:

- What is a Report Type?
- How do we check the Report Type used in an existing report?
- How important is it to select the correct report type when we create a new report?

All of these questions will be covered in this chapter.

Salesforce reports, including all standard reports and custom reports, are built on a report type. A report type is the foundation of a report. Once the report is created, you cannot change the report type, but if you have many reports that need to change the report type, you can engage a developer or consultant to write a script for you, but we will not discuss these advanced topics in this book. For now, if you need to change the report type, you need to recreate it as a new report.

The Report Type defines the set of records and fields available to a report based on the relationships between a primary object and the related objects defined. Ideally, to maintain report type; including report type creation, edit, and delete should fall under the Salesforce admin job scope, not the standard user. As a system admin, you need to think about the number of report types deployable and available for the user to use. Too many report types available will cause your user to get confused as which report type to use and what the difference is between each of them, so make sure that you balance it as required.

When a custom object is enabled for a report, Salesforce will auto-create a report type with **Report Type Name** equal to the **Plural Name** of the object name, and this report type will be stored in the **Other Reports** category folder.

 To use a custom object for a report type, make sure that you select **Enable Reports** for the object.

In order to understand report types easily, let's have an example--we have a custom object called **Expense** with **Plural Label Expenses,** you can use other custom objects too for testing. The object has a Lookup relationship field to Opportunity, and it has also been activated for **Enable Reports** and **Track Field History**. Let's have a quick look at the details in the Custom Object setup:

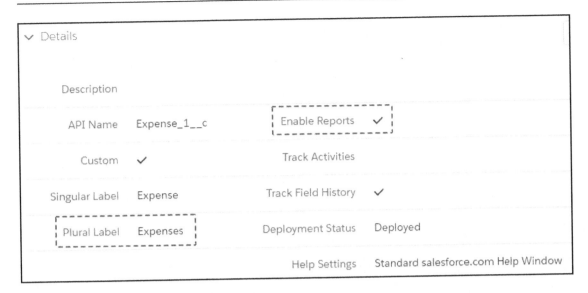

Navigate to the **Reports** tab and create a new report; you will see that a custom report type or multiple report types related to **Expense** has been created:

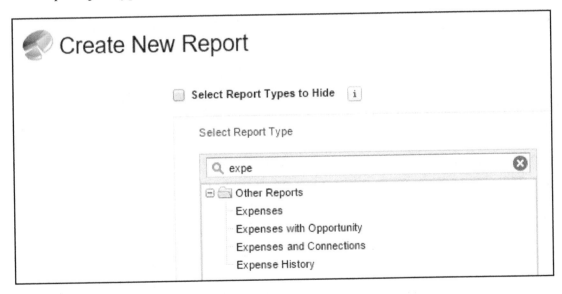

You can type in the report type name for a quick search.

In my organization, typing **expense** in the search text box filter four report types related to the Expense object. It may differ in your org., so it is okay if you do not see the same result, but you should see at least one report type. Let's analyze the four report types in my org.:

- **Expenses**: This report type will contain all fields related to the Expense object
- **Expenses with Opportunity**: This report type is automatically created because in my organization I have a Lookup field to Opportunity from the Expense object
- **Expenses and Connections**: This report type was created because in my organization, I have configured Salesforce to Salesforce connection
- **Expense History**: This report type is created as **Track Field History** is activated; refer to the preceding screenshot

Report type categories

Report type categories are stored and presented in folders. This will help us find the right report type quickly when creating a new report. Depending on the Salesforce edition you subscribe to, you will get different report type categories.

You cannot create a new report type category, but you can create a custom report type and store it in one of the categories provided; it is always a good practice to store a custom report type in the right category.

Over the years, you may have too many reports types created, but many of them are seldom used or are only used once; as an admin, you can delete these report types or hide them from the user selection when creating a new report; this includes both standard and custom report types.

Here is a comparison between hiding and deleting the report type:

Action	Delete	Hide
Restore report type	Not possible	Just unhide it
Existing reports	All delete	No effect
Start from	**Setup** menu	**Reports** tab
Applicable to	Custom report type	All report types

Personally, I prefer to hide rather than delete custom report types just in case the report type is needed one day in the future or used by existing reports.

Deleting a custom report type will delete all existing reports built with the report type, including reports stored in all user private folders. So be cautious when deleting a report type, and make sure that it is no longer used.

Best practices for deleting a custom report type are as follows:

1. Hide the report type.
2. Run a report to check how many active reports are using the identified report type. We will look into this in detail later in this chapter.
3. Rename the report type with a prefix (for example, **to be deleted** with today's date). The purpose of this action is to delete the report type after x months only if there are no active reports used.

The Report Type category structure is a pretty similar to the Standard Report Folder, but do not get confused between the two.

The standard report folder contains all standard reports provided by Salesforce out-of-the-box; you will not be able to overwrite it, but you can modify it and save the report as a new report into a custom public report folder or your personal report folder.

The **Report Type** category stores all report types, including the standard and custom report types. You can store custom report types into any **Report Type** category, but you cannot create or add a new **Report Type** category.

Hands-on exercise for hiding a report type

Use case: We have too many report types available and this causes our user to get confused about which report type to use and the differences between some of the report types. Instead of deleting the custom report type, which will auto-delete the reports created with that report type, let's just hide those existing report types that are no longer needed.

1. to the **Reports** tab.
2. Click on the **New Report** button.
3. Click on the **Select Report Types to Hide** checkbox.
4. Click on the + icon before the report category name to expand all report types in that category. For this exercise, click on **Accounts & Contacts**.
5. A report type with a green checkmark means the report type is available to use when creating a new report, while the one with a yellow cross means it is not available for use.

6. Click on the report type name to toggle from visible to hide and from hide to visible. For this exercise, click on **Contacts with Assets**; the icon will change from a green tick to a yellow cross, and all existing reports built on that report will be not deleted, if the report is used as a data source report for a dashboard component, hiding the report type will not affect the dashboard too. Consider the following screenshot:

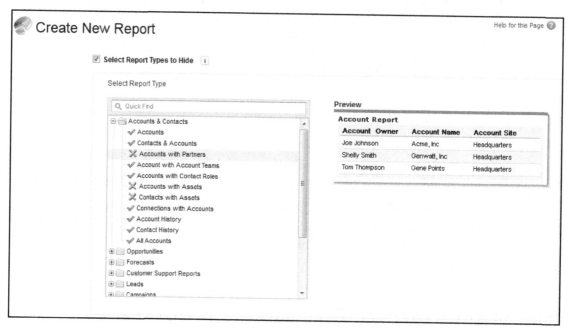

7. Click on **Select Report Types to Hide** again to unselect it; all report types hidden will no longer be visible for all users to use when creating a new report.

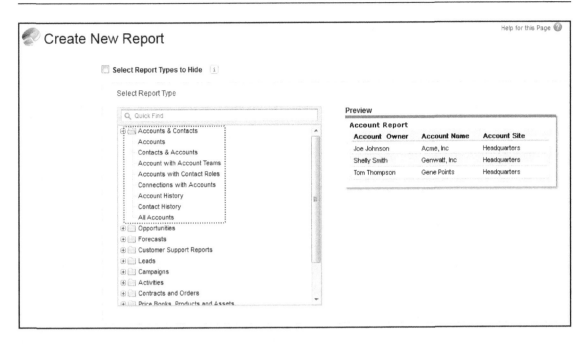

Standard Report Type

When you click on the **New Report** button from the **Reports** tab, you will be presented with a list of the **Report Type** categories as shown in the following screenshot:

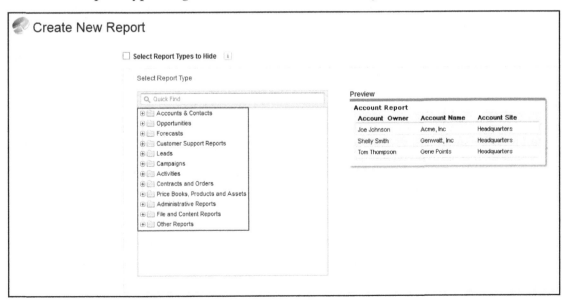

There are two types of Standard Report Types:

- The report type that comes with Salesforce for standard objects, such as **Contacts & Accounts**. You can easily distinguish this report type, as it will have a **Preview** when you select that report type when creating a new report.

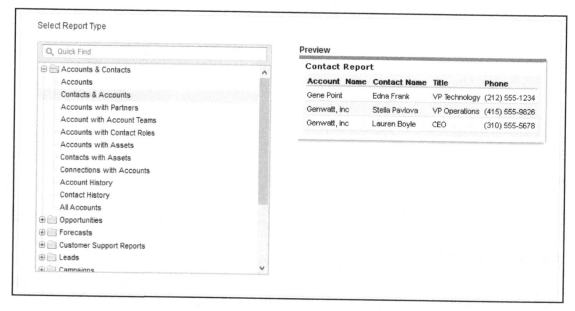

- The report type is autogenerated when you enable the **Allow Report** option for a custom object. This report type will not have **Preview**, but it will just say **No preview available**.

When you relate an object to another object and both objects are enabled for reports, the following options will happen depending on the relationship. In the following example, we will use Customer (custom object) as the parent object and Claim (custom object) as the child object. Both objects have been enabled for the report. Let's look closer at both Master-Detail Relationship and Lookup Relationship and see what will happen with the report type when the relationship between these objects is built.

The Lookup relationship

When you add a Lookup field relationship between objects, the following behavior will happen related to the report type:

- When you activate **Enable Reports** for a claim object, the system will auto-create the **Claims** report type.
- When you relate **Claim** to the customer object as a child with a Lookup relationship, the system will add the customer field to the claims report type. The user will see the additional customer name field available for the claims report type, but no other fields from the customer object will be available for the report. The **Claims** report type will contain all the claims recorded with or without customer:

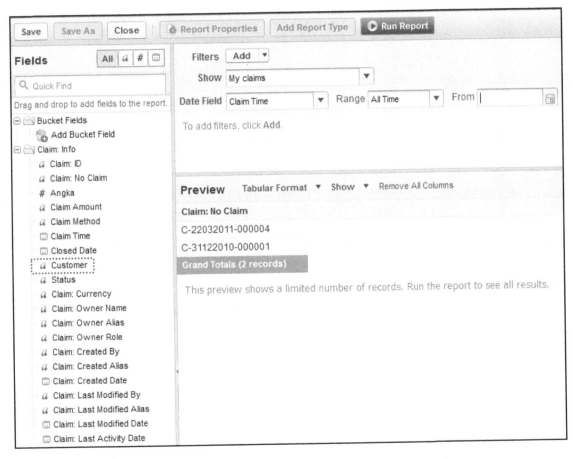

- There will be no change in the existing **Customers** report type because **Customer** is the parent object.
- A new report type called **Claims with Customer** will be created in the **Other Reports** category. This report type will contain all fields available from both **Claim** and **Customer** objects.

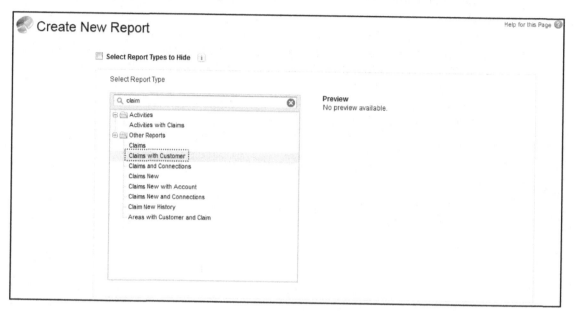

- This report type will show the **Claims with Customer** record only; this also means that the **Claims** record without Customer will not be in the report generated.

The Master-Detail Relationship

When you add a Master-Detail Relationship between objects, the following behavior will happen related to the report type:

- When you activate **Enable Reports** for the Claim object, the system will auto-create the **Claims** report type.
- When you relate **Claims** to the **Customers** object as a child with a Master-Detail Relationship, the existing **Claims** report type will be removed because the **Claim** object became the child of the Customer object in a master-detail relationship.
- There is no change in the existing **Customers** report type because customer is the parent object.

- A new report type called **Customers with Claims** will be created in the **Other Reports** category folder. Note the difference with the report type auto-created in **Lookup Relationship** discussed earlier. This report has all fields available from both **Customer** and **Claim** objects and will show **Customer with Claim** only; this also means **Customer without Claim** records will be not in the report generated:

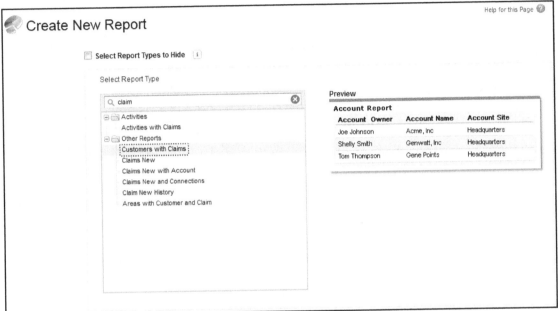

Let's summarize the preceding relationship in the matrix:

Description	Lookup	Master-Detail Relationship
Claim Report Type	No change, only add the **Customer** field name	**Claim** report type will be removed
Customer Report Type	No change	No change
New Report Type Created	**Claims with Customer** with all fields from both objects, only show claim records with customer; here, the primary object is **Claim**	**Customers with Claims** with all fields from both objects, only show customers records with claim; here, the primary object is **Customer**

The Custom Report type

A report type defines the set of records and fields available to a report. The source of a report type can be only from an object, or it can include related objects. The report type also determines only those records that meet the criteria defined in the report displayed in it.

When the standard report types provided do not meet your reporting needs, your admin can create a custom report type. The custom report type supports multi-level object relationships, defined from the parent level object as the Primary object and related to the child object and grandchild object, not the other way.

Let's look at an example--you have an object relationship of **Customer** > **Claim** > **Claim Payment**; in this relationship, you can build a custom report type **Customer** with **Claim** and Claim Payment, not Claim Payment Customer with **Claim** and **Customer**.

Using **Customer** and **Claim** objects discussed in the Standard Report Type, in the Master-Detail Relationship, the **Customers with Claims** report type will be auto-created. See the following illustration, the grey area would be the report result when using this report type:

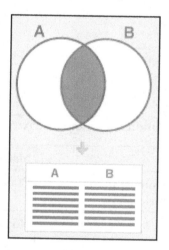

In the preceding figure, A is the customer object and B is the Claim object. The **Customers with Claims** standard report type will be auto-created by the system when you relate the objects. This report type will generate reports for **Customers with Claim** only, and **Customers without Claim** will not be available in the report using the report type. If you need to generate a report to produce all customers, you can use the **Customers** report type, but **Claim** fields will be not available in the report.

In this scenario, the custom report type comes into the picture. We can create a custom report type customers with or without claims. This report type will produce customer information with claim information even if the customer does not have any claims. This report type will generate reports with all customer data. See the gray area in the following screenshot:

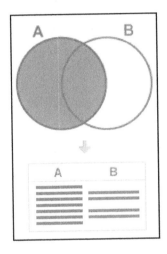

With the custom report type, we can define a Primary object and relate it to the child objects, where:

- The record in the primary object must have at least one record of a related object
- The record in the primary object may or may not have records of a related object

Custom report types start from the top-level object as the **Primary object**; they support only one child object per hierarchy but allow you to create multiple levels of parent and child hierarchies.
With the custom report type, you can define which objects' fields can be made available for report columns. If a field is removed from the custom report type, that particular field will be removed from all reports built with that report type.

Hands-on exercise for creating a Custom Report type

This exercise is applicable only to the system admin or the user with the **Manage Custom Report Types** permission. In this exercise, we will create a new custom report type where **Customer** is the Primary object, it may or may not have **Claim**, and claim may or may not have claim payment. Make sure all objects have been created and enabled for reporting.

1. Navigate to **Setup** | **Feature Settings** | **Analytics** | **Reports & Dashboards** | **Report Types** (or you can easily find the menu by entering `report types` in the **Quick Find** textbox in the **Setup** menu) and click on the **New Custom Report Type** button.

2. In **Primary Object**, the selected object will be in the top hierarchy for the report type; in this exercise, select **Customers**.

 Once the record type is saved, you cannot change the primary object.

3. Enter **Report Type Label** and the **Report Type Name**. The label can be up to 255 characters long; for this exercise, label it `Customers with/without Claims with/without Payment`. The name will be auto-populated, you can modify it, but just leave it for this exercise.

4. Enter **Description** for the custom report type; you can enter up to 1,000 characters. This description is mandatory and will be shown when users select the report type to create a report. Provide a meaningful description so users have a good idea of which data is available for reports, for example, `All customers with Claim information`.

5. Select **Store in Category**; always store the report type in the correct category; for users to find the report type easily, select **Other Reports**.

6. Select **Deployment Status**; click on the **Next** button to continue.

- **In Development**: The report type with this status is only available for the system admin and users with the **Manage Custom Report Types** or **Customize Application** permission. Select this option during the design and testing phase. The report type and its reports are hidden from all other users.

- **Deployed**: This report type and its report will be available for everyone. Change to this option after it is tested and you are ready to let all users to access it.

7. Click on the **Next** button to continue.

8. Customers will be shown as a Primary object; click on **(Click to relate to another object)** to relate to a child object. In our exercise, select **Claims** and then do the same to relate Claims to **Claim Payments**.

9. Click on the **Save** button to finish it. Consider the following screenshot:

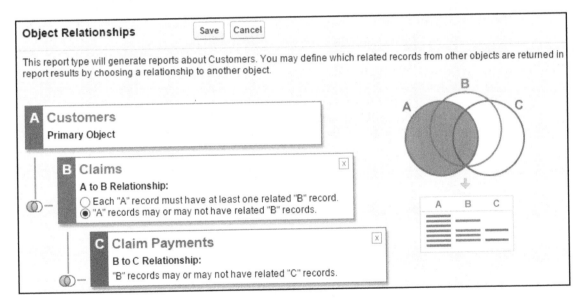

Custom report types start from the top-level object as the Primary object, for example, **Customer with Claims**; this report will get all customers with and without claim. But how about if you would like to report all claims and the customer information regardless of whether it linked to customer or not - **Claim with Customers**.

You still can use the custom report type for this scenario. Set claims as the primary object without relating to another object and then use **Add fields related via lookup** » to add fields from the customer object.

Hands-on exercise for extending Custom Report types

Let's modify the **Customers with/without Claims with/without Payment** report type created earlier with the following requirements:

- The claim object also has a Lookup relationship to the **Policy** custom object. We would like to get status field from **Policy** object.
- Because of privacy, the management decides not to make a field called **Tier** under the **Customer** object available for the user to use in the report.

With these requirements, let's open and edit the report type created:

1. Open the report type created by navigating to **Setup** | **Feature Settings** | **Analytics** | **Reports & Dashboards** | **Report Types** (or you can easily find the menu by entering `report types` in the **Quick Find** textbox in the **Setup** menu) and click on the report type name.

2. Now, you should see the **Fields Available for Reports** section in that report type. Click on the **Edit Layout** button to add the **Policy Status** field to the report type; by default, policy-related fields will not be available for the report type as shown in the following screenshot:

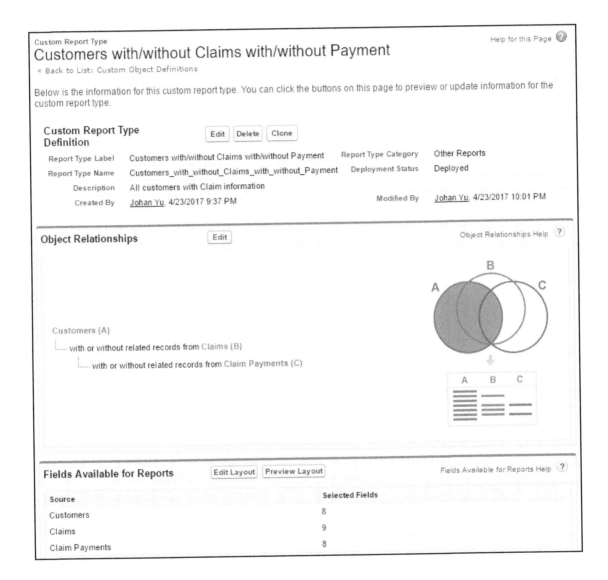

3. Change the View to **Claim Fields** and then click on **Add fields related via lookup** » below the Lookup. Because **Policy** is a lookup field from the Claim object, you should see the **Policy** » link here. Consider the following screenshot:

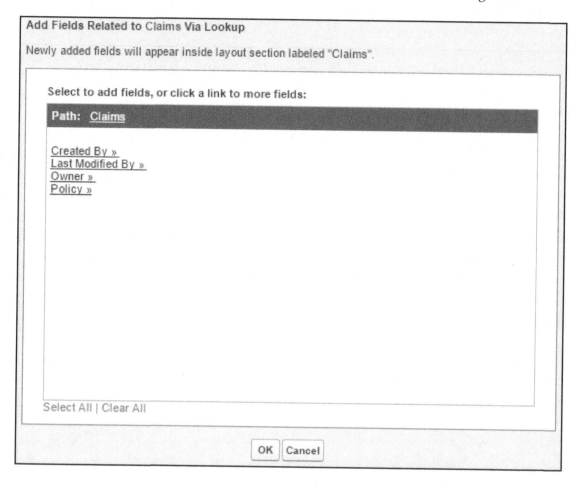

4. Select the checkbox next to **Status** and then click on the **OK** button.
5. Now you should see Status (with the magnifying glass icon) added to the Claims section.

6. Next, we would like to remove the **Tier** field from **Customers**; just drag and drop the **Tier** field to the **Customers Fields** panel on the right-hand side as shown in the following screenshot:

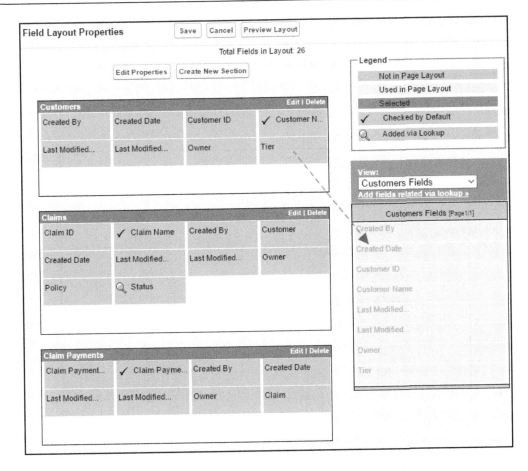

7. Click on the **Save** button.
8. Note that, in the **Fields Available for Reports** section, the **Customers** field now becomes seven fields and **Claims** becomes 10 fields.

Hands-on exercise for using a Custom Report type

In this exercise, we are going to use the report type created and edited in the preceding exercises:

1. Click on the **Reports** tab and then click on the **New Report...** button.
2. Type customer into the **Quick Find** textbox under **Select Report Type**.
3. Select **Customers with/without Claims with/without Payment** and then click on the **Create** button.

4. Note these in the left-hand side panel in the **Fields** panel:
   - There are three field groups: **Customers**, **Claims**, and **Claim Payments**. This is similar to the report type setup field layout.
   - We do not see **Tier** under the **Customers** group.
   - We see **Policy: Status** under the **Claims** group. Consider the following screenshot:

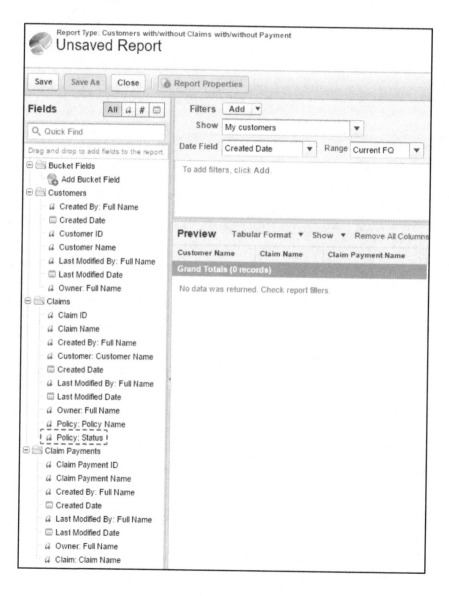

5. There are three fields added by default when you select this report type--
Customer Name, **Claim Name**, **Claim Payment Name**. The following screenshot
shows that there are three fields checked. So, if you would like to add more
default fields, for example, **Policy: Status**, double-click on the field and select the
Checked by Default checkbox. Consider the following screenshot:

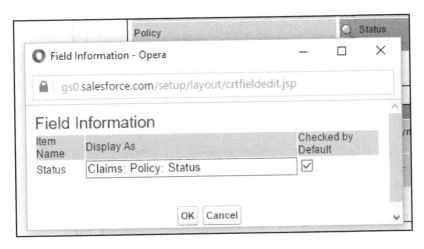

6. We do not plan to store this report, so we can just ignore the report builder from
here. However, if you would like to save the report, feel free to save it to your
personal report folder.

Limitations and benefits of Custom Report types

As we went through this chapter, we can make use of custom report types for the following:

- Filtering the report result related to the child object
- Extending the report with look fields from the parent object
- Hidden fields will not be available for the report
- Setting default fields added when creating a new report

Here are some limitations when implementing a custom report type:

- A custom report type can contain up to 60 object references.
- You can add up to 1,000 fields to each custom report type.
- The maximum report type name length is 50 characters, including spaces.

- There are a few standard fields not available for the custom report type, such as **Product Schedule** fields, the **Age** field on cases and opportunities, and so on.
- If you add fields after the report type created to an object related to the report type, the new fields added will not be available by default for the report type. The admin needs to manually add these fields to the report type.
- You can associate up to four level of object relationships for a report type, where each level containing one object only.

Tips on Custom Report types

To fully make use of a custom report type with less maintenance, here are a few tips you should be aware of as an admin when implementing a report type:

- When new fields are created in an object, scan through all the existing report types if the new fields added need to be added to that report type.
- Always using a name that reflects what the content and filter of the report type are. In the exercise discussed earlier in this chapter, we used **Customers with/without Claims with/without Payment** as the name, which explains what the primary object is and how it relates to the child object.
- Always add a meaningful **Description.** The description is mandatory and it will be visible to users who create reports.
- Custom report types are added to the bottom of the Report Category. If you are the one who creates the report type, alert your users with the permission to create a report.
- Remember to change the report type status to **Deployed**; otherwise, your users will not see the report when built; refer to the *Hands-on exercise for creating a Custom Report type*, section.
- If the current report type needs to have a significant change, such as adding or editing object relationships, it is advisable to clone the report type to a new one so it will not affect existing reports built with that report type.
- Change the field section folder name when needed. By default, the section folder name will follow the object name. This name will appear in the report builder, so when you change it from the report type setup, the section folder name will change in the report builder too.
- Hide the unused report type easily (the standard and custom report type) so your user is not confused by so many report types. Some of them may no longer be needed, which you can delete after being hidden for a few months provided you are sure they are not used in active reports.

Summary

In this chapter, we went through report types in detail and explored why a report type is so important when building a report. We also saw that the system will autogenerate a new report type for a custom object when you enable an object for the report.

There are two well-known types of relationships in Salesforce: Lookup and Master-Detail for when you relate an object to another object. We discussed how this will affect report types. We shared how to extend fields from the parent object and also remove fields not available for the user to use in the report.

Lastly, we shared the benefits and limitations of using a custom report type and realized that one of the limitations is that most people will experience that when new fields are added, they will be not available in the report type. The admin needs to manually add them and while using a standard report type, all fields for the objects will be auto-added when new fields are added.

In the next chapter, we will discuss more advanced features related to reports, including the custom summary formula, bucket fields, adding a chart to a report, adding a chart to a page layout, and scheduling a report.

6

Advanced Report Configuration

You learned about report types in detail in Chapter 5, *Understanding Report Types*. In that chapter, we introduced what a report type is and why the report type is so important for building reports. We also discussed the report type category, standard report type, custom report type and ended with a hands-on exercise to create a custom report type, extend a custom report type, and apply it by creating a new report.

In this chapter, we will onto bucket fields and custom summary formula. It is not like a report type, where you have to select a report type when creating a report, but bucket fields and custom summary formulas are optional; you may use or not use them. But in many scenarios, we can take advantage of these features to build an advanced report, such as to show the growth trends month-by-month in percentages using a custom summary formula.

By the end of this chapter, you will fully understand the benefits of bucket fields and how to use a custom summary formulas, which will help you when building reports. Both bucket fields and custom summary formulas are applicable in both Classic and Lightning, and there are no differences in configuring them in a Classic and Lightning environment.

Throughout this chapter, we will provide notes and tips to help you to understand important items. The following topics will be covered:

- Using a bucket field to categorize data for reporting
- Introducing and creating a custom summary formula
- Functions available in a custom summary formula
- Relative functions: PARENTGROUPVAL and PREVGROUPVAL

Categorizing data in reports

In Chapter 4, *Creating and Managing Reports*, we used the **Summary** format to group reports into multiple levels with available fields. The report generated will be shown in groups, with the number of groups depending on the values returned for the field used for grouping. This means that if there is no value returned in the report, that value will not be shown in the grouping at all. For example, if you group by month, you may see that some months are missing if there are no records for those months.

How about if we need to categorize multiple values of a field into one category? Creating a formula field with a CASE() function may be a solution, but think about how often that formula field will be used, or will that formula field be used for one report only? Is the category standard for the entire organization or only for a report? Furthermore, only the system admin will be able to create the formula field.

If the answer is only for one or a very small number of reports and not standard for the whole organization, then creating a new formula field is not a good solution; furthermore, there is a maximum number of formula fields that you can create in an object. Bucket fields come into the picture for both these scenarios.

Bucket fields

So what is a bucket field? It is an incredibly powerful functionality offered by Salesforce in reporting. It lets you quickly categorize values for a field in a report without the need to have a custom formula field at the object level. When you create a bucket field, you define multiple categories into groups depending on the record values; this bucket field will not affect other reports or the object itself.

For example, you have the following values in the **Account Type**:

- **Prospect**
- **Customer - Direct**
- **Customer - Channel**
- **Channel Partner / Reseller**
- **Installation Partner**
- **Technology Partner**
- **Other**

You need to categorize all account types containing Customer as **Customer**, all **Account Type** containing Partner as **Partner**, all **Account Type** containing Prospect as **Prospect**, and the rest as **Other**. Using a bucket field, you will get a new field without having to create a custom formula field in the Account just for this purpose. For this scenario, the bucket field will contain the following values:

- **Prospect**
- **Customer**
- **Partner**
- **Other**

These values will be available only for the particular report configured.

Bucket fields are available in most report formats: **Tabular**, **Summary**, and **Matrix**. However, the **Joined** report does not support bucket fields. When you change the report format to another format, the bucket fields will stay. If you have a report with bucket fields, then change the report format into a Joined report and bucket fields will be removed.

 You can add up to five bucket fields in a report. Each bucket field can contain up to 20 buckets.

You can use the following field types as a source for the bucket field:

- **Number, Currency, Percent**
- **Picklist**
- **Text**
- **Lookup**

This includes the **Formula** field and the **Roll-Up Summary** field, which return the field type as shown earlier.

The following field types cannot be used as the source field for a bucket field:

- Date and Date/Time--Although this is not supported in bucket fields, you can still get a concept a similar to bucket fields using the Group By feature discussed in **Summary** and **Matrix** reports
- Checkbox--You can create a custom formula field that returns 1 or 0 or a custom formula field that returns the text **Yes/No** or **True/False** and use that custom formula field in your Bucket field
- Email

- Phone
- Picklist (Multi-Select)
- Text Area, Long Text Area, and Rich Text Area
- URL

Hands-on exercise for adding a bucket field to a report

In this exercise, we are going to create an Account report and categorize all Account Types containing Customer as Customer, all Account Type containing Partner as Partner, all Account Type containing Prospect as Prospect, and the rest as Other:

1. Navigate to the **Reports** tab and click on the **New Report...** button.
2. Select the **Accounts** report type and click on the plus sign under the **Accounts & Contacts** category.
3. Click on the **Create** button to continue.
4. Change **Show** to **All Accounts**.
5. Change the **Date Field Range** to **All Time**.
6. Click on **Remove All Columns** to clear the report without any columns. This link is useful when you would like to have a new report without any default field.
7. Add **Account Name** and **Account Owner** by double-clicking on the field from the left-hand side panel.
8. Double-click on **Add Bucket Field** (or drag it to the report area) in the top-left panel under **Bucket Fields.**
9. Set **Source Column** to **Type.**
10. In **Bucket Field Name**, enter Type (Core).
11. Click on the **New Bucket** button and type in **Customer.** Repeat this same for **Partner** and **Prospect**.
12. Select all **Type contains Customer** and click on the **Move To** button. Then, select **Customer**, and you will notice a bucket label added to the picklist field selected. Repeat for **Partner** and **Prospect**.

13. Tick **Show Unbucketed values as "Other."** to categorize the rest as **Other**. This is shown in the following screenshot:

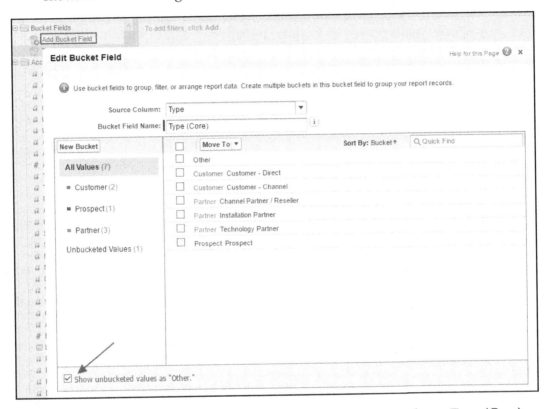

14. Click on the **OK** button to continue. You will notice a new column **Type (Core)** added to the report with a bucket icon before the label.

15. Click on the **Save** button and enter the following details:
    - **Report Name** as `Account with Bucket Fields`
    - **Report Folder** as `My Personal Custom Reports`
    - Click on the **Save** button again

16. Click on the **Run Report** button to generate the report. This is how the report would look like:

ACCOUNT NAME	ACCOUNT OWNER ↑	TYPE (CORE)
United Oil & Gas, UK	Alvin Lee	Customer
United Oil & Gas Corp.	Alvin Lee	Customer
Element Industry Ltd	Alvin Lee	Prospect
Accurate Glass	Alvin Lee	Customer
Mass-100	Alvin Lee	Other
PMA Manufacturing	Johan Yu	Prospect

17. Click on the **Save As** button:
      • **Report Name** as **Account with Bucket Fields**
      • **Report Folder** as **My Personal Custom Reports**

You can treat the bucket field as a normal field, you can use bucket field for following items:

  • Used as a grouping in the **Summary** and **Matrix** report
  • Used as a report filter
  • Used for report sorting
  • Available when we export a report; we will discuss an Export report later in this chapter
  • Included in field search results when you type in the left-hand side panel to filter a field

Creating a bucket field depending on the source field type

In the preceding example, we used the picklist field as the source field; however, different field types will have different ways to define the bucket field.

In the following sections, we will discuss how we create bucket fields using a different types of fields as the field source.

The picklist field

By creating a bucket field with picklist as the field source, you will be able to categorize the picklist values into a smaller category. Some points to note when using the picklist field as the source field type for the bucket field are as follows:

- Select the picklist value and move it into a bucket
- One picklist cannot be categorized for more than one bucket
- Not all picklist fields can be used as a source for the bucket, such as a record type
- If you do not select **Show unbucketed values as "Other."**, all values not captured in the bucket will be as shown in the following screenshot:

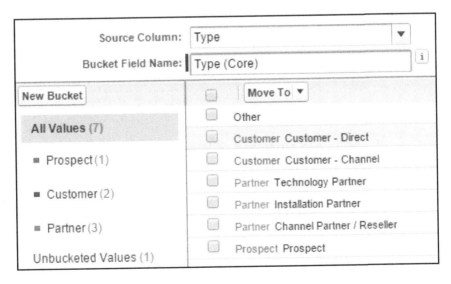

The Currency, Number, and Percent fields

By creating a bucket field with currency, number, and percent as the field source, you will be able to sort data that can be described in terms of numbers. Some points to note when using these field types for bucket fields are as follows:

- You need to have a minimum of two buckets for small and big range values
- You can add many bucket ranges up to a total of 20 buckets
- If you do not tick **Treat empty** <field name>**values in the report as zeros**, blank values of the source column will be shown as follows:

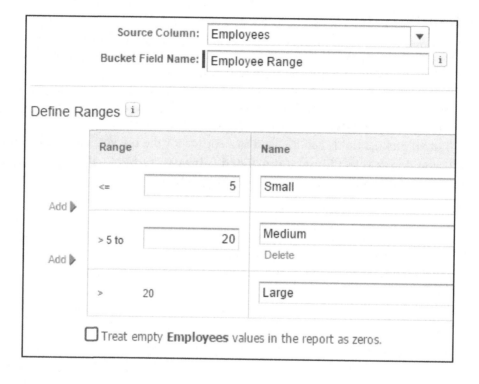

The Text and Lookup fields

Creating a bucket field with text and lookup fields as the field source, you will be able to categorize based on values that consist of words or phrases. Some points to note for a bucket with this source field type are as follows:

- Search the text value of the source column; all values containing the search keyword will be shown; it is case-insensitive. Or, click on the **Enter Values** tab to enter values manually and move into the bucket
- Select the search result and move it to the bucket
- If you do not tick **Show unbucketed values as "Other."**. All values not captured in the bucket will be shown as is:

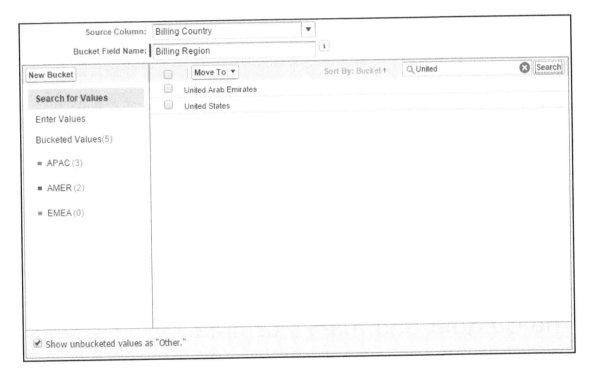

Editing a bucket field

You can edit a bucket field by hovering your mouse over the bucket field in the top-left panel and then clicking on the pencil icon. You can delete a bucket field by clicking on the trash bin icon next to the pencil icon.

Clicking on the pencil icon will open the bucket field window; to remove selected values from the bucket field value, perform the following steps:

1. Click on the bucket; it will show all values selected for that bucket.
2. Click on the checkbox to select the value.
3. Click on the **Move To** button and then click on **Unbucketed Values** or a different bucket. Consider the following screenshot:

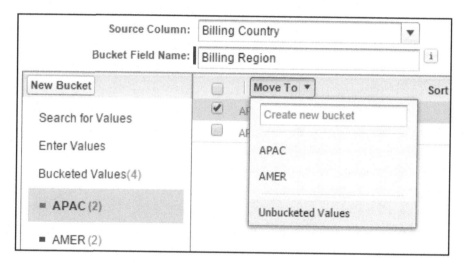

The Custom Summary Formula

Do not confuse a custom summary formula in the report with a formula field for an object. They are totally different things and not related at all, although they both have a formula.

The custom summary formula is only available in the **Summary**, **Matrix**, and **Joined** reports. Use a custom summary formula to calculate additional totals based on the numeric fields available in the report or the record count. The same holds true with the bucket field discussed earlier in this chapter. A custom summary formula created in a report will not affect any other places and is not related to other reports.

When you need to get a value from a Lookup or Master-Detail Relationship object, the formula field is the answer; you cannot use the custom summary formula in the report for this purpose. So whenever you need to get a field value from the parent lookup object for any usage (including for the report), create a formula field and then hide it from the page layout. However, only the system admin will be able to create the formula field.

When you create a custom summary formula, you need to define the format to return and also define how many decimal points are to be returned. Here are the format options to be returned by the custom summary formula:

- Currency
- Number
- Percent

Only the following field types can be used in the formula for the custom summary formula:

- Currency
- Number
- Percent
- Record Count
- You also can use the formula field and the roll-up summary fields that are returned in the preceding field types
- Similar to the summarizing field option in the report, you can use these in the custom summary formula: **Sum**, **Max**, **Min**, and **Average**; for example, `Account.Number_of_Branch__c:SUM`

The Custom Summary Formula in Summary and Matrix reports

In the **Summary** report, the custom summary formula can be displayed at:

- **All summary levels**: This would be similar to field summarize
- **Grand summary only**: This is the same with the grand total

- **Grouping**: This has levels 1 or 2 or 3 (depending on how many levels of grouping are added to the report)

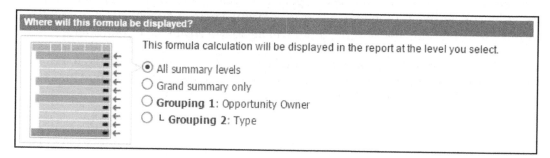

The preceding screenshot is taken from a **Summary** report with two levels of grouping, **Opportunity Owner** and **Type**.

For the **Matrix** report, the custom summary formula can be displayed at:

- **All summary levels**.
- **A specific row/column grouping level...**; selecting this option will give you the option to use the field or Grand Summary for both row (A) and column (B) groupings. If you have more than one level of row or column grouping, you can select any of them.

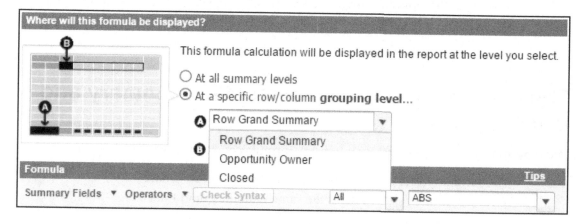

The preceding screenshot is taken from a **Matrix** report with two levels of row grouping (marked as **A**), **Opportunity Owner** (first level) and **Closed** (second level), and one level of column grouping (marked as B): **Type**.

Points to note from the summary formula field are as follows:

- The summary formula is always shown in the last column of the report; if you have multiple formulas, they will be ordered by the formula creation date and time
- You cannot summarize the summary formula field

 If you change the report format, the summary formula field in the report will be deleted, so be careful.

Hands-on exercise for adding a simple summary formula

Let's consider a use case: in a **Summary** report, add the total amount of Open opportunities in the **Grand Total** level. Assuming that a **Roll-Up Summary** field in **Account** from opportunity called **Total Amount of Open Opportunities** has been created, here are the roll-up summary field details:

Account Custom Field   Help for
Total Amount of Open Opportunities
Back to Account Fields

Custom Field Definition Detail   [Edit] [Set Field-Level Security] [View Field Accessibility]

Field Information

Field Label	Total Amount of Open Opportunities	Object Name	Account
Field Name	Total_Amount_of_Open_Opportunities		
API Name	Total_Amount_of_Open_Opportunities__c		
Description			
Help Text			
Created By	Johan Yu, 4/28/2017 7:43 AM	Modified By	Johan Yu, 4/28/2017 7:48 AM

Roll-Up Summary Options

Data Type	Roll-Up Summary	Summary Type	SUM
Summarized Object	Opportunity		
Field to Aggregate	Opportunity: Amount		
Filter Criteria	Closed EQUALS False		

1. Go to the **Reports** tab and click on the **New Report...** button.
2. Select the **Accounts** Report Type and click on the plus sign under the **Accounts & Contacts** category.
3. Click on the **Create** button to continue.
4. Change **Show** to **All accounts.**
5. Change the **Date Field Range** to **All Time.**
6. Change the format to **Summary** and click on **Remove All Columns**.
7. Add **Account Name** and **Type** to the report from the **Fields** panel.
8. Drag **Account Owner** to the grouping area.
9. Double-click on **Add Formula** in the left-hand side panel under **Fields**. This is shown in the following screenshot:

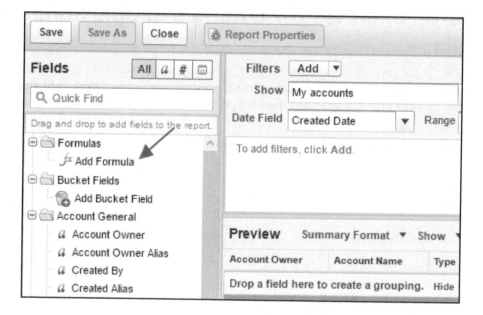

10. Enter **Column Name** as `Total Open Opportunities.`
11. Enter **Description** as `Total Amount of Open Opportunities.`
12. Select **Format** as **Currency** and **Decimal Places** as **2**.

13. Select **Grand summary only**.
14. In the **Formula** field, navigate to **Summary Fields** | **Total Amount of Open Opportunities** | **Sum**. Consider the following screenshot:

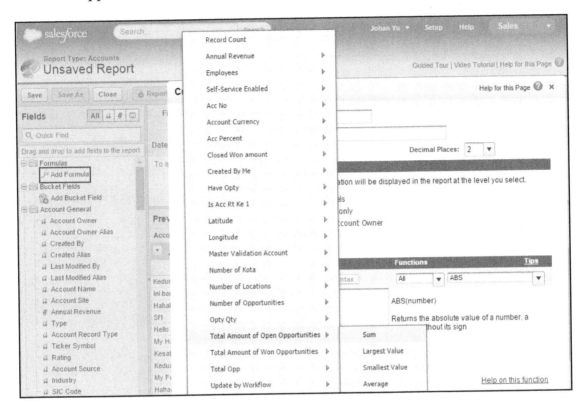

15. The formula will be automatically filled with **Account.Total_Amount_of_Open_Opportunities__c:SUM**.
16. Click on the **OK** button and note the **Total Open Opportunities** option added in the formula and in the report column.
17. Note that the formula summary field is always added in the last column of the report and you cannot move it to the left.
18. Save the report as **Open Opportunities.**
19. Click on **Run Report.**

Here is the report result:

ACCOUNT OWNER ↑	ACCOUNT NAME ↑	TYPE	TOTAL OPEN OPPORTUNITIES

REPORT

Open Opportunities

Total Records	Total Open Opportunities
17	$1,250,000.00

ACCOUNT OWNER ↑	ACCOUNT NAME ↑	TYPE	TOTAL OPEN OPPORTUNITIES
Alvin Lee (4 records)	Accurate Glass	Customer - Channel	
	Element Industry Ltd	Prospect	
	United Oil & Gas, UK	Customer - Direct	
	United Oil & Gas Corp.	Customer - Direct	
Subtotal			-
Johan Yu (13 records)	Burlington Textiles Corp of America	Customer - Direct	
	Dickenson plc	Customer - Channel	
	Edge Communications	Customer - Direct	
	Express Logistics and Transport	Customer - Channel	
	GenePoint	Customer - Channel	
	Grand Hotels & Resorts Ltd	Customer - Direct	
	King Inc	Customer - Direct	
	PMA Manufacturing	Prospect	
	Pyramid Construction Inc.	Customer - Channel	
	Quality Materials	Customer - Channel	
	Super Force Inc	Customer - Direct	
	United Oil & Gas, Singapore	Customer - Direct	
	University of Arizona	Customer - Direct	
Subtotal			-
GRAND TOTAL (17 RECORDS)			$1,250,000.00

20. Now let's change the formula by hovering the mouse over the **Total Open Opportunities** formula and then clicking on the pencil icon.

To edit or delete the formula, when the report is in the report builder, hover the mouse over the formula and click on the pencil icon or the trash bin icon; this is the same with the bucket field.

21. Change from **Grand summary only** to **All summary levels**. This is shown in the following screenshot:

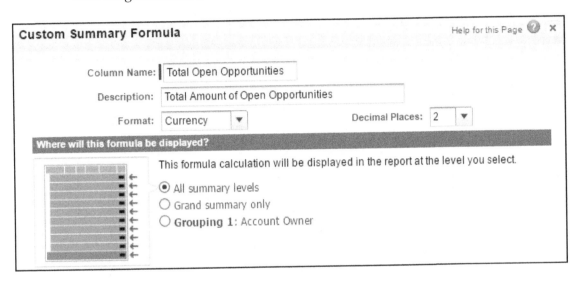

22. Click on the **OK** button and then click on **Run Report.**

23. Take a look at the changes in the following screenshot; the **Subtotal** value for **Account Owner** is now populated:

REPORT
Open Opportunities

Total Records	Total Open Opportunities
17	$1,250,000.00

ACCOUNT OWNER ↑	ACCOUNT NAME ↑	TYPE	TOTAL OPEN OPPORTUNITIES
Alvin Lee (4 records)	Accurate Glass	Customer - Channel	
	Element Industry Ltd	Prospect	
	United Oil & Gas, UK	Customer - Direct	
	United Oil & Gas Corp.	Customer - Direct	
Subtotal			$395,000.00
Johan Yu (13 records)	Burlington Textiles Corp of America	Customer - Direct	
	Dickenson plc	Customer - Channel	
	Edge Communications	Customer - Direct	
	Express Logistics and Transport	Customer - Channel	
	GenePoint	Customer - Channel	
	Grand Hotels & Resorts Ltd	Customer - Direct	
	King Inc	Customer - Direct	
	PMA Manufacturing	Prospect	
	Pyramid Construction Inc.	Customer - Channel	
	Quality Materials	Customer - Channel	
	Super Force Inc	Customer - Direct	
	United Oil & Gas, Singapore	Customer - Direct	
	University of Arizona	Customer - Direct	
Subtotal			$855,000.00
GRAND TOTAL (17 RECORDS)			$1,250,000.00

But since the **TOTAL AMOUNT OF OPEN OPPORTUNITIES** is a roll-up summary field in Account, we can just add the field to the report and summarize it, and we will get a similar report result:

REPORT
Open Opportunities

Total Records	Total Total Amount of Open Opportunities	Total Open Opportunities
17	$1,250,000.00	$1,250,000.00

ACCOUNT OWNER ↑	ACCOUNT NAME ↑	TYPE	TOTAL AMOUNT OF OPEN OPPORTUNITIES Sum	TOTAL OPEN OPPORTUNITIES
Alvin Lee (4 records)	Accurate Glass	Customer - Channel	$0.00	
	Element Industry Ltd	Prospect	$0.00	
	United Oil & Gas, UK	Customer - Direct	$0.00	
	United Oil & Gas Corp.	Customer - Direct	$395,000.00	
Subtotal			$395,000.00	$395,000.00
Johan Yu (13 records)	Burlington Textiles Corp of America	Customer - Direct	$0.00	
	Dickenson plc	Customer - Channel	$15,000.00	
	Edge Communications	Customer - Direct	$35,000.00	
	Express Logistics and Transport	Customer - Channel	$200,000.00	
	GenePoint	Customer - Channel	$60,000.00	
	Grand Hotels & Resorts Ltd	Customer - Direct	$265,000.00	
	King Inc	Customer - Direct	$0.00	
	PMA Manufacturing	Prospect	$0.00	
	Pyramid Construction Inc	Customer - Channel	$100,000.00	
	Quality Materials	Customer - Channel	$0.00	
	Super Force Inc	Customer - Direct	$80,000.00	
	United Oil & Gas, Singapore	Customer - Direct	$0.00	
	University of Arizona	Customer - Direct	$100,000.00	
Subtotal			$855,000.00	$855,000.00
GRAND TOTAL (17 RECORDS)			$1,250,000.00	$1,250,000.00

In this case, it is not necessary to create a summary formula unless you need to hide the amount of each Opportunity and just get the total. The sample in this hands-on does not show the real power of the report formula summary; except for the normal Summarize field, we cannot configure it, and it will always show at all levels. Let's look at a better usage of summary formula in the next hands-on exercise.

Hands-on exercise for working with a summary formula

Let's consider a use case: in a **Summary** report, add **Total Amount of Closed Opportunities** in all summary levels. Assuming that roll-up summary fields in Account from Opportunity called **Total Amount of Opportunities** and **Total Amount of Open Opportunities** have been created and the detail for **Total Amount of Open Opportunities** field has been discussed in the previous hands-on, here is the roll-up summary field detail for **Total Amount of Opportunities**:

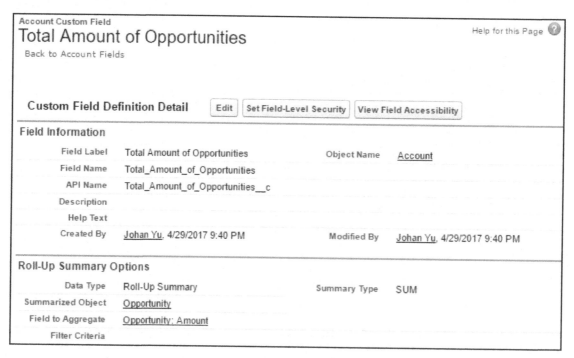

Account Custom Field
Total Amount of Opportunities
Back to Account Fields

Help for this Page

Custom Field Definition Detail   Edit | Set Field-Level Security | View Field Accessibility

Field Information

Field Label	Total Amount of Opportunities	Object Name	Account
Field Name	Total_Amount_of_Opportunities		
API Name	Total_Amount_of_Opportunities__c		
Description			
Help Text			
Created By	Johan Yu, 4/29/2017 9:40 PM	Modified By	Johan Yu, 4/29/2017 9:40 PM

Roll-Up Summary Options

Data Type	Roll-Up Summary	Summary Type	SUM
Summarized Object	Opportunity		
Field to Aggregate	Opportunity: Amount		
Filter Criteria			

1. Create a new custom summary formula field similar to the one we created in the hands-on exercise earlier and name it `Total Closed Opportunities`, with this formula: **Account.Total_Amount_of_Opportunities__c:SUM - Account.Total_Amount_of_Open_Opportunities__c:SUM**

2. For the sake of clarifying for this exercise, let's add both **Total Amounts of Opportunities** and Total Amount of Open Opportunities roll-up summary fields to the report and then summarize them with **Sum**. Consider the following screenshot:

REPORT				
Closed Opportunities				

Total Records	Total Total Amount of Opportunities	Total Total Amount of Open Opportunities	Total Closed Opportunities	
17	$6,086,000.00	$1,250,000.00	$4,836,000.00	

ACCOUNT OWNER ↑	RECORD COUNT	TOTAL AMOUNT OF OPPORTUNITIES Sum	TOTAL AMOUNT OF OPEN OPPORTUNITIES Sum	TOTAL CLOSED OPPORTUNITIES
Alvin Lee	4	$3,511,000.00	$395,000.00	$3,116,000.00
Johan Yu	13	$2,575,000.00	$855,000.00	$1,720,000.00
GRAND TOTAL	17	$6,086,000.00	$1,250,000.00	$4,836,000.00

3. In the preceding report, **Total Amount of Closed Opportunity** (summary formula) is equal to **Total Amount of Opportunity** (roll-up summary field) minus **Total Amount of Open Opportunity** (roll-up summary field). We use the **Subtract operator** between summary formulas, and we can also use this technique for the other formulas:

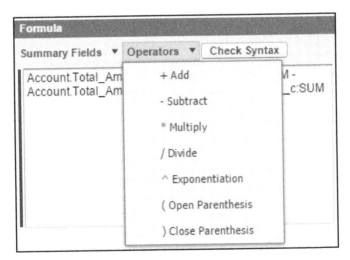

If you notice the area on the right of **Formula** in the **Custom Summary Formula** editor, there are many functions that you can use to enhance your formula; they are categorized as **All**, **Logical**, **Math**, and **Summary**. We will not discuss each function available, but let's look at a sample in the next section.

Using the IF() function

The IF() function is categorized under the Logical function and the syntax for this formula is **IF(logical_test, value_if_true, value_if_false)**.

This function checks whether a condition returns true. If it does, it will return the first value defined; otherwise, it will return the second value, for example, IF (RowCount > 4, WON:SUM, CLOSED:SUM).

This formula will return a total number of WON opportunities if the number of records is more than four rows; otherwise, it will return the total number of CLOSED opportunities. WON and CLOSED are available from the Opportunity report type.

You don't really have to type WON:SUM and CLOSED:SUM or other fields you would like to use, but from the **Custom Summary Formula** window, navigate to **Summary Fields** | <field name>| **Sum.**

Once you click on **Sum**, it will automatically populate in the formula; just make sure that you place the cursor in the formula editor.

Let's look at the report result using the preceding formula:

REPORT					
Opportunity Check Count					

Total Records: 9   Check Count: 5

OPPORTUNITY OWNER ↑	OPPORTUNITY NAME ↑	STAGE	AMOUNT	CHECK COUNT
Alvin Lee (4 records)	United Oil Installations	Negotiation/Review	$270,000.00	
	United Oil Office Portable Generators	Negotiation/Review	$125,000.00	
	United Oil Plant Standby Generators	Closed Won	$675,000.00	
	United Oil Refinery Generators	Closed Lost	$270,000.00	
Subtotal				2
Johan Yu (5 records)	Edge Emergency Generator	Id. Decision Makers	$35,000.00	
	Edge Installation	Closed Won	$50,000.00	
	Edge SLA	Closed Won	$60,000.00	
	Project Motor Head	Closed Won	$100,000.00	
	Project Motor Links in Kentica	Closed Won	$75,000.00	
Subtotal				4
GRAND TOTAL (9 RECORDS)				5

Let's analyze the preceding report; **Check Count** is a summary formula:

- For **OPPORTUNITY OWNER Alvin Lee**, since there are four record, the formula will return the number of closed opportunities for **Alvin Lee**, which is 2. In this exercise one opportunity is **Won** and one opportunity is **Lost**.
- For **OPPORTUNITY OWNER Johan Yu**, there are five records; the formula will return the number of won opportunities for **Johan Yu**, which is 4.
- For the **GRAND TOTAL**, the total records are nine; the formula will return the number of won opportunities in total, which is 5: one opportunity from **Alvin Lee** and four opportunities from **Johan Yu**.

Using the MAX() function

The MAX function is categorized as the **Math** function; the syntax for this formula is *MAX(number,number,...)*.

This function returns the greatest of all arguments, for example, `MAX(Opportunity.Projected_Revenue__c:SUM, AMOUNT:SUM)`.

The same is true with the `IF()` function explained earlier; you can just point and click to get the preceding formula populated. In this sample, we use the opportunity report type, and the `MAX()` function returns the maximum value by comparing the sum of a custom field called **PROJECTED REVENUE** with the sum of **AMOUNT**. A sample report is shown as follows:

REPORT

Opportunity Max

Total Records	Total Amount	Total Projected Revenue
9	$1,660,000.00	$1,530,000.00

OPPORTUNITY OWNER ↑	OPPORTUNITY NAME ↑	AMOUNT Sum	PROJECTED REVENUE Sum	MAX AMOUNT
Alvin Lee (4 records)	United Oil Installations	$270,000.00	$275,000.00	
	United Oil Office Portable Generators	$125,000.00	$120,000.00	
	United Oil Plant Standby Generators	$675,000.00	$500,000.00	
	United Oil Refinery Generators	$270,000.00	$300,000.00	
Subtotal		$1,340,000.00	$1,195,000.00	1,340,000
Johan Yu (5 records)	Edge Emergency Generator	$35,000.00	$40,000.00	
	Edge Installation	$50,000.00	$50,000.00	
	Edge SLA	$60,000.00	$65,000.00	
	Project Motor Head	$100,000.00	$110,000.00	
	Project Motor Links in Kentica	$75,000.00	$70,000.00	
Subtotal		$320,000.00	$335,000.00	335,000
GRAND TOTAL (9 RECORDS)		$1,660,000.00	$1,530,000.00	-

Let's analyze the preceding report; **MAX AMOUNT** is a summary formula:

- We set the **MAX AMOUNT** summary field to display only at the grouping level, and that's why it does not show in **GRAND TOTAL**

- Because this is a summary formula, it will not compare the **AMOUNT** value with the **PROJECTED REVENUE** value in record level but only compare it in the **Summary**
- For **OPPORTUNITY OWNER Alvin Lee**, **AMOUNT** is greater than **PROJECTED REVENUE**, so **MAX AMOUNT** is equal to **AMOUNT**
- For **OPPORTUNITY OWNER Johan Yu**, **PROJECTED REVENUE** is greater than **AMOUNT**, so **MAX AMOUNT** is equal to **PROJECTED REVENUE**.

Function formulas

There are two functions in Salesforce available only in the summary formula and considered the most powerful report formula. They are categorized under the Summary functions: PARENTGROUPVAL and PREVGROUPVAL.

The PARENTGROUPVAL() function

The PARENTGROUPVAL() function returns the value of a specified grouping; the grouping level is higher than the formula display level.

The formula syntax is different depending on the report format:

- In the **Summary** and **Joined** reports: *PARENTGROUPVAL(summary_field, grouping_level)*
- In the **Matrix** report: *PARENTGROUPVAL(summary_field, parent_row_grouping, parent_column_grouping)*

Using the PARENTGROUPVAL() function in Summary report

For the **Summary** report, the PARENTGROUPVAL() function is not applicable when you select the formula displayed as **All summary levels** or **Grand summary only**. The only formulas displayed as field grouping can use this function.

Next, we need to populate the value for both parameters **Summary Fields** and grouping level. Let's start with the grouping level parameter; I'll tell you why I start with grouping level instead of the **Summary Fields** parameter.

Let's look at a hands-on exercise to populate the parameters; in this exercise, we have a **Summary** report with two levels of field grouping; the first level is **OPPORTUNITY OWNER** and the second level is **TYPE**:

1. Make sure that you select the formula to be displayed as the field grouping, not all summary or grand summary; because the report has two levels of field grouping, we will have two options. They are **Grouping 1: Opportunity Owner** and **Grouping 2: Type**; let's select **Grouping 2: Type** for this exercise.

2. Place your mouse in the **Formula** editor and select the **PARENTGROUPVAL** function from the dropdown.

3. If you have only one level of field grouping in the summary report, the parent grouping_level parameter is always **GRAND_SUMMARY**, while if you have more than one level as in this exercise (two levels of grouping), we will have the option of **GRAND_SUMMARY** and **field name** of the first level grouping for the parent grouping level, which is Opportunity Owner in our exercise.

4. The field name for the first-level grouping in the parent grouping level will be enabled when the formula to be displayed is selected with the second-level grouping. In summary, the availability of the parent grouping level is one level higher than the selected formula to be displayed. Compare the following screenshots; the first one is when **Grouping 2: Type** is selected:

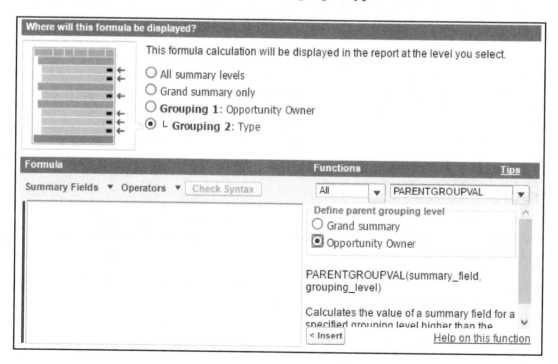

Compare this with the following screenshot. When **Grouping 1: Opportunity Owner** is selected, **Opportunity Owner** becomes disabled in the parent grouping level:

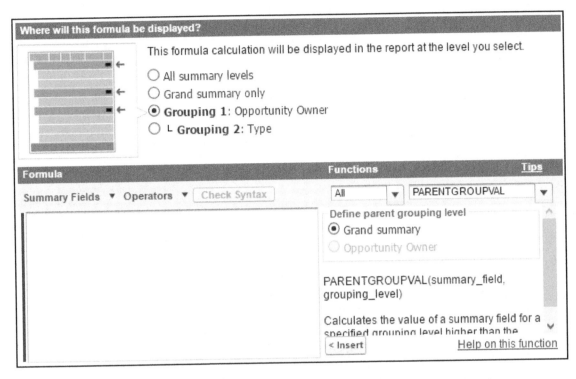

5. Let's select **Grouping 2: Type** for this exercise and select **Opportunity Owner** as the parent grouping level from the radio button.

6. Click on the **< Insert** button, and you will get the formula added in our sample here: **PARENTGROUPVAL(summary_field, FULL_NAME)**.

7. Delete the **summary_field** text and change it with the correct field summary. To populate the **summary_field** parameter, place your cursor before the comma, click on **Summary Fields**, select the field name you would like to use (for example, **Amount**), and select the action (for example, **Sum**). Now your formula should be *PARENTGROUPVAL(AMOUNT:SUM, FULL_NAME)*.

Here is the final formula. Look at the arrows in the following screenshot for the relationship between the grouping levels:

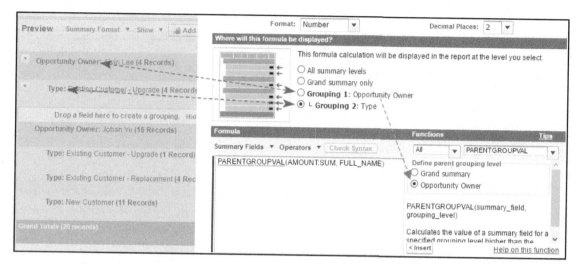

Next, let's create a new **Summary** report:

1. Group the report by **CLOSE DATE** (Group Dates by Calendar Month) and then group by **Opportunity Owner**.
2. Add a summary formula and name it **Amount by Close Date**; add this formula and display at **Opportunity Owner** (Grouping 2) with formula as *PARENTGROUPVAL(AMOUNT:SUM, CLOSE_DATE).*:
3. Add the summary formula created to the report.
4. Add the **Amount** field and summarize it with **Sum**. This is shown in the following screenshot:

CLOSE DATE ↑	OPPORTUNITY OWNER ↑	OPPORTUNITY NAME ↑	AMOUNT Sum	AMOUNT BY CLOSE DATE
June 2016 (3 records)	Alvin Lee (1 record)	Pyramid Emergency Generators	$100,000.00	
	Subtotal		$100,000.00	$265,000
	Johan Yu (2 records)	Element Stage 1A	$85,000.00	
		Element Stage 1B	$80,000.00	
	Subtotal		$165,000.00	$265,000
Subtotal			$265,000.00	-
July 2016 (3 records)	Alvin Lee (1 record)	Element Phase IIa	$38,000.00	
	Subtotal		$38,000.00	$213,000
	Johan Yu (2 records)	Project Motor Head	$100,000.00	
		Project Motor Links in Kentica	$75,000.00	
	Subtotal		$175,000.00	$213,000
Subtotal			$213,000.00	-
GRAND TOTAL (6 RECORDS)			$478,000.00	-

Let's analyze the report from the screenshot:

- In **June 2016**, Total Amount is **$265,000.00**. We see that this value is the same as the value from the summary formula; this means the value of the summary formula from one level above, which is subtotal of Close Date.
- In **July 2016**, Total Amount is **$213,000.00**, which is the same value in the summary formula.
- The value of the formula will be available in **Opportunity Owner** (which is level 2) grouping in the report, and the parent grouping level is **CLOSE_DATE**.

Next, let's create another similar formula in the same report:

1. Name is **Amount by Grand Total**.
2. Select and display the summary formula at **Opportunity Owner (Grouping 2)**.
3. Select the parent grouping level as **Grand summary**.
4. Formula is *PARENTGROUPVAL(AMOUNT:SUM, GRAND_SUMMARY)*.

CLOSE DATE ↑	OPPORTUNITY OWNER ↑	OPPORTUNITY NAME ↑	AMOUNT Sum	AMOUNT BY CLOSE DATE	AMOUNT BY GRAND TOTAL
June 2016 (3 records)	Alvin Lee (1 record)	Pyramid Emergency Generators	$100,000.00		
	Subtotal		$100,000.00	$265,000	$478,000.00
	Johan Yu (2 records)	Element Stage 1A	$85,000.00		
		Element Stage 1B	$80,000.00		
	Subtotal		$165,000.00	$265,000	$478,000.00
Subtotal			$265,000.00		
July 2016 (3 records)	Alvin Lee (1 record)	Element Phase IIa	$38,000.00		
	Subtotal		$38,000.00	$213,000	$478,000.00
	Johan Yu (2 records)	Project Motor Head	$100,000.00		
		Project Motor Links in Kentica	$75,000.00		
	Subtotal		$175,000.00	$213,000	$478,000.00
Subtotal			$213,000.00		
GRAND TOTAL (6 RECORDS)			$478,000.00		

Let's analyze the preceding screenshot:

- Note that the summary formula value is the same as the value of **GRAND TOTAL**.
- The summary formula is shown in the **Opportunity Owner** grouping, which is the Grouping 2 we configured, and the value is a copy from **GRAND_SUMMARY** (this is two levels above **Opportunity Owner** in the hierarchy).
- However, if you change the formula to show in **Close Date** (Grouping 1), the value would be the same from **GRAND TOTAL** (this is one level above Close Date). Refer to the following screenshot:

CLOSE DATE ↑	OPPORTUNITY OWNER ↑	OPPORTUNITY NAME ↑	AMOUNT Sum	AMOUNT BY CLOSE DATE	AMOUNT BY GRAND TOTAL
June 2016 (3 records)	Alvin Lee (1 record)	Pyramid Emergency Generators	$100,000.00		
	Subtotal		$100,000.00	$265,000	-
	Johan Yu (2 records)	Element Stage 1A	$85,000.00		
		Element Stage 1B	$80,000.00		
	Subtotal		$165,000.00	$265,000	-
Subtotal			$265,000.00	-	$478,000.00
July 2016 (3 records)	Alvin Lee (1 record)	Element Phase IIa	$38,000.00		
	Subtotal		$38,000.00	$213,000	-
	Johan Yu (2 records)	Project Motor Head	$100,000.00		
		Project Motor Links in Kentica	$75,000.00		
	Subtotal		$175,000.00	$213,000	-
Subtotal			$213,000.00	-	$478,000.00
GRAND TOTAL (6 RECORDS)			$478,000.00		-

From the preceding examples, we can easily understand that the PARENTGROUPVAL() function gets the summary value from one or more levels above, and that's why it is called **parent group value**.

Next, let's use the PARENTGROUPVAL() function in real actions; we would like to know the percentage of total opportunity for each month compared to the total. For sure, you can't do this without a custom summary formula, and here is the report result:

CLOSE DATE ↑	OPPORTUNITY OWNER ↑	RECORD COUNT	AMOUNT Sum	% OF TOTAL
June 2016	Alvin Lee	1	$100,000.00	-
	Johan Yu	2	$165,000.00	-
Subtotal		3	$265,000.00	55.44%
July 2016	Alvin Lee	1	$38,000.00	-
	Johan Yu	2	$175,000.00	-
Subtotal		3	$213,000.00	44.56%
GRAND TOTAL		6	$478,000.00	-

The subtotal for **June 2016** is **55.44%**; this is calculated by *265,000 / 478,000*100*. The same is for **July 2016** which is **44.56%**, which is calculated by *213,000 / 478,000*100*. The formula behind this is pretty simple and not much different from the one we used earlier: *AMOUNT:SUM / PARENTGROUPVAL(AMOUNT:SUM, GRAND_SUMMARY)*; in short, this formula will divide the monthly subtotal by the **GRAND TOTAL**.

Using the PARENTGROUPVAL() function in the Matrix report

In the **Matrix** report, the syntax for this function is *PARENTGROUPVAL(summary_field, parent_row_grouping, parent_column_grouping)*.

The same is true with the **Summary** report; the `PARENTGROUPVAL()` function is not applicable when you select the formula displayed as **All summary levels**. This function is applicable only when you select **At a specific row/column grouping level.**...

The grouping level parameter in the **Summary** report is split into two parameters in the **Matrix** report: **parent_row_grouping and parent_column_grouping**.

Let's create a new Opportunity report with the **Matrix** format, filter the report by **Close Date** of 3 months, and then group by **Calendar Month (column)** and **Stage (row)**. Refer the following screenshot:

	CLOSE DATE	APRIL 2016	MAY 2016	JUNE 2016	Total
STAGE		AMOUNT Sum	AMOUNT Sum	AMOUNT Sum	AMOUNT Sum
Prospecting		$0.00	$0.00	$80,000.00	$80,000.00
Qualification		$0.00	$0.00	$100,000.00	$100,000.00
Id. Decision Makers		$0.00	$50,000.00	$0.00	$50,000.00
Closed Won		$60,000.00	$0.00	$85,000.00	$145,000.00
Closed Lost		$270,000.00	$0.00	$0.00	$270,000.00
Total		$330,000.00	$50,000.00	$265,000.00	$645,000.00

Let's consider a use case: we would like to know the percentage of each Stage compared to the **GRAND TOTAL**:

1. Create a formula summary called `Total Amount` and show it in **Column Grand Summary**. Refer the following screenshot:

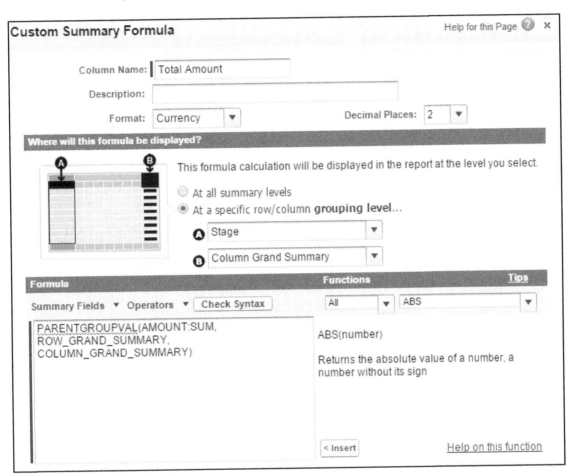

Do not worry about how to get the keyword for the parameters; refer to the hands-on exercise in PARENTGROUPVAL() for the preceding **Summary** report; when you click on the **< Insert** button, the keyword will be automatically populated; then, add **AMOUNT:SUM** as **summary_field**. Run the report and you should see your report as something similar to what is shown in the following screenshot:

STAGE	CLOSE DATE APRIL 2016 AMOUNT Sum	TOTAL AMOUNT	MAY 2016 AMOUNT Sum	TOTAL AMOUNT	JUNE 2016 AMOUNT Sum	TOTAL AMOUNT	Total AMOUNT Sum	TOTAL AMOUNT
Prospecting	$0.00		$0.00		$80,000.00		$80,000.00	$645,000.00
Qualification	$0.00		$0.00		$100,000.00		$100,000.00	$645,000.00
Id. Decision Makers	$0.00		$50,000.00		$0.00		$50,000.00	$645,000.00
Closed Won	$60,000.00		$0.00		$85,000.00		$145,000.00	$645,000.00
Closed Lost	$270,000.00		$0.00		$0.00		$270,000.00	$645,000.00
Total	$330,000.00		$50,000.00		$265,000.00		$645,000.00	

The **TOTAL AMOUNT** column here does not have much meaning; it just copies **GRAND TOTAL** to **TOTAL AMOUNT** for each stage, while we would like to know the percentage of each **Stage** compared to **GRAND TOTAL**.

2. Edit the report and change the summary formula:
   - Change the format to **Percent**
   - Change the formula to *AMOUNT:SUM / PARENTGROUPVAL (AMOUNT:SUM, ROW_GRAND_SUMMARY, COLUMN_GRAND_SUMMARY)*

So, we are dividing **Column Total** to **GRAND TOTAL** and showing the percentage. Here is the report:

STAGE	CLOSE DATE APRIL 2016 AMOUNT Sum	TOTAL AMOUNT	MAY 2016 AMOUNT Sum	TOTAL AMOUNT	JUNE 2016 AMOUNT Sum	TOTAL AMOUNT	Total AMOUNT Sum	TOTAL AMOUNT
Prospecting	$0.00		$0.00		$80,000.00		$80,000.00	12.40%
Qualification	$0.00		$0.00		$100,000.00		$100,000.00	15.50%
Id. Decision Makers	$0.00		$50,000.00		$0.00		$50,000.00	7.75%
Closed Won	$60,000.00		$0.00		$85,000.00		$145,000.00	22.48%
Closed Lost	$270,000.00		$0.00		$0.00		$270,000.00	41.86%
Total	$330,000.00		$50,000.00		$265,000.00		$645,000.00	

With a simple change to **Custom Summary Formula**, you can move the formula to **Row Grand Summary** to get a percentage for each month by comparing it to **GRAND TOTAL**:

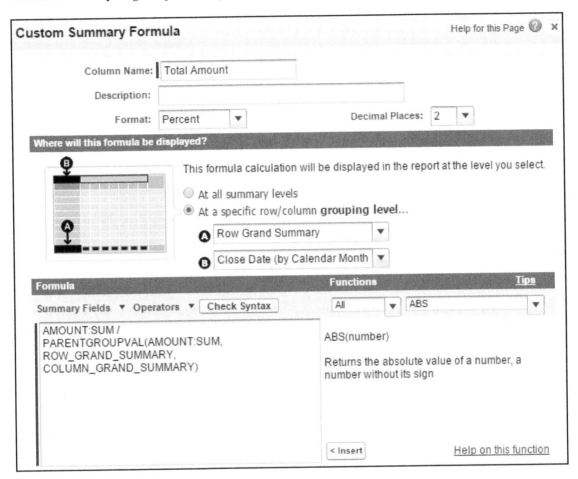

Notice that A and B have changed; the formula stays the same, and here is the report:

CLOSE DATE	APRIL 2016		MAY 2016		JUNE 2016		Total	
STAGE	AMOUNT Sum	TOTAL AMOUNT	AMOUNT Sum	TOTAL AMOUNT	AMOUNT Sum	TOTAL AMOUNT	AMOUNT Sum	TOTAL AMOUNT
Prospecting	$0.00		$0.00		$80,000.00		$80,000.00	
Qualification	$0.00		$0.00		$100,000.00		$100,000.00	
Id. Decision Makers	$0.00		$50,000.00		$0.00		$50,000.00	
Closed Won	$60,000.00		$0.00		$85,000.00		$145,000.00	
Closed Lost	$270,000.00		$0.00		$0.00		$270,000.00	
Total	$330,000.00	51.16%	$50,000.00	7.75%	$265,000.00	41.09%	$645,000.00	

This report shows the percentage of the total amount for each month compared to the **GRAND TOTAL**.

The PREVGROUPVAL() function

The PREVGROUPVAL() function returns the value of the previous grouping on the same hierarchy level. This allows you to prepare reports that show, for example, the month-to-month opportunity comparison; the main difference with the PARENTGROUPVAL() function is the return value from the higher hierarchy level.

The formula syntax for the PARENTGROUPVAL() function is the same for all report formats: *PREVGROUPVAL(summary_field, grouping_level [, increment]).*

There is not much difference in the navigation and tips to get the formula parameters for the PARENTGROUPVAL() function compared to the PARENTGROUPVAL() function. The only difference in the syntax is an additional optional parameter **incremental**. If we skip this parameter, it will use the default value, which is **1**. The increment is the number of columns or rows before the current summary; the minimum and the default value is **1**, while the maximum is **12**.

Although the syntax is almost similar to the PARENTGROUPVAL() function, the functionality is totally different. Both functions serve a different purpose to make our report powerful.

The same is the case with the PARENTGROUPVAL() function; this function is not applicable when you opt to display this formula: At **All summary levels**, **Grand summary only**. It will work only for field level groupings for the **Summary** report and **specific row/column grouping level** for the **Matrix** report.

To get the keyword for the parameter in the `PREVGROUPVAL()` function, perform the following steps:

- Select **PREVGROUPVAL** from the drop-down function menu
- For the **Summary** report, just like **PARENTGROUPVAL**, you can select the field under eligible grouping levels; if you have more than one level of grouping, we will see this the detail later in the hands-on exercise
- Click on the **< Insert** button; you will get the formula created with the parameters selected, for example, *PREVGROUPVAL (summary_field, CLOSE_DATE)*
- Click on **Summary Fields** and select the field you want and the action, for example, **AMOUNT:SUM**
- The increment parameter will not be added by default when you click on **< Insert** button; you can add it manually when needed

Using the PREVGROUPVAL() function in Summary report

Let's create a **Summary** report:

1. Use the **Opportunity** report type.
2. Group by **Stage** and **Close Date** (Group Dates by **Calendar Month**).
3. Add the summary formula and name it `Prev Month Won` with this formula: *PREVGROUPVAL(AMOUNT:SUM, CLOSE_DATE)*.
4. In this exercise, I'll filter the report to show the only Opportunity for 2 months of **Close Date**; This is only for simplicity in order to reduce data in the report, see the following screenshot for details:

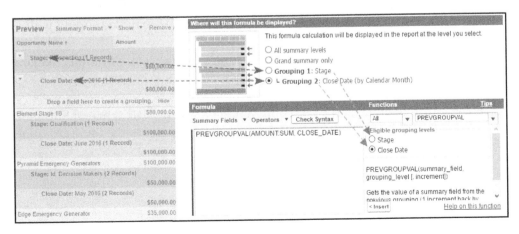

5. Add the formula summary to the **Summary** report.

6. Add the **Amount** field and summarize it with **Sum**. You would see something similar to this report:

STAGE ↑	CLOSE DATE ↑	OPPORTUNITY NAME ↑	AMOUNT Sum	PREV MONTH WON
Prospecting	May 2016	Element Stage 1A	$85,000.00	
		Grand Hotels Kitchen Generator	$15,000.00	
	Subtotal		$100,000.00	-
	June 2016	Element Stage 1B	$80,000.00	
	Subtotal		$80,000.00	$100,000.00
Subtotal			$180,000.00	-
Qualification	June 2016	Pyramid Emergency Generators	$90,000.00	
	Subtotal		$90,000.00	$80,000.00
Subtotal			$90,000.00	-
Id. Decision Makers	May 2016	Edge Emergency Generator	$35,000.00	
	Subtotal		$35,000.00	$90,000.00
Subtotal			$35,000.00	-

Let's analyze the preceding report:

- The first subtotal is **Prospecting** for **May 2016**, the total **Subtotal** is **$100,000.00** because this is the first grouping, so there is no value return by the PREVGROUPVAL() function

- The second subtotal is **Prospecting** for **June 2016**, the total **Subtotal** is **$80,000.00**; now the PARENTGROUPVAL() function will point to the first grouping with **$100,000.00**

- The third subtotal is **Qualification** for **June 2016**, the total **Subtotal** is **$90,000.00**, the PARENTGROUPVAL() function will point to the second grouping with **$80,000.00**

- The fourth Subtotal is **ID. Decision Makers** for **May 2016**, the total **Subtotal** is **$35,000.00**; the PARENTGROUPVAL() function will point to the third grouping with **$90,000.00**

What we have just seen is based on the grouping order, not based on the value of the grouping.

Let's make a minor change from existing report to the formula, from *PREVGROUPVAL(AMOUNT:SUM, CLOSE_DATE)* to *PREVGROUPVAL(AMOUNT:SUM, STAGE_NAME)*, see the following screenshot:

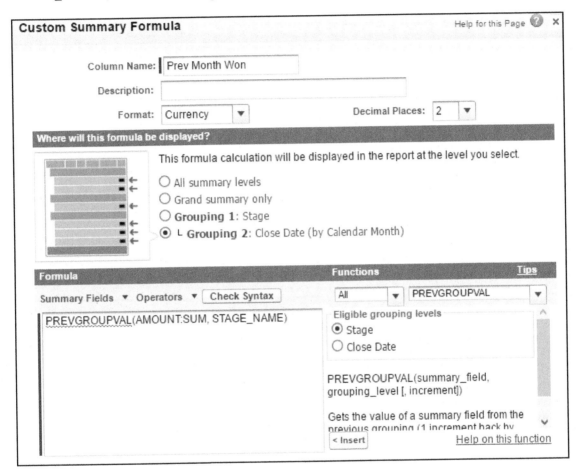

Here is the report generated; compare it with the earlier result:

STAGE ↑	CLOSE DATE ↑	OPPORTUNITY NAME ↑	AMOUNT Sum	PREV MONTH WON
Prospecting (3 records)	May 2016 (2 records)	Element Stage 1A	$85,000.00	
		Grand Hotels Kitchen Generator	$15,000.00	
	Subtotal		$100,000.00	-
	June 2016 (1 record)	Element Stage 1B	$80,000.00	
	Subtotal		$80,000.00	-
Subtotal			$180,000.00	-
Qualification (1 record)	June 2016 (1 record)	Pyramid Emergency Generators	$90,000.00	
	Subtotal		$90,000.00	$180,000.00
Subtotal			$90,000.00	-
Id. Decision Makers (1 record)	May 2016 (1 record)	Edge Emergency Generator	$35,000.00	
	Subtotal		$35,000.00	$90,000.00
Subtotal			$35,000.00	-

The difference here is that the previous group value will come from the **STAGE Subtotal** instead of the **Close Date Subtotal**, as shown in the earlier report.

Next, let's use the earlier formula and add an increment parameter with 2; the formula changes from *PREVGROUPVAL(AMOUNT:SUM, CLOSE_DATE)* to *PREVGROUPVAL(AMOUNT:SUM, CLOSE_DATE, 2)*. The following screenshot shows a **Summary** report with the PREVGROUPVAL formula:

STAGE ↑	CLOSE DATE ↑	OPPORTUNITY NAME ↑	AMOUNT Sum	PREV MONTH WON
Prospecting (3 records)	May 2016 (2 records)	Element Stage 1A	$85,000.00	
		Grand Hotels Kitchen Generator	$15,000.00	
	Subtotal		$100,000.00	-
	June 2016 (1 record)	Element Stage 1B	$80,000.00	
	Subtotal		$80,000.00	-
Subtotal			$180,000.00	-
Qualification (1 record)	June 2016 (1 record)	Pyramid Emergency Generators	$90,000.00	
	Subtotal		$90,000.00	$100,000.00
Subtotal			$90,000.00	-
Id. Decision Makers (1 record)	May 2016 (1 record)	Edge Emergency Generator	$35,000.00	
	Subtotal		$35,000.00	$80,000.00
Subtotal			$35,000.00	-

In the preceding report, note that the total **PREV MONTH WON** will get a value from two previous subtotals because we add the incremental parameter with 2.

Let's look at one more sample with a **Summary** report and use the `PARENTGROUPVAL()` function:

CLOSE DATE ↑	RECORD COUNT	AMOUNT Sum	PREV MONTH AMOUNT
June 2016	2	$170,000.00	-
July 2016	3	$213,000.00	$170,000.00
September 2016	2	$355,000.00	$213,000.00
October 2016	1	$440,000.00	$355,000.00
GRAND TOTAL	8	$1,178,000.00	-

The preceding report does not have a value for August 2016; the `PREVGROUPVAL()` function will not know if any month is missing or a value has been jumped, so in **Summary**, the value returned from the `PREVGROUPVAL()` function is not based on the value in the group but only based on the value of the previous group order.

Using the PREVGROUPVAL() function in Matrix report

Let's use the PREVGROUPVAL() function in the Matrix report.

We would like to know the percentage of growth for **Total Amount** for each month:

1. Create a **Matrix** report and group by **Close Date** (by **Calendar Month**) as the row grouping and **Stage** as the column grouping.
2. Hide **Remove Count**, and hide **Details**. Filter only **Open** and **Won** opportunities.
3. Create a formula summary called Month by Month; group it as **Closed Date** (by **Calendar Month**) and **Column Grand Summary**.
4. Set the summary format to **Percent** with two decimal points.
5. Enter this formula: (AMOUNT:SUM - PREVGROUPVAL(AMOUNT:SUM, CLOSE_DATE)) / PREVGROUPVAL(AMOUNT:SUM, CLOSE_DATE):

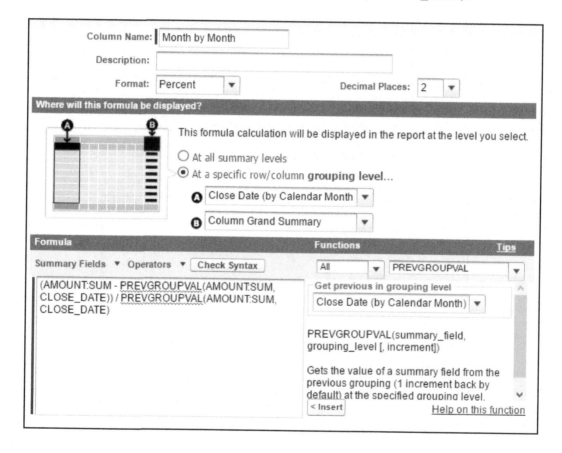

The summary formula will be added next to amount subtotal for each month; from here, we can easily check the month by month percentage and see that it increases for all Open and Won Opportunities:

STAGE	QUALIFICATION		ID. DECISION MAKERS		CLOSED WON		Total	
	AMOUNT		AMOUNT		AMOUNT		AMOUNT	
CLOSE DATE	Sum	MONTH BY MONTH	Sum	MONTH BY MONTH	Sum	MONTH BY MONTH	Sum	MONTH BY MONTH
March 2016	$0.00		$15,000.00		$22,000.00		$37,000.00	-
April 2016	$27,000.00		$0.00		$40,000.00		$67,000.00	81.08%
May 2016	$55,000.00		$50,000.00		$0.00		$105,000.00	56.72%
June 2016	$80,000.00		$10,000.00		$0.00		$90,000.00	-14.29%
Total	$162,000.00		$75,000.00		$62,000.00		$299,000.00	

Note that there are no value shown in the formula for March 2016 because it is the first value. In **April 2016**, an increase of **81.08%** is compared to the previous group, which is **March 2016**. **May 2014** sees an increase of **56.72%** compared to **April 2016**, and the last group shows a **-14.29%** decrease compared to the group earlier. As mentioned earlier, the PREVGROUPVAL() function will not know the value of the previous group. In this sample, it just shows nicely because there is no skipped month in the report.

Summary

In this chapter, we explored the bucket fields and **Custom Summary Formulas** in detail. With the bucket field, we can categorize data for report purpose, and nothing needs to be done on the field in the object. This will eliminate the admin right to create a custom field, and if that field only serves for one or two reports. However, bucket fields are not used to replace formula fields; you can't have a formula calculation in the bucket field; you can have it to group values into a bucket.

Bucket fields only work for certain field types, and different field types will have different ways configured for the bucket value; you can use the range for currency, number, and percentage but not for others.

The **Custom Summary Formula** is not the same as a custom formula field. You can't retrieve a value from another object using a **Custom Summary Formula**, and a **Custom Summary Formula** only lives in that report; it does not affect another report, object, or field, and you can't use it from other reports.

A **Custom Summary Formula** is not available in the **Tabular** report and when you change the report type with the summary formula, the existing summary formula will be deleted, so be aware of this.

There are many functions available in **Custom Summary Formulas**; the value will be returned as a number, currency, or percentage only, and you can configure the decimal place returned. The formula accepts a limited type of field only, but this includes the formula field and the roll-up summary field.

The PARENTGROUPVAL() and PREVGROUPVAL() functions are available only in **Custom Summary Formulas**. You can't find them in another formula in Salesforce; they are very powerful functions. You can use the PARENTGROUPVAL() function to retrieve the group value from the parent group hierarchy and use the PREVGROUPVAL() function to retrieve the value from the previous group in the same level of the hierarchy.

In the next chapter, we will discuss more features related to reporting, adding a chart to a report, and embedding a chart from a report into the parent record page.

Adding Charts in Reports and Pages

7

Starting from Chapter 4, *Creating and Managing Reports*, you learned to create and manage reports, continued with report types in Chapter 5, *Understanding Report Types*, and then used bucket fields and **Custom Summary Formula** in Chapter 6, *Advanced Report Configuration*.

In this chapter, we will continue by adding a chart to a report, and we will discuss multiple types of charts available in Salesforce Lightning and the types of report formats that support the addition of a chart, and we will walk through at a hands-on exercise on adding and working with charts in a report.

Next, we will discuss how to add the chart from the report to the record page, for example, opportunities or cases related to an account in an account page; the chart here will be filtered by the account opened, and we will also cover a hands-on exercise on this.

By end of this chapter, you will be fully equipped with knowledge of the types of charts in a report and will learn how to add and edit charts. You will also understand how to add charts in a report to the record page layout.

Throughout this chapter, we will provide notes and tips to help you understand important items. The following topics will be covered:

- Types of charts in a Lightning report
- Adding a chart to a report
- Adding embedded charts to the record page

Adding a chart to a report

Adding a chart to a report is a good practice; the audience will get a quick glimpse of the report's content and will find it easy to understand the data with visualization. You can add a chart to any type of report format except a **Tabular** report. However, the **Tabular** report with **Row Limit** and **Dashboard Settings** allows the report to be used as a data source report for dashboard. We will discuss dashboards in Chapter 9, *Building Dashboards in Lightning Experience*.

 You can add only one chart for a report, no matter what the chart type is. **Tabular** reports do not support charts.

If you are switching from Classic, you need to be in the report builder by editing/customizing the report when you would like to add a chart in a report or modify an existing chart in Classic. However, the whole concept is changed in Lightning; you add or modify an existing chart when you view the report; in fact, you cannot add or modify a chart while creating or editing a report in the report builder.

Another difference with Classic is that a chart created is locked based on the user who configures the chart in the report builder, while in Lightning, every user can add or change the chart when they view the report, even the users who do not have permission to create reports. However, users who are able to edit the report will be able to save the changes, including charts added or modified. If you migrate from Classic, you don't need to worry about the existing charts added; they will work nicely in Lightning.

Here is a summary of changes related to charts in reports between Classic and Lightning:

Action	Classic	Lightning
Add or edit chart	From the report builder (need to edit the report)	When the report runs (the view mode).
Change chart or hide chart when running report	Not possible; chart is locked.	Users are able to change the chart as they want, including hiding a chart added in the report.
Add chart when running report	Not possible; the added chart must be from report builder.	Users are able to add charts by themselves, even for users who do not have permission to edit the report. If the user does not have permission to edit the report, they cannot save the added or edited chart.

Types of charts in reports

There are eight types of charts available in Salesforce Lightning reports. Note that a chart in reports is not the same as the dashboard component. We will discuss dashboards in Chapter 9, *Building Dashboards in Lightning Experience*.

Each chart format has its own extra features, such as an inline chart, and you can enable the cumulative value; in a stacked bar chart, you can set all bar lengths to 100%, and so on.

Let's understand each type of chart available in Salesforce.

The Horizontal Bar chart

The Horizontal Bar chart shows values as horizontal lengths, so this format is good for comparing values. Select a Horizontal Bar Chart format when you have many values on the y-axis, for example, a pipeline report based on **Sum of Amount** and **Sum of NRR Amount** for each sales representative. If we have 20 sales representatives, the charts will still look good and not be too crowded.

When you hover your mouse above the chart, it will show you more detailed information of the bar, including the x-axis value, the y-axis value, and the percentage of the bar compared to the total. See the following screenshot for a Horizontal bar chart, including information popup when you hovering the mouse over a bar:

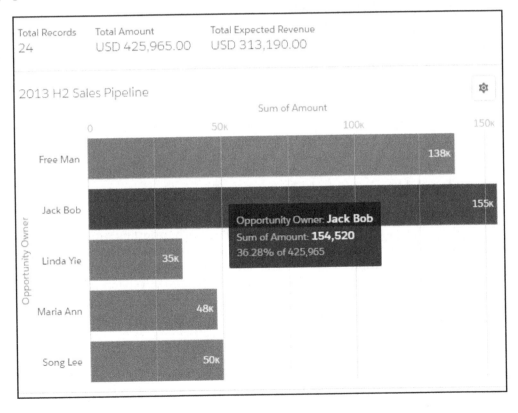

The Vertical Bar chart

The Vertical Bar chart is similar to the Horizontal Bar chart. This chart is useful when the number of groupings is not too high, such as Calendar Month in a Year. Just like with the Horizontal Bar chart, here too you can add multiple bars based on the summarizing field in the reports. You can hover your mouse to see the details of each bar here too. The following is a sample screenshot taken from a Pipeline report, with Vertical Bar chart grouped by Close Date Month and Opportunity Owner:

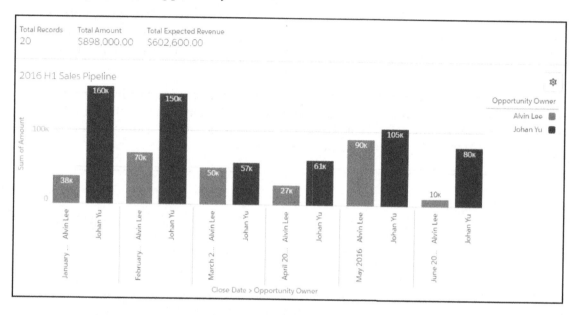

The Stacked Horizontal Bar chart

Use a stacked bar chart when you have multiple groupings and are interested in the proportions between values in each grouping as well as each grouping's total. The chart displays a single bar for each status, broken down by campaign, with each campaign shown in a different color. For example, to compare an Open Pipeline by Stage in a report, set the total amount as the x- axis and the calendar months as the y-axis. When you hover your mouse over a group in a chart, it will show the x-axis, the y-axis, and the group information. The following chart is a Horizontal bar chart grouped by Close Date Month and Stage:

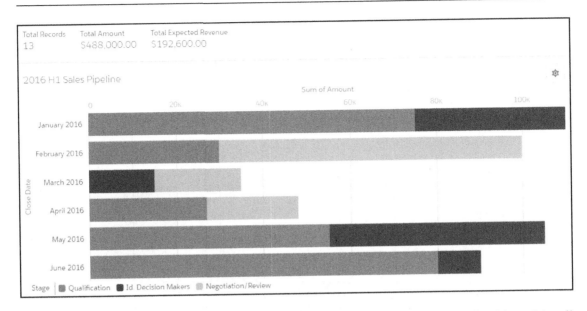

With a Stacked Bar Chart, you will have the option to set **Stack** to **100%**; by enabling this, all bars will have the same length. The preceding Horizontal bar chart if modified to Horizontal Stacked Bar chart will be as shown in the following screenshot:

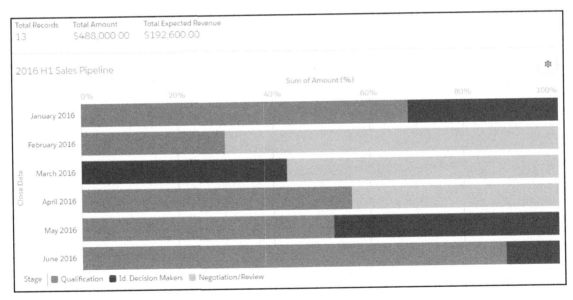

The Stacked Vertical Bar chart

The Stacked Vertical Bar chart is pretty much the same as the Stacked Horizontal Bar chart. It will change the bar to vertical, and the x-axis and the y-axis are swapped. The following screenshot is the same as the preceding one, but is a Vertical stacked bar chart:

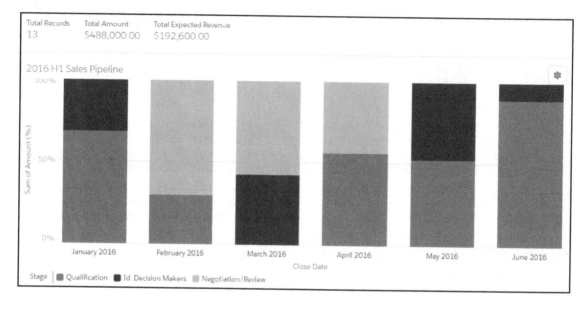

The Line chart

A Line chart is good for showing changes in the values of an item over a series of points in time. Following is a sample of Opportunity line chart grouped by Opportunity Owner:

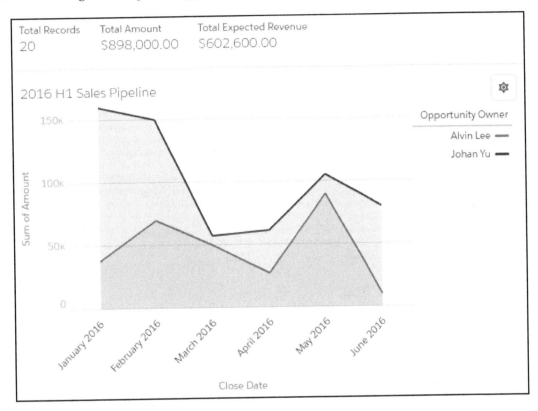

You can configure a Line chart to show as Cumulative; this is a good option when you would like to show the total number of items over a period of time. The following screenshot shows a Line chart with cumulative values:

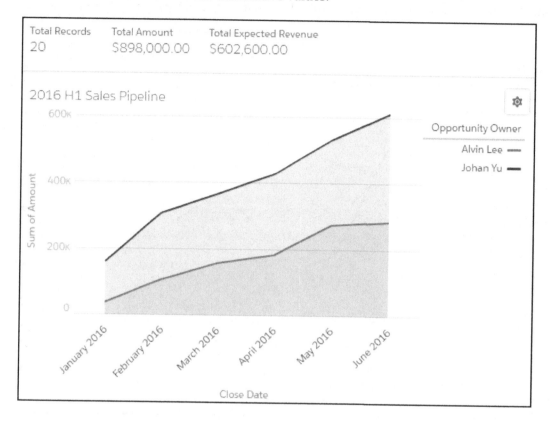

The Donut chart

With the Donut chart, the user is able to see the biggest portion and the smallest portion at a glance; on top of that, it shows the total amount and the amount for each group, for example, the pipeline report by stage with the total value. Just like the stacked bar chart, when you hover your mouse over the group, it will show you the group name and the group amount. The following sample shows a Donut chart with groups by month of Close Date:

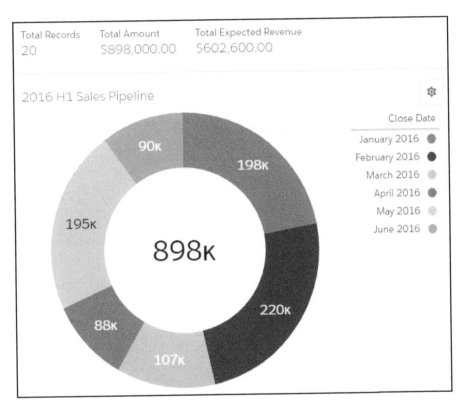

The Funnel chart

The Funnel chart is good for showing values of groups in an order based on a grouping field. For example, see the following sample screenshot for the total value of each Opportunity Stage with the order of the Sales Process:

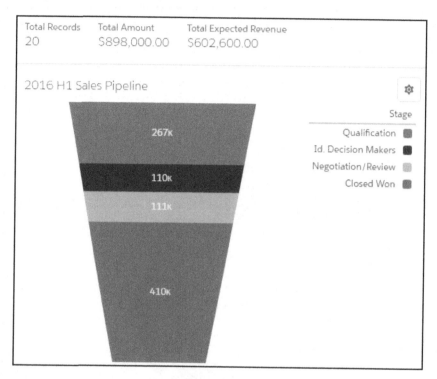

The Scatter chart

The Scatter chart shows data grouped by summarized values, so you need to have at least one grouping in your report, and each dot will represent a group summary too. For example, the Scatter chart will show Opportunity Pipeline by Amount and also by the number of quantity within a month and also by Opportunity Owner. You can hover your mouse over the dot to get detailed information. See the following sample showing Scatter chart with information when hovering the mouse over a dot:

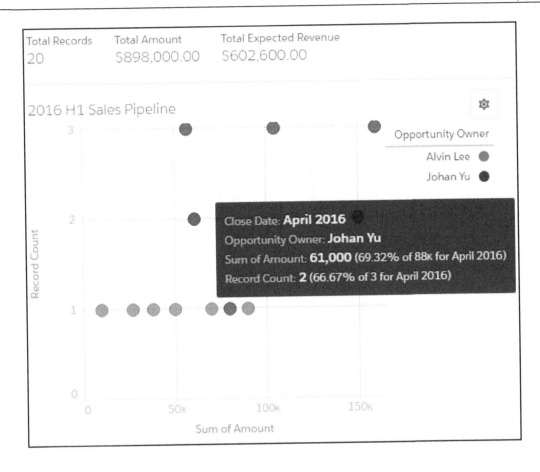

Total Records
20

Total Amount
$898,000.00

Total Expected Revenue
$602,600.00

2016 H1 Sales Pipeline

Opportunity Owner

Alvin Lee ●
Johan Yu ●

Close Date: **April 2016**
Opportunity Owner: **Johan Yu**
Sum of Amount: **61,000** (69.32% of 88k for April 2016)
Record Count: **2** (66.67% of 3 for April 2016)

Record Count

Sum of Amount

Hands-on exercise for adding a chart to a report

In this exercise, we will create an **Opportunity** report group by Opportunity **Stage** in the **Summary** format. Let's walk through the steps:

1. Navigate to the **Reports** tab and click on the **New Report** button.
2. Select the **Opportunities** report type and click on the plus sign under the **Opportunities** category.
3. Click on the **Create** button to continue.
4. Change **Show** to **All opportunities**.
5. Change the **Date Field Range** to **Previous FY**.

6. Click on the **Remove All Columns** link to clear all default fields added to a report and then click on the **OK** button to confirm.
7. Change the report format to **Summary.**
8. Drag these fields into the report: **Opportunity Name, Amount**, and **Expected Revenue**. To find the field name quickly, type the field name in the field textbox and double-click on the field to get it added to the report.
9. Drag the **Stage** field to the grouping drop zone.
10. Summarize **Amount** and **Expected Revenue** with **Sum.**
11. Click on **Show** and then click on **Details** to hide the report details.
12. Click on the **Save** button and enter the following information:
    - Report Name is `Previous FY Opportunities by Stage`
    - Report Folder is **My Personal Custom Reports**
    - Click on the **Save** button
    - Click on the **Run Report** button

13. You should see something similar to what is shown in the following screenshot; this is a standard Salesforce report:

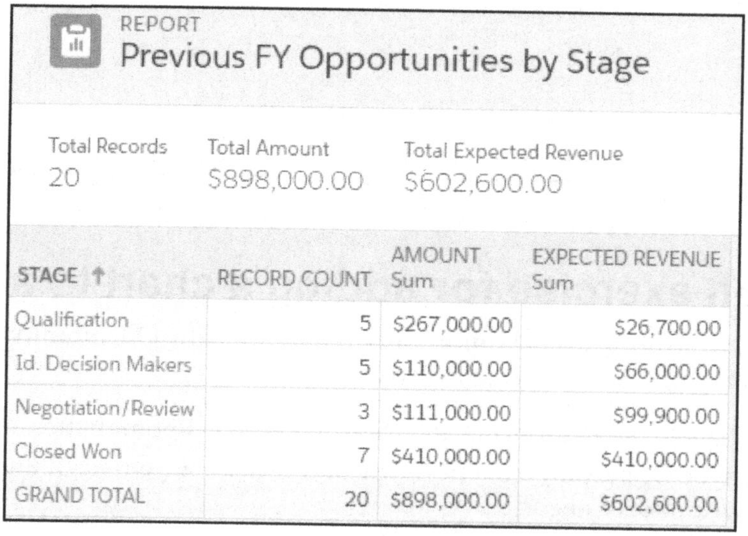

REPORT
Previous FY Opportunities by Stage

Total Records	Total Amount	Total Expected Revenue
20	$898,000.00	$602,600.00

STAGE ↑	RECORD COUNT	AMOUNT Sum	EXPECTED REVENUE Sum
Qualification	5	$267,000.00	$26,700.00
Id. Decision Makers	5	$110,000.00	$66,000.00
Negotiation/Review	3	$111,000.00	$99,900.00
Closed Won	7	$410,000.00	$410,000.00
GRAND TOTAL	20	$898,000.00	$602,600.00

14. Now we are going to add a chart to this report; click on the pie chart icon in the top-right section next to the report name; by default, it will generate a Horizontal bar chart:

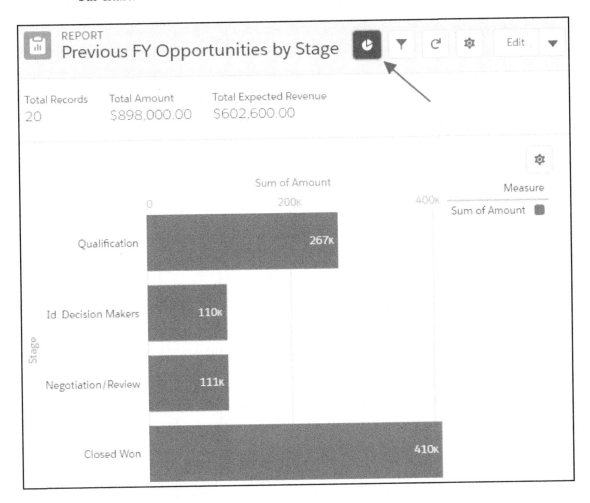

15. If you are happy with this chart, click on **Save** under the arrow next to the **Edit** button:

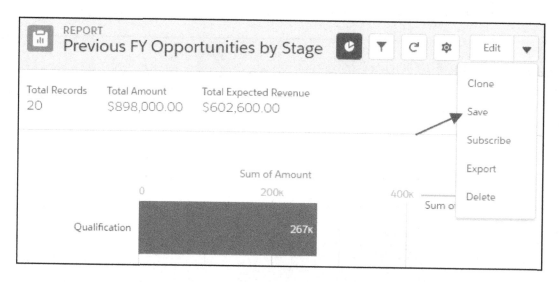

16. Let's customize this chart as a **Donut** chart.

17. Click on the gear icon, the one just above the chart on the right-hand side, not the gear icon next to the **Edit** button:

- Under **Display As**, select **Donut**.
- Add **Chart Title** as `Previous FY Opportunity`.
- Under **Value**, we can select **Sum of Amount**, **Sum of Expected Revenue**, and **Record Count**; remember that in Step 10, we use the sum for both fields; for now, just leave it is **Sum of Amount**.
- Under **Sliced By**, you can change the chart color by clicking on the color icon.
- By default, **Show Values** is ticked; let's leave it as it is.
- You can select to display **Legend Position** on the right-hand side or at the bottom. This is shown in the following screenshot:

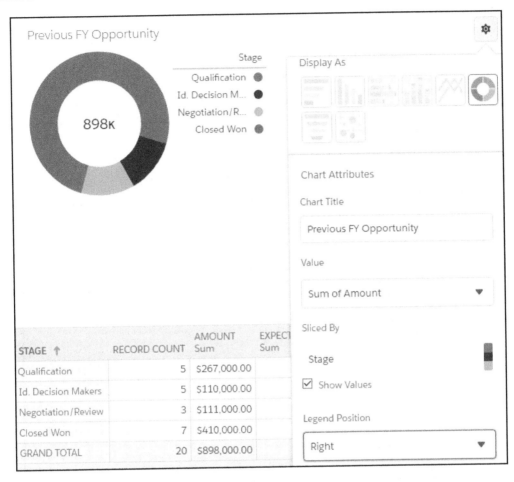

18. Click anywhere in the chart to show the result. Remember to save the report. This will include the chart that we just configured; otherwise, the added chart will not be stored and will not be there when you or someone else opens the report in the future.

19. Now let's save the report as a new report and change the chart format to **Line**.

20. Click on the **Edit** button, click on the **Save As** button, Report Name as `Previous FY Opportunities by Stage /Line`, and continue by clicking on the **Save and Run Report** button.

21. Click on the gear icon in the report; if you hover over the icon, it will show a pop-up label--**Edit Chart**.

22. Select the line icon; leave all values as it is and just tick the Cumulative checkbox.

23. Click anywhere in a report to close the **Edit Chart** panel.

24. The report will be shown immediately; don't forget to save the report again for the new Line chart:

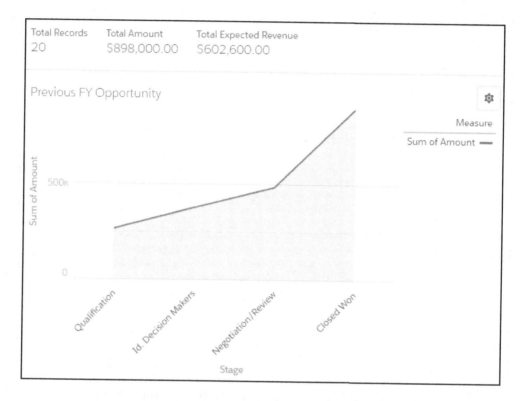

25. Next, let's modify the report to have a second grouping of **Opportunity Owner**. Click on the **Edit** button and drag **Opportunity Owner** into a grouping zone under **Stage**.

26. Click on the **Run Report** button; you should now see **Opportunity Owner** added as the second level grouping after **Stage**.

27. Click on the gear icon in the report, scroll to the bottom in the **Edit Chart** panel, take note of the **Add** drop-down, and then select **Group**.

28. Because we only have only one additional group, **Opportunity Owner**, it will be added by default. Consider the following screenshot:

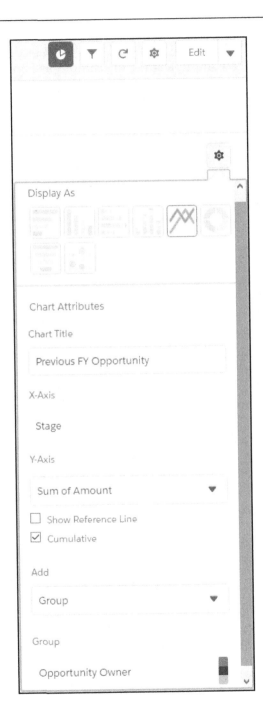

29. Click anywhere in a report to close the **Edit Chart** panel.
30. Now you should see multiple lines; my sample, as I only have two owners, so it just shows two lines. Remember to click on **Save** to save the report changes. Consider the following screenshot:

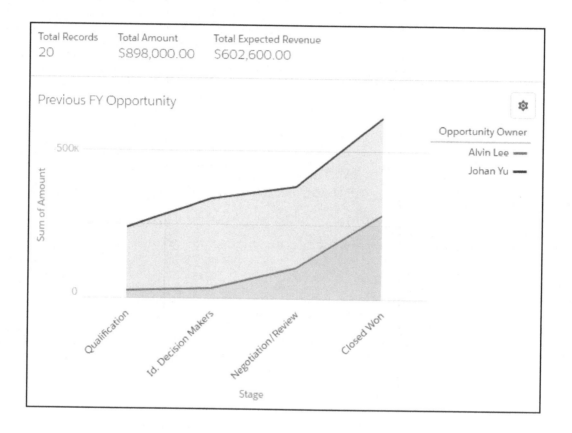

Embedding a report chart in an object page

Wouldn't it be nice if you could present in the chart all opportunities for an account, directly on the **Account** page and group by **Opportunity Stage**? The same is having a chart showing tickets raised by the account related to Customer Support on the **Account** page, or for other custom objects. This is a great feature out-of-the-box from Salesforce for embedding report charts into standard or custom object pages.

Instead of showing all records based on the standard report result, embedded charts allow us to filter only records related to the record or record the parent record in the page layout, for example, on the **Account** page, only opportunities related to the account. By looking at the chart here, the user will quickly see all **Opportunities** for the **Account** at a glance:

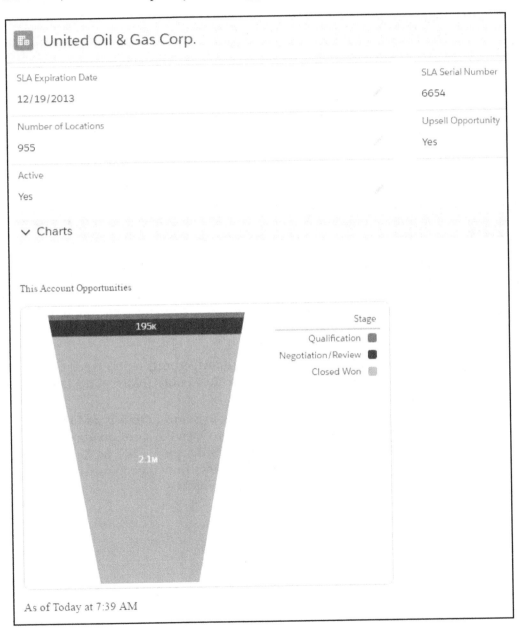

Some points to note in relation to the embedded chart in the record page are as follows:

- To add the chart to the page layout, you need to edit the page layout so only admins or users with the **Customize Application** permission are able to perform this
- You can only add up to two charts in a page layout
- The chart shown on the record page is based on the chart added in the **Summary** or **Matrix** report
- You cannot modify the chart type in the page layout
- You can set the chart to auto-refresh when the user opens the page layout
- When the user clicks on the chart in the page layout, it will drill down to the data by opening the report and automatically filtering the report based on the record where the user opens the record.

Hands-on exercise for adding a chart to a page layout

Let's consider a use case: adding an embedded chart of opportunity and the number of cases in the **Account** page layout.

1. Create an **Opportunity** report, group the report by **Stage**, add **Amount**, summarize it, and save the report to a public folder, add a **Vertical Bar Chart**, and save the report again.
2. Create a case report from the **Custom Support Reports** report type category, group the report by **Status**, save the report to a public folder, add a **Donut Chart**, and save the report again.
3. Edit the account page layout by navigating to **Setup** | **Objects and Fields** | **Object Manager** | **Account** | **Page Layouts**. Open the corresponding page layout and look for **Report Charts in** the left-hand side menu. Click on **Report Charts** and find the report in the right-hand side panel; only the report with the chart will be shown here, and stored in the public folder:

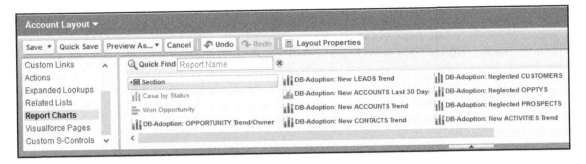

4. You will see the chart type as the icon for the report.

5. Drag both reports into the report area. I prefer to create a new section for a better user experience.

6. Once the component has been added to the page layout, click on the Properties icon to modify it:

   - **Size: Small, Medium, Large**.
   - **Appearance**: **Show title from report, Hide chart with error**.
   - **Data**: Filter and refresh. Refer the following screenshot:

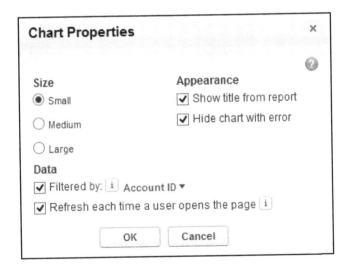

7. The filter is one of the most important items here, as it is used to determine data shown in the chart. For both reports, select the **Filtered by Account ID**.
8. Enable **Show Title** from report, **Hide chart with error.**
9. Tick **Refresh each time a user opens the page**; otherwise, it will refresh once every 24 hours.
10. Click on the **OK** button and then click on the **Save** button in the page layout to save the changes:

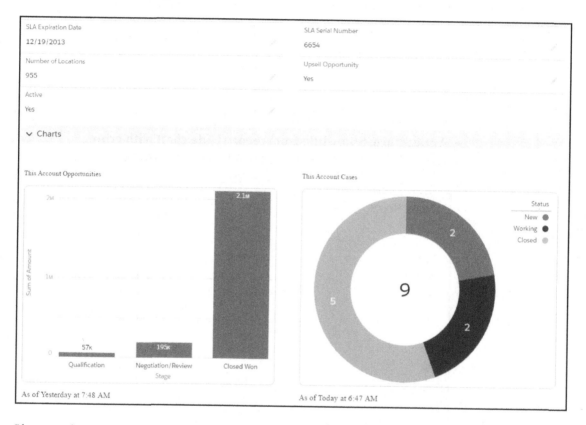

If a user does not have access to the report and **Hide chart with error** is enabled, they will see a blank area in the page layout, but if it is not enabled, they will see an error message. For example, take a look at the following screenshot:

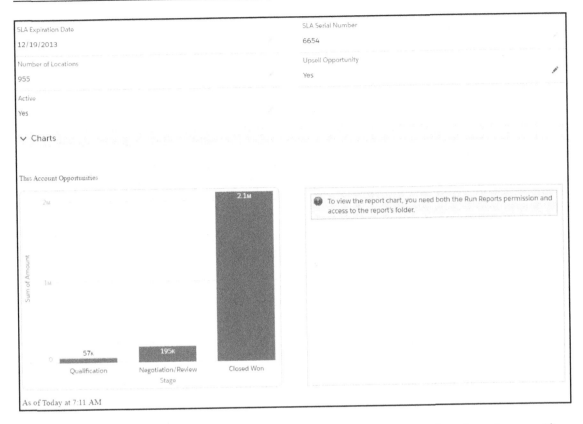

So make sure that the report is visible to everyone in the company unless there is a specific reason for not doing so.

At the bottom of the chart, you will see when the chart was last refreshed. If you did not tick **Refresh each time a user opens the page** for the chart, click on the chart here and you should see the **Refresh** button and the **Go to Report** button.

You can add chart to other page layouts, including custom objects with the relationship:

- For a Master-Detail Relationship, you do not need to change anything; the detail field for the page layout does not have to be in the report or chart to have the option to filter by the parent field.
- For a Lookup Relationship, make sure the parent field is available for the report type; otherwise, create a new report type to accommodate it. The same goes for the Master-Detail relationship; you do not need to add that field in the report or chart.

Summary

In this chapter, we went through the types of chart available in Salesforce Lightning. Anyone able to run the report will be able to add or modify the chart on-the-fly when running the report. This includes users without the permission to create and customize the report. We also discussed report formats that support the addition of a chart.

If a chart is added to the report and the report is stored in public folders, we can embed the chart into the record page layout. We can have up to two charts in a page record. Only the system admin or a user with a customizing application permission is able to add a chart to the page layout. You have the option to set the chart to auto-refresh in 24 hours or get it refreshed manually by the user.

In the next chapter, we will discuss how to work with reports. Reports in Lightning offer many features for us the explore; we can then analyze the data generated from them.

Working with Reports

In our daily work, most of us deal with running a report rather than creating or editing the report. Therefore, it is important to equip ourselves with the knowledge to work with reporting in the Lightning Experience, including tips to make our job more effective and efficient.

In this chapter, we will discuss how to work with a report, including opening a report, searching a report, and adding a report to favorites. Then, we will continue with navigating a report and components that you need to be aware of when running a report, including adding a chart, the show or hide report option, and change and remove report filters.

By the end of this chapter, you will be fully equipped with the working knowledge of Salesforce reporting in Lightning, including subscribing reports for report delivery by email.

Throughout this chapter, we will provide notes and tips to help you to understand important items. The following topics will be covered:

- Opening and searching reports
- Navigating to a report and report components
- Subscribing reports

Opening a report

Let's start with opening a report in Salesforce Lightning; remember that reports are stored in the report folder, either in a private or public folder. Private reports are only accessible by the user who saves the report into the **My Personal Custom Reports** folder. We have discussed this in depth in Chapter 2, *Concepts and Permissions in Reports and Dashboards*, please refer to that chapter for a refresher on permissions.

There are multiple ways to open a report in Salesforce Lightning. First, click on the **Reports** tab.

The Reports tab

You will see two main panels here: the left-hand side panel and the right-hand side panel. The left-hand side panel contains categories of **Reports** and **Folders**, and the right-hand side panel will show a list of reports or folders related to the menu selected in the left-hand side panel.

The Reports menu

Once you click on the **Reports** tab, you will see all things related to reports. There are two main categories on the left panel, which are **Reports** and **Folders**. Under the **Reports** category, there are multiple menus which will filter the reports shown in the right-hand side panel. Consider the following screenshot:

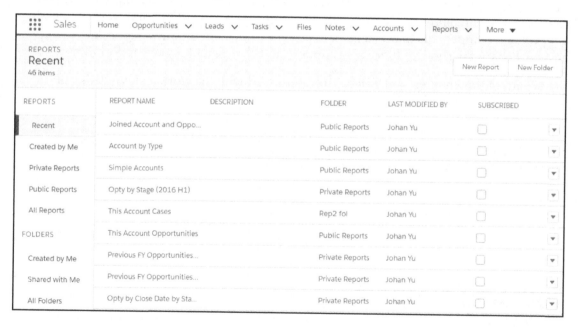

From the preceding screenshot, there are five menus under **Reports**:

- **Recent**: This is the default selection after clicking on the **Reports** tab. When this is selected, the right-hand side panel will list all reports recently opened by that user, so my recent list will be different from my colleague's list.
- **Created by Me**: Clicking on this will show all reports created by the user, including reports stored in private and public folders.
- **Private Reports**: This includes all reports stored by the user into the **My Personal Custom Reports** folder.
- **Public Reports**: These are reports stored in the **Unfiled Public Reports** folder; all users with the run report permission will be able to run reports stored in this folder.
- **All Reports**: This will show all reports the user has access to, from both private and public reports. If your organization has too many reports that are no longer used, it is a good practice to delete them periodically, so the list will be not too big here.

When you select any menu here, the right-hand side panel will list all reports based on the menu selected on the left-hand side. There will be five columns and one action column in this panel: **REPORT NAME, DESCRIPTION, FOLDER, LAST MODIFIED BY,** **SUBSCRIBED,** and an arrow icon for the dropdown of actions. You will be able to sort the list by **REPORT NAME, FOLDER, LAST MODIFIED BY,** and **SUBSCRIBED**. The **SUBSCRIBED** column will be visible only when the user has a **Subscribe report** permission.

Let's see the action menu available for each report:

REPORTS Recent 70 items					New Report	New Folder
REPORTS	REPORT NAME	DESCRIPTION	FOLDER	LAST MODIFIED BY	SUBSCRIBED	
Recent	Account by Type		Public Reports	Johan Yu	☐	▼
Created by Me	Account with Bucket Fields		Private Reports	Johan Yu	☐	Run
Private Reports	Opty History		Public Reports	Johan Yu	☐	Edit
Public Reports	Opportunity Historical Tre...		Public Reports	Johan Yu	☐	Subscribe
All Reports	Opportunity by Stage (Asia)		Asia Sales	Johan Yu	☑	Export
FOLDERS	Opportunity by Stage and ...		Public Reports	Johan Yu	☐	Delete

For the actions menu in the last column for each report, the menu visibility will depend on the user permission:

- **Run**: This is the same as clicking on the report name to run the report.
- **Edit**: This option will be visible only when the user is able to edit the report.
- **Subscribe**: This option will be visible if the user has the **Subscribe report** permission.
- **Export**: This option will visible if the user has an Export report permission.
- **Delete**: This option will be visible if the user is able to delete the report based on user accessibility in the report folder. The user will be able to delete all reports in their private folder.

The Folders menu

As with the **Reports** category, under he **Folders** category, there are multiple menus which will filter the folders shown in the right-hand side panel. Consider the following screenshot:

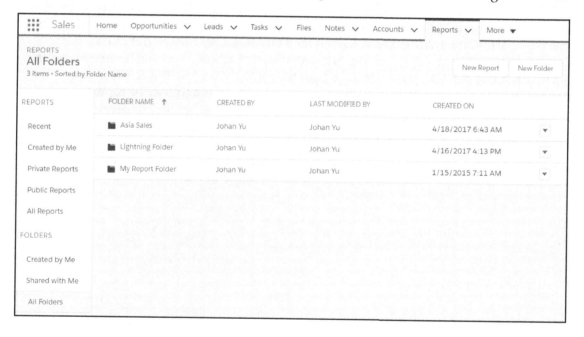

There are three menus under **Folders**:

- **Created by Me**: This will list all the report folders that you create
- **Shared with Me**: This will list all the report folders created by someone else but shared with you
- **All Folders**: This will list all the report folders you have access to, either created by yourself or someone else

When you select any menu here, the right-hand side panel will list all the report folders based on the menu selected on the left-hand side. There will be four columns and one action column. The columns would be **FOLDER NAME**, **CREATED BY**, **LAST MODIFIED BY**, **CREATED ON**, and an arrow icon for the dropdown of action.

Click on the arrow in the last column in the folder row; this will show the **Delete** menu if the user has permission to delete the folder. For users with permission to delete the folder, the user will be able to delete the report folder from here, but only for folders without any reports in that folder; otherwise, the user will receive an error message.

You also can sort the list by any column by hovering your mouse over the header and clicking on the column header. Click once to sort by ascending order, and click again to sort by descending order.

The favorites icon

In the top-right section of the screen, before **Global Actions** (the + icon), take a look at the star icon with an arrow next to it, that is for adding to favorites, while the arrow next to it is used to open the item that has been added to favorites. Favorites let you quickly access important records, lists, groups, dashboards, and other frequently used pages in Salesforce, including reports.

Favorites are similar to bookmarks in a web browser but better because your favorites are available no matter which device or browser you use to log into in Lightning Experience. So, each user will have their own list of favorites.

Hands-on exercise for adding an item to favorites

Let's consider a use case: because you always deal with reports, specifically a report called **Opty by Stage (2016 H1)**, add the reports tab and the report as a **Favorite**.

You can add the **Reports** tab as a favorite item by following these steps:

1. Click on the **Reports** tab.
2. Click on the star icon.
3. The system will pop up with the **"Reports" was added to your favorites** message. Consider the following screenshot:

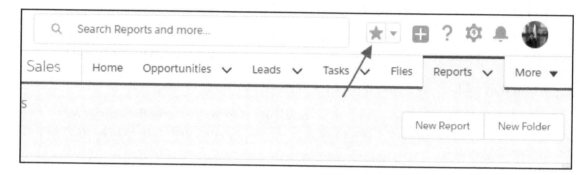

4. Once added, confirm that it has been added by clicking on the arrow next to the star in the favorite icon. Refer the following screenshot:

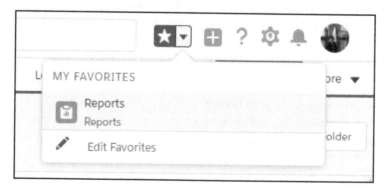

5. Now you should see **Reports** with the report icon under **MY FAVORITES**.
6. If you click on **Reports** from here, it is the same as you clicking on the **Reports** tab.
7. You can rename or delete it by clicking on the **Edit Favorites** link.

Instead of just adding the **Reports** tab as a favorite, you can add an individual report as a favorite too. Let's follow these steps:

1. Open an existing report. In my case, I will open a report called **Opty by Stage (2016 H1)**.
2. Click on the star icon.
3. The system will pop up with the **"Opty by Stage (2016 H1)" was added to your favorites** message.
4. Click on the arrow next to the star in the favorite icon, and you should see that **Opty by Stage (2016 H1)** is added to **MY FAVORITES** as shown in the following screenshot:

Once **Reports** is added into favorites, it will be listed under **MY FAVORITES** of the **Reports** tab too. Instead of clicking on the **Reports** tab, click on the arrow next to the **Reports** tab to show reports in **MY FAVORITES** and **RECENT RECORDS** for recently opened reports. Consider the following screenshot:

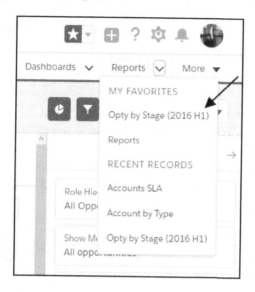

This step can be applied to **Dashboards**, **Account**, or any other records and tabs. The items added to favorites will be shown as **MY FAVORITES** in the object tab too. This is shown in the following screenshot:

Ideally, you should just add the item you most often use as a favorite; too many favorites is not a good practice. This is pretty similar to bookmarking, but favorites allow you to access your reports and other records from any browser and from any computer within Lightning.

The search textbox

When you click on the **Reports** tab, notice that the search box here has default text in the box **Search Reports and more...**, while in the **Accounts** tab, the search box changes to **Search Accounts and more...**. When opening a record or in the **Home** tab, the message would be "**Search Salesforce**". Does this mean you can search a report when only you are in the **Reports** tab? The answer is no. You can search a report from the search box from any tab, and not necessarily from the **Reports** tab.

When you type in the search box, Salesforce will auto-search, filter, and show the results. In the following screenshot, I typed `sla`; it will show all records with that keyword, including a report. Note that the icons are different between objects, and there is a label of the object below the record name:

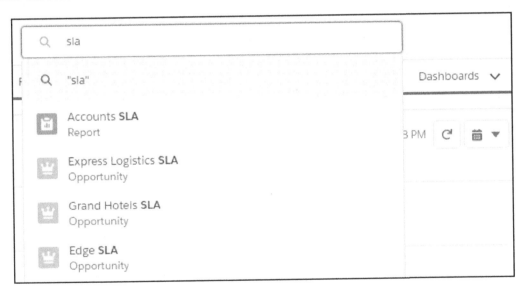

But if you hit the *Enter* button or click on the magnifying glass, the system will show all results on the Search Results page as shown in the following screenshot:

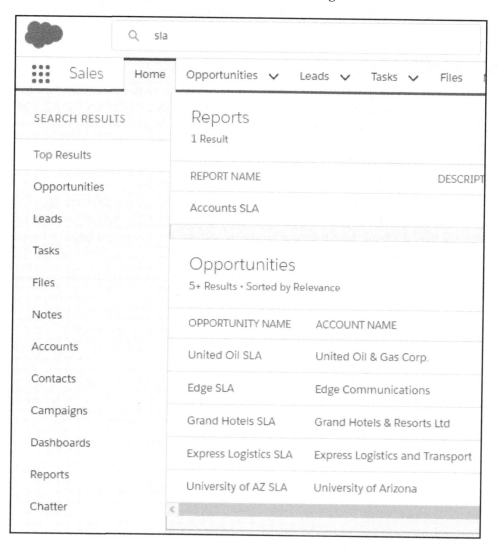

Navigating to a report

When you open a report, what items can we customize in the report result without edit the report? The following screenshot is taken from a pipeline report in Lightning experience:

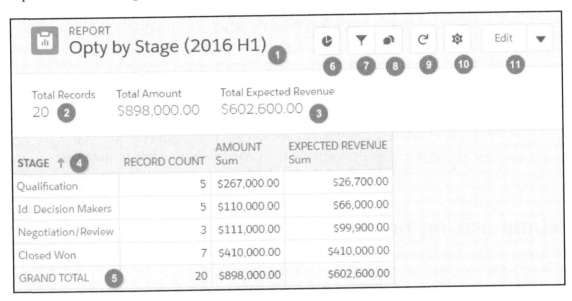

Let's start by looking all the components in a :

1. **Title**: This is purely just the report title that is derived from report name, and when you change the report name, the title will automatically follow.
2. **Total Records**: This is the number of records returned by the report. You can hide this by disabling **Record Count** under **Settings** (the gear icon), as shown in the preceding screenshot.
3. **Summarize**: For each field's summarization, the total will be shown here. If a field has two summarize options configured, such as **Sum** and **Average**, you will see two values for the same field. You can hide these values from **Settings** (the gear icon) marked with number **10** in the preceding screenshot, but you can't choose to show or to hide just a value; it is all or nothing.
4. **Details**: This is the report content. If you hide the details in a **Tabular** report, then it will show nothing, while in the **Summary** and **Matrix** report, it will show the values of field used for grouping.
5. **GRAND TOTAL**: You can opt to hide this total number from Settings (the gear icon). Check number 10 in the preceding screenshot.

6. **Chart**: Click on this to add or hide or change a chart in a report. We discussed charts in depth in `Chapter 7`, *Adding Charts in Reports and Pages*.

7. **Filter**: Click on the icon to hide or show the filter panel, denoted by number **7** in the preceding screenshot.

8. **Collaborate**: This will be visible only if **Chatter Feed Tracking** for report is enabled, we will discuss **Chatter Feed Tracking** for collaboration in `Chapter 11`, *Advanced Tips and Tricks for Reports and Dashboards*.

9. **Refresh**: Click on the icon to refresh the data shown in the report, denoted by number **9** in the preceding screenshot.

10. **Settings**: To show/hide the report result, the options available here will depend on the report format.

11. **The action button**: If a user has more than one permission for the report open, there will be an arrow next to the button, and this button will include **Edit**, **Clone**, **Save**, **Subscribe**, **Export**, and **Delete**.

Summarizing fields

When your report has summarized fields configured in a report and **GRAND TOTAL** (under **Settings**) is enabled, all summarized fields will be shown next to the report title:

REPORT
Opty by Stage (2016 H1)

Total Records	Total Amount	Total Expected Revenue	Average Expected Revenue
20	$898,000.00	$602,600.00	$30,130.00

STAGE ↑	OPPORTUNITY NAME	AMOUNT Sum	EXPECTED REVENUE Sum	Avg
Qualification (5 records)	Edge Emergency Generator	$75,000.00	$7,500.00	
	United Oil Emergency Generators	$30,000.00	$3,000.00	
	Element Stage 1A	$55,000.00	$5,500.00	
	Element Stage 1B	$80,000.00	$8,000.00	
	United Oil Refinery Generators	$27,000.00	$2,700.00	
Subtotal		$267,000.00	$26,700.00	$5,340.00

The preceding screenshot shows that **Amount** is summarized with **Sum**, while **Expected Revenue** is summarized with **Sum** and **Average**; this is valid for all formats of reports.

Filters

To hide the filters panel on the right-hand side, just click on the arrow in the top-right section of the panel or click on the filters icon; toggling it again will bring back the filters panel.

In Lightning, all users with the permission to run the report will be able to change the default filter, such as **Show Me**, date range, and all additional filters not locked, even users who do not have permission to create and customize reports.

Let's discuss this in the following screenshot:

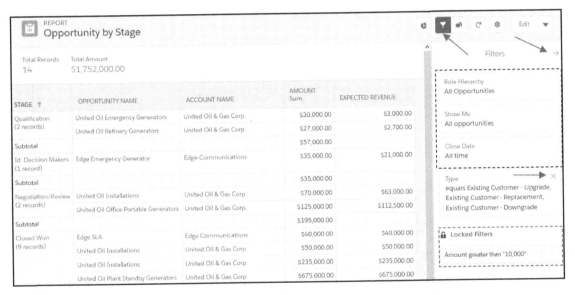

This report **Opportunity by Stage** is an **Opportunity** report type. For a report with report type as **Opportunity**, you will see an additional default filter, **Role Hierarchy**, while other report types will not have it, they will only have filters for **Show Me** and **Date**. The user is able to change the filter when running the report. There is no need to edit the report; just click on the filter name to modify the filter values.

The following default filters would be the additional filters added by the report creator; the creator can leave it for the user to change the filter values or lock the filter. The **Type** field in the preceding report is not locked, so the running user is able to change or remove it from the filter, click on the filter to edit, or cross the icon in that filter to remove the filter. The following screenshot shows all filters added to the report, including **Locked Filters**:

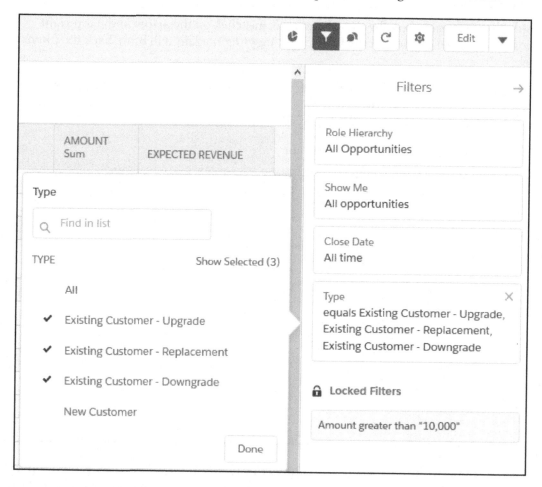

The next filter **Amount** is locked, so the user will be not able to delete it. All the changes here will not be saved and will not affect other users unless the user has an edit permission and clicks on **Save** from the action button.

The Collaborate field

If **Chatter Feed Tracking for Report** is enabled, this icon will be visible to all users able to open the report. To enable this, navigate to **Setup | Feature Settings | Feed Tracking**, look for **Report** in the left-side panel and tick **Enable Feed Tracking**.

By default, it will have **Post** and **Poll** for collaboration. The same is the case with all other **Chatter** posts; you can mention other users using @ followed by the username. Other users can **like**, **comment**, and **bookmark** the post, while for the user who posts in **Chatter** feed, the user also will be able to **Delete** and **Edit** the post.

Report settings

For the **Matrix** and **Summary** reports, the user will have options to show or hide--**Details**, **Subtotals**, **Grand total**, and **Record counts**. Consider the following screenshot:

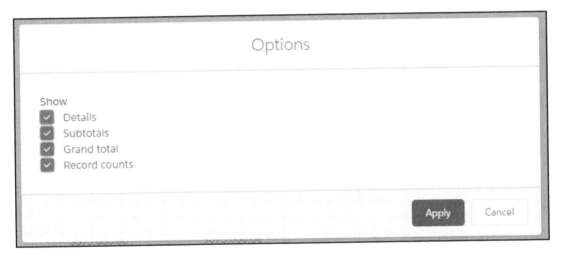

For **Tabular** reports, options are limited to showing or hiding **Details** and **Grand total**. Consider the following screenshot:

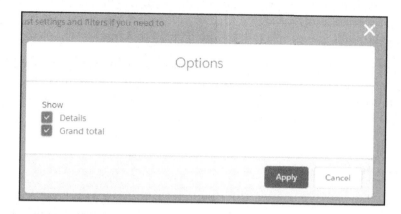

When the **Record Count** is hidden in **Summary** and **Matrix** reports, it will be hidden at the top as well. Hiding **Grand total** will hide the values from the bottom of the report as well as at the top, below the title. **Subtotals** are only available for the **Summary** and **Matrix** reports, which totally makes sense because there are no subtotals in the **Tabular** report.

The action button

These are complete actions you can perform in an open report. Consider the following screenshot:

Depending on the user permissions, the user will see different actions; let's quickly explain each of the action available:

- **Edit**: This is used to edit the report in the report builder
- **Clone**: This is used to clone to a new report; you will have the option to store it as a private report, make it public, or store it to a specific folder
- **Save**: This saves the report with any changes made, such as adding a chart
- **Subscribe**: This subscribes a report for email delivery on a schedule; we will discuss this in the next section
- **Export**: This is used to export a report into comma-delimited `.csv` or Excel format `.xls`
- **Delete**: The report deleted will be available in the Recycle Bin for 15 days and can be restored at that time

Subscribing reports

In Lightning Experience, you can subscribe to up to five reports and receive refreshed report results by email on a schedule that you set--**Daily**, **Weekly**, or **Monthly**.

To subscribe to reports, you need to have the **Subscribe to Reports** permission granted from **Profile** or **Permission Set**. On top of that, there are two more additional permissions related to this:

- **Subscribe to Reports: Add Recipients**
- **Subscribe to Reports: Set Running User**

These permissions require the **Subscribe to Reports** permission to be enabled.

This is a sample of an email sent to you when you subscribe for a report; you can click on the report title to open the report directly in Salesforce or click on the record name, such as **Account Name** or **Opportunity Name**, to open the report in Salesforce:

Opportunity by Stage

As of 5/8/17 at 11:00 PM · Viewing as Johan Yu · Report subscription started by Johan Yu

All opportunities·Close Date: Custom·Amount greater than "10,000"·Type equals Existing Customer - Upgrade,Existing Customer - Replacement,Existing Customer - Downgrade

Total Records Total Amount
14          $1,752,000.00

Stage↑	Opportunity Name	Account Name	Amount Sum	Expected Revenue
Qualification (2 records)	United Oil Emergency Generators	United Oil & Gas Corp.	$30,000.00	$3,000.00
	United Oil Refinery Generators	United Oil & Gas Corp.	$27,000.00	$2,700.00
			$57,000.00	
Id. Decision Makers (1 record)	Edge Emergency Generator	Edge Communications	$35,000.00	$21,000.00
			$35,000.00	
Negotiation/Review (2 records)	United Oil Installations	United Oil & Gas Corp.	$70,000.00	$63,000.00
	United Oil Office Portable Generators	United Oil & Gas Corp.	$125,000.00	$112,500.00
			$195,000.00	
Closed Won (9 records)	Edge SLA	Edge Communications	$40,000.00	$40,000.00
	United Oil Installations	United Oil & Gas Corp.	$50,000.00	$50,000.00
	United Oil Installations	United Oil & Gas Corp.	$235,000.00	$235,000.00
	United Oil Plant Standby Generators	United Oil & Gas Corp.	$675,000.00	$675,000.00
	United Oil SLA	United Oil & Gas Corp.	$120,000.00	$120,000.00
	United Oil Standby Generators	United Oil & Gas Corp.	$120,000.00	$120,000.00
	Edge Installation	Edge Communications	$50,000.00	$50,000.00
	Project Motor Links in Kentica	Burlington Textiles Corp of America	$75,000.00	$75,000.00
	Project Motor Head	Burlington Textiles Corp of America	$100,000.00	$100,000.00
			$1,465,000.00	
Grand Total (14 records)			$1,752,000.00	

Hands-on exercise for subscribing to a report in Lightning Experience

Let's consider a use case: you have a weekly sales pipeline meeting with your team every Monday morning at 9:00 am. To make sure you are well prepared when you reach the office, you would like the system to email you and your assistant, Alvin Lee, the pipeline report every Monday morning at 8:00 am:

1. Assume you have the **Subscribe to Reports** permission and the **Subscribe to Reports: Add Recipients** permission.
2. If you see the report under the **Reports** tab, click on the arrow and then click on **Subscribe**, or you also can open the report to confirm and then click on the **Subscribe** button.
3. Select these:
   - Frequency as **Weekly**
   - Days as **MON**
   - Time as **8:00 AM**

   Under **Email Results**, select send to **ME**, and your assistant's name.

4. Click on the **Save** button and you're done.
5. If you need to change the schedule or email delivery recipients, click on the **Subscribe** button again and change as necessary. Click on **Save** when done, or click on the **Cancel** button to ignore the changes made.

6. You and Alvin Lee will receive the email with a report every Monday morning. Consider the following screenshot:

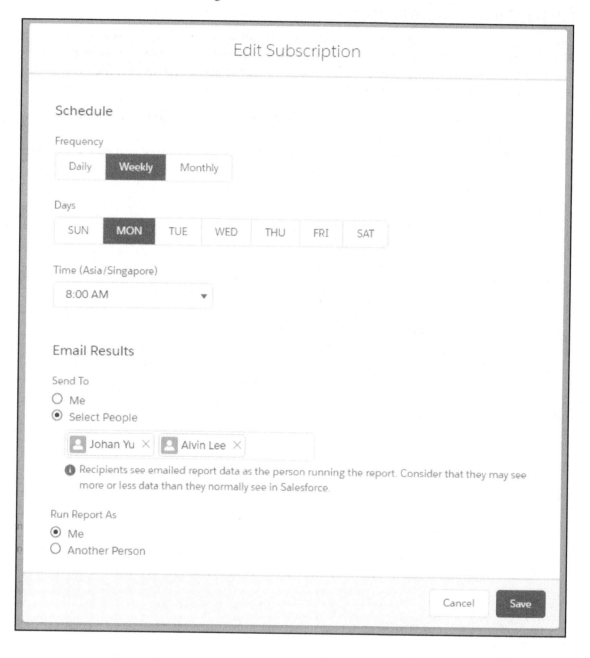

Summary

In this chapter, we worked with reports, including opening a report, searching for a report, and adding a report to favorites. You also learned how to navigate a report and discussed each component available when running a report.

We walked through the **Reports** tab, where we will be presented with the recently opened reports; click on the header to sort the reports, and there are a few menu options under **Reports**. Under the **Reports** category is the **Folders** category, where we can check the folder that you created, the folders shared with you, and all the folders you have access to.

Next, we also learned about the action menu which is available for each report. Where they are available depends on the user permission in general and user access related to the specific report.

You also learned about subscribing to a report. For report delivery to an email, you need to have permissions to subscribe to the report, and there are up to five reports you can subscribe to.

In the next chapter, we will start working with dashboards, where the report serves as the data source for the dashboard component.

9
Building Dashboards in Lightning Experience

Dashboards offer data visualization at a glance. The audience would be able to see the summary of the data in a graphical layout, including charts, matrix, and tables.

In Salesforce, a dashboard is one of the most interesting features. It consists of many components. It allows you to present many components in a wide blank canvas, so your audience can compare each of the components easily; for example, sales between the western region versus the eastern region, comparing last month sales with sales 2 months ago, and so on.

In this chapter, we will discuss the Lightning dashboard in detail, and you will be introduced to the **Dashboards** tab, with a navigation around the dashboard view, the dashboard builder, dashboard components, and the data source to support each component.

The way a dashboard works is not the same as a report. Reports show the current data, while dashboards show a snapshot of the data on which it was last refreshed.

By end of this chapter, you will be fully equipped with working knowledge of the Salesforce dashboard in Lightning, from creating a dashboard to scheduling dashboard refresh; this includes the schedule to deliver the dashboard refreshed by email.

Throughout this chapter, we will provide notes and tips to help you to understand important items. The following topics will be covered:

- Opening and searching a dashboard
- Navigating a dashboard
- The dashboard builder
- Dashboard refresh
- Dashboard components

Introducing dashboards in Salesforce

A dashboard is visualization data that displays the key metrics based on the criteria in reports, a running user, and with the option of dashboard filters. A powerful dashboard consumes multiple reports that often have a common theme, such as global sales, customer support, and so on. Dashboards visualize data stored in Salesforce and help you identify trends, sort out quantities, and measure the impact of their activities.

Built-on components

A dashboard is usually built on many dashboard components. We can mix types of charts or tables of dashboard components in a dashboard. Each dashboard component always needs to have one report as the data source. However, we can use the same report as the data source for multiple components within the same dashboard (for example, use the same report in both a bar chart and pie chart), or we can use it in different dashboards.

Dashboard accessibility

Similar to reports, dashboards are also stored in folders, but they are different types of folders. The folder controls who can access the dashboards, not the dashboard itself. If you have access to the dashboard folder, you can view all the dashboards in that folder. As dashboards are built on components and each component needs a report served as the data source, so the dashboard running user needs to have access to the report too.

Running user

Different from reports, each dashboard has a running user defined, who will use the security settings in determining the data to display in the dashboard. If the running user is a specific user, all dashboard viewers will see the dashboard data based on that user, including data security and hierarchy. For this reason, when you create a report, you need to choose the right running user for the dashboard to show the correct data. For example, set the **Country Manager** as the running user for a country sales performance dashboard; this will allow all users to see the overall country sales performance. When you build a performance leaderboard for the team, all users will see the same data, so make sure to set the dashboard viewer as the **Country Manager**.

Dynamic dashboards

Dynamic dashboards are totally different from the standard dashboards explained earlier. With dynamic dashboards, data shown in the dashboard will follow the running user visibility, which is always the logged-in user. This way, each user sees the dashboard according to his or her own access level. We'll cover dynamic dashboards in detail in Chapter 10, *Learning Advanced Dashboard Configuration*.

Users with specific permission will be able to change the running user when they run the dashboard; this is only if the dynamic dashboard is configured to allow that. This is very useful for the top management in analyzing data by changing the running user, but there is no need to change the dashboard or reports filter.

The new experience

If you switch from Classic, Salesforce has to redesign the whole dashboards experience in Lightning, but existing dashboards built in Classic will work in Lightning without the need to migrate or reconfigure. Lightning Experience introduces a new dashboard builder and offers the flexibility to create components of different sizes:

- **Flexible dashboard components size**: You can drag the corners and sides of the dashboard components to resize them. The components can have a size from one column and one row to as big as you want. The charts and all other items, such as legends, will be automatically resized when you resize the component size. You can configure the chart starting from chart type, chart title, chart axis, and others, by clicking on the pencil icon. Consider the following screenshot:

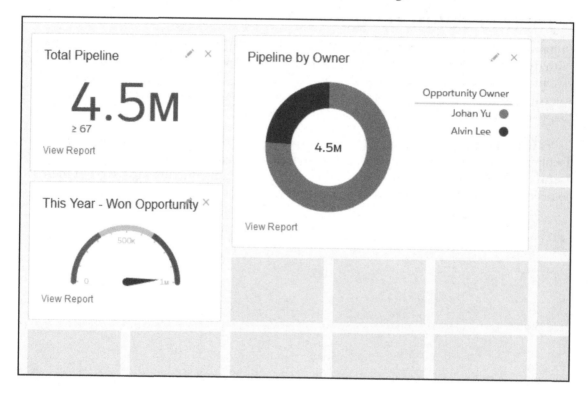

- **Drag and drop dashboard components**: You can arrange the dashboard components' position by dragging and dropping the components. Consider the following screenshot:

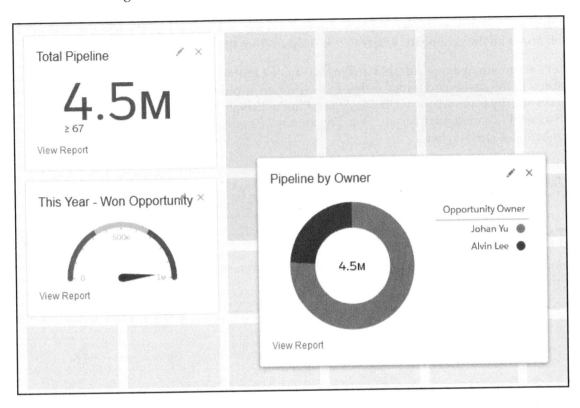

- **Dashboards with more than three columns**: In Lightning Experience, you can have a dashboard with up to nine columns, whereas in Classic, we only have a maximum of three columns.

Opening a dashboard

If you have the **Run Report** permission, you will be able to view a dashboard that you have access to, from the **Dashboards** tab, from the search result, or from the favorite icon. Similar to reports, dashboard accessibility is controlled by the folder that stores that dashboard.

From the dashboards tab, if you have the **Create and Customize Dashboards** permission, you will be able to create a new dashboard by clicking on the **New Dashboard** button, or to edit existing dashboards stored in folders that you have edit access. Check Chapter 2, *Concepts and Permissions in Reports and Dashboards* and Chapter 3, *Implementing Security in Reports and Dashboards* for a complete reference on the permissions for dashboards and in relation with the dashboard folder that is used to store the dashboard.

Let's start with opening a dashboard in Salesforce Lightning; remember that dashboards are stored in the dashboard folder, either in the private or public folder. Private reports are only accessible by users who save the dashboard in the **Private Dashboards** folder; we have discussed this in depth in Chapter 2, *Concepts and Permissions in Reports and Dashboards*, so we will not repeat it here.

There are multiple ways to open a dashboard in Salesforce Lightning. First, click on the **Dashboards** tab.

The Dashboards tab

Here is a screenshot taken after clicking on the **Dashboards** tab; let's go through all the components here:

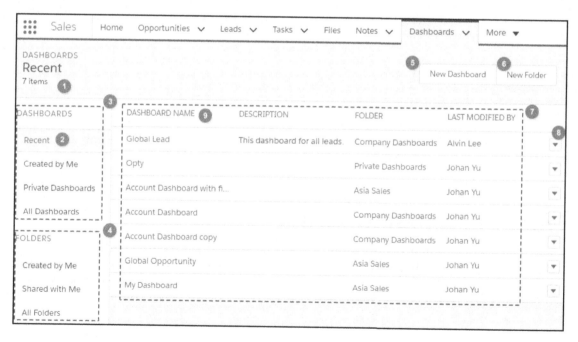

1. Title (denoted by **1**): This will show the menu selected, the number of items for that folder, and information if the list of dashboards is sorted with a column (if any).
2. Recent (**2**): When you click on the **Dashboards** tab, it will show a list of the dashboards you recently opened by default.
3. The **DASHBOARDS** menu (**3**): There are four menus in the dashboards area.
4. The **FOLDERS** menu (**4**): There are three menus in the folders area.
5. The **New Dashboard** button (**5**): Click on this button to create a new dashboard; this is visible only when you have the permission to create and customize the dashboard.
6. The **New Folder** button (**6**): Click this button to create a new folder for the dashboard; this is visible only when you have the permission to create dashboard folders.
7. Dashboards or folder area (**7**): This is the list of dashboards or folders depending on the selected menu on the left-hand side.
8. The action button (**8**): From here, you will be able to view (the same as clicking on the dashboard name), edit, or delete a dashboard or delete the folder. Visibility of the menu depends on user permissions.
9. Sort (**9**): You can sort the dashboard or folder list in an ascending or descending order by clicking on the header.

Similar to the **Reports** tab or the other objects tab in Lightning, if you click on the arrow next to the **Dashboards** tab, it will show the dashboards that you have added to your favorites and the list of dashboards you recently opened. Adding a dashboard to favorites is similar to adding a report or other records to favorites; refer to `Chapter 8`, *Working with Reports*. The following screenshot shows the **Dashboards** tab menu when you click on the arrow icon next to the **Dashboards** tab, including **MY FAVORITES** and **RECENT RECORDS**:

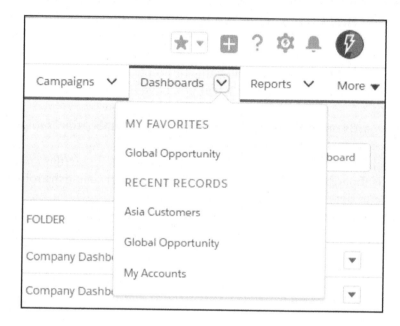

The DASHBOARDS menu

After you click on the **Dashboards** tab, you will see two main panels: the left-hand side panel and the right-hand side panel. The left-hand side panel contains categories of the **DASHBOARDS** and **FOLDERS** menus, and right-hand side panel will show a list of dashboards or folders related to the menu selected in the left-hand side panel. This is shown in the following screenshot:

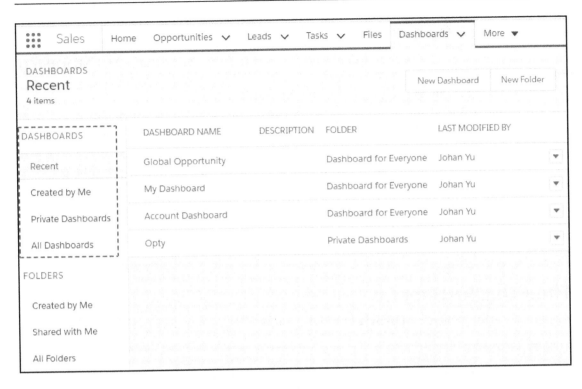

There are four menus under **DASHBOARDS**:

1. **Recent**: This is default selection after clicking on the **Dashboards** tab. When this is selected, the right-hand side panel will list all the dashboards recently opened by that user, so my recent list will be different from my colleague's list.

2. **Created by Me**: Clicking on this will show all the reports created by the user, including dashboards stored in private and public folders.

3. **Private Dashboards**: This includes all the dashboards stored by the user into his or her **Private Dashboards** folder.

4. **All Dashboards**: This will show all dashboards the user has access to, including both private and public dashboards. If your organization has too many dashboards that are no longer used, it is a good practice to delete them periodically, so the list will not be too big here.

When you select any menu here, the right-hand side panel will list all the dashboards based on the menu selected on the left-hand side. There will be four columns and one action column in this panel: **DASHBOARD NAME**, DESCRIPTION, **FOLDER**, **LAST MODIFIED BY**, and arrow icon for the dropdown of actions. You will be able to sort the list by **DASHBOARD NAME**, **FOLDER**, and **LAST MODIFIED BY**.

For the actions menu in the last column for each report, the menu visibility will depend on the user permission:

- **View**: This is the same as clicking on the report name to view the dashboard.
- **Edit**: This option will be visible only if the user is able to edit the dashboard.
- **Delete:** This option will be visible only if the user is able to delete the report based on user accessibility in the folder. The user will be able to delete the dashboard in his or her private folder.

The FOLDERS menu

As with the arrangement of **DASHBOARDS**, you will find a few menus under **FOLDERS**:

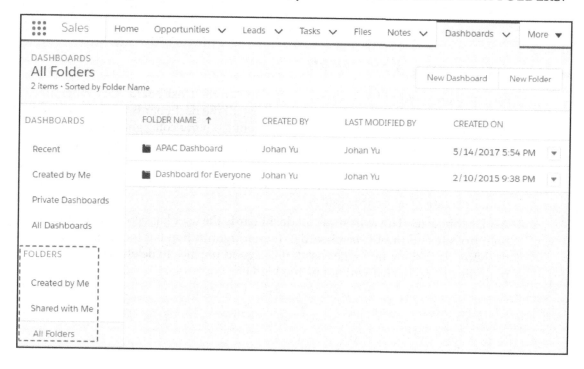

There are three menus under **FOLDERS**:

1. **Created by Me**: This will list all the dashboard folders you create.
2. **Shared with Me**: This will list all the dashboard folders created by someone else but shared with you.
3. **All Folders**: This will list all the dashboard folders you have access to, either created by yourself or someone else.

When you select any menu here, the right-hand side panel will list all the report folders based on the menu selected on the left-hand side. There will be four columns and one action column. The columns will be **FOLDER NAME, CREATED BY, LAST MODIFIED BY, CREATED ON**, and the arrow icon for the dropdown of actions.

Clicking on the arrow in the last column in the folder row will show the **Delete** menu if the user has permission to delete the folder. For users with permission to delete the dashboard folder, the user will be able to delete the dashboard folder from here, but only for folders without any dashboards in that folder; otherwise, the user will get an error message.

You also can sort the list by any column by hovering your mouse over the header and clicking on the column header. Click once to sort by ascending order, and click again to sort by descending order.

The favorites icon

By now, you should be familiar with the favorites icon; just for a quick recap, you can add any records, including reports and dashboards as your personal favorites. Simply click on the star icon when the report or dashboard opens; you can do this for **Account, Opportunities**, or any other records.

Once added, you can access records, reports and dashboards easily from anywhere within the Lightning environment because it is located in the top area and is always visible. Consider the following screenshot:

The search textbox

Similar to reports or any other records, you can search the dashboard from the **global** search textbox; just enter the whole dashboard name or partial name if you do not remember the complete dashboard name.

Make sure that you are not in the **SETUP** menu when searching for the dashboard; otherwise it will not search any records but will just search for metadata in the **SETUP** menu, such as user, profile, objects, and so on. Refer to the following screenshot:

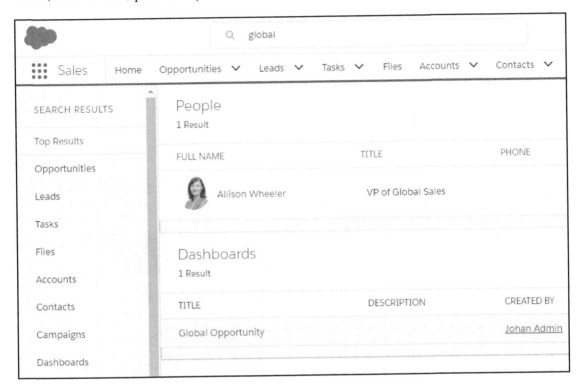

Navigating to a dashboard

Interactive dashboard components give viewers more information and links to data-supplying reports. Let's look at all the items in a dashboard:

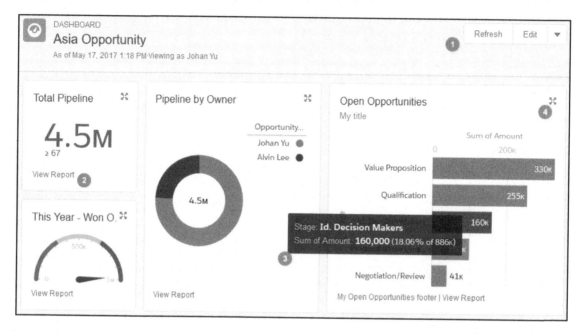

1. **Refresh, Edit, Clone, New Dashboard**, or **Delete**: The buttons and drop-down menu at the top of each dashboard provide one-click access to administrative tasks.
2. **View Report** underlying a component: Would you like to get the data behind a metric or a chart? Click on **View Report** to drill into the data.
3. **Hover over charts to get more information:** Hovering over a chart segment reveals more information about the chart.
4. **Expand dashboard components to get the big picture:** Click on the expand icon to see a larger version of the component and continue with the **View Report** button to drill into the data.

Dragging and dropping in the Dashboard Builder

The **Dashboard Builder** is a drag and drop interface to create and modify dashboards. You can use it to customize the whole dashboard, a column in the dashboard, or a component in the dashboard.

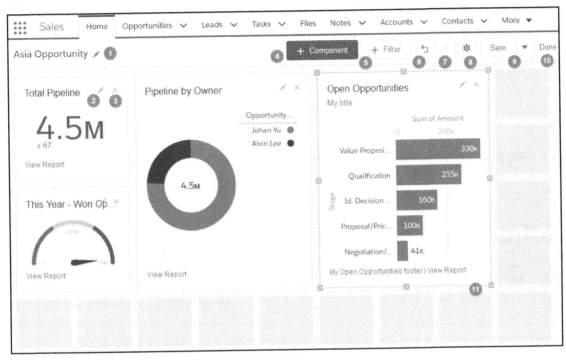

Let's go through all the items in the Dashboard Builder from the preceding screenshot:

1. Editing the dashboard title (denoted by **1**): You can easily change the dashboard title from the pencil icon.
2. Editing the components (**2**): Clicking on this pencil icon changes the component type, sort, max values displayed, title, subtitle, and footer.
3. The **Delete** component (**3**): Click on this cross icon to delete the component.
4. The add **+ Component** button (**4**): Click on this to add a new component to the dashboard.
5. The add **+ Filter** button (**5**): Click on this to add a filter for the whole dashboard.
6. The undo button (**6**): Click on this to undo items that have changed but haven't been saved.
7. The redo button (**7**): Click on this to redo items.

8. The edit properties button (**8**): Click on this to edit the dashboard properties: title, description, folder, View Dashboard as, and enable Dynamic Dashboard.

9. The **Save**, **Save As**, and **Delete** buttons (**9**) : The **Save** button saves and overwrites an existing dashboard, the **Save As** button saves the dashboard as a new dashboard, and the **Delete** button deletes the dashboard.

 A deleted dashboard can be recovered from the Recycle Bin within 15 days, but as of the Summer '17 release, the Recycle Bin does not exist in Lightning Experience yet, so you need to switch to Classic to undelete.

10. The **Done** button (**10**): Click on this to close the dashboard editor: If you haven't saved the changes made, the system will prompt you to save or discard the changes.

11. Resize and move (**11**): Drag a component corner to resize the component or hold the component to move it.

Refreshing dashboards

Dashboards are not the same as reports. When you open a report, the report data will be generated based on current data. On the other hand, for dashboards, when you open a dashboard, it will show the data as of the latest dashboard refreshed by any users or by a schedule.

All users able to view the dashboard will be able to refresh the dashboard by simply clicking on the **Refresh** button after opening the dashboard. Even users who do not have permission to edit the dashboard are able to refresh the dashboard. Once refreshed, the other user that sees the dashboard will be based on latest refreshed data.

Notice that in the following screenshot, information under the dashboard title will show us the data used for the dashboard, which is the same with the latest dashboard refresh:

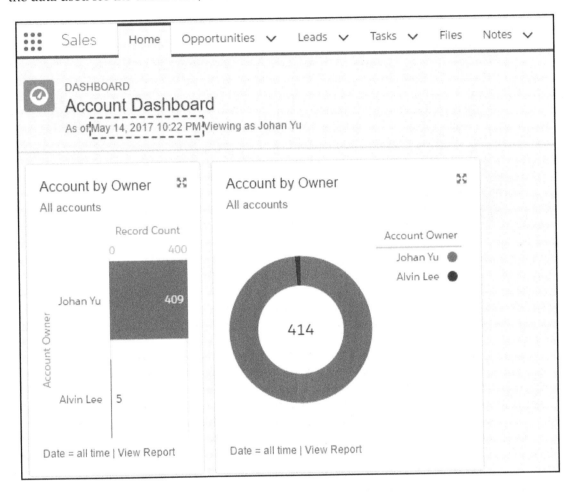

But if the dashboard hasn't been refreshed in 24 hours, it lets you know with a helpful warning message with an exclamation icon, as shown in the following screenshot:

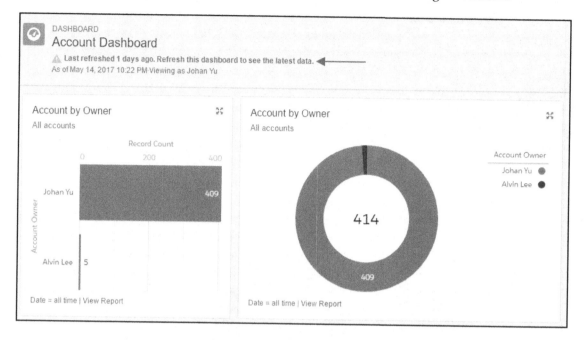

If you switch from Classic to Lightning and have the Visualforce Component developed by your vendor or consultant, the Visualforce Component is no longer supported in Lightning. This will cause you to not be able to refresh the dashboard. To resolve this, remove the Visualforce Component and you should be able to refresh the dashboard in Lightning Experience.

Scheduling a dashboard refresh

This is a very useful feature to get the system to auto refresh a dashboard on a schedule. You can also configure the system to email the dashboard to you and your team. Unfortunately, this feature is not available in Lightning until the Summer '17 release, so you need to switch to Classic to configure this.

To schedule refresh a dashboard, perform the following steps:

1. Open the dashboard from Classic.
2. Click on the arrow near the **Refresh** button. This is not available for free editions of Salesforce.
3. Click on **Schedule Refresh...**. Consider the following screenshot:

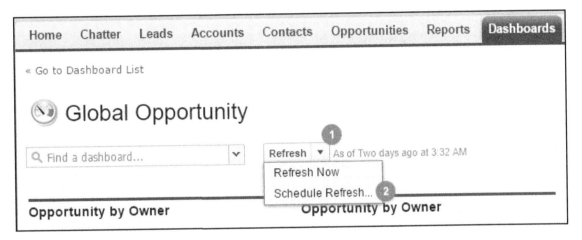

Next, you need to configure the following:

4. **Email Dashboard**: Use this if you (and your team) would like to get emails with the dashboard when it is auto-refreshed.
5. **Frequency**: **Daily**, **Weekly**, **Monthly**.
6. **Start Date** and **End Date**.

7. **Preferred Start Time**. Consider the following screenshot:

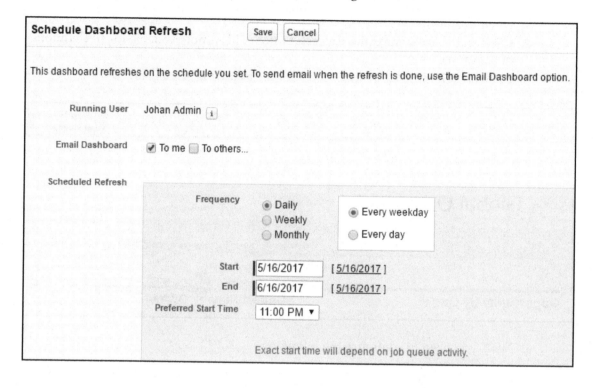

Here is a sample of an email delivered along with a dashboard refresh in a schedule:

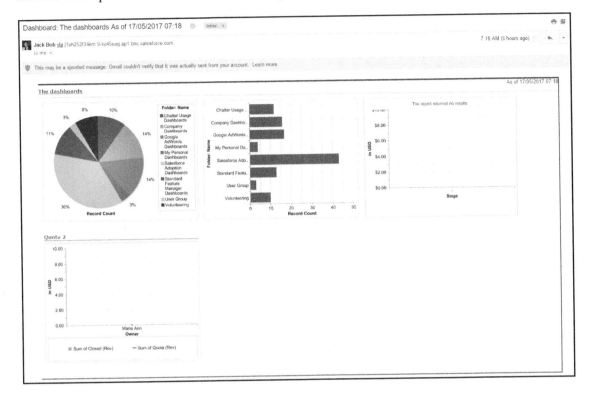

If you click the dashboard title from the email, it will open the dashboard in the web browser and it should show the same data and refresh date time as the email delivered:

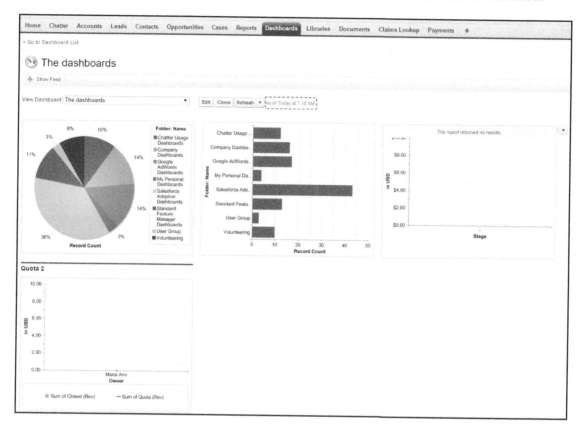

For the dashboard created in Lightning Experience, you will not able to edit it in Salesforce Classic - the Edit button will not be visible. The same is the case with the dashboard created in Classic; then, you edit and save in Lightning, and you can't edit it again in Classic. You should consider cloning the dashboard and saving it in Lightning Experience. With this, you can still edit the original dashboard in Salesforce Classic when required.

To check whether all dashboards have been scheduled for auto-refresh, navigate to **Setup** | **Monitor** | **Jobs** | **Scheduled Jobs** (from Classic), or **Setup** | **Environments** | **Jobs** | **Scheduled Jobs** (from Lightning). You can delete the schedule from here.

Creating your first dashboard

If you switch from Classic to Lightning, a dashboard is one of the things that attract most people to switch to Lightning. In Classic, you can have up to three columns for dashboard components, while in Lightning, you can have up to nine columns for the components, although the maximum number of components for a dashboard stays the same, which is 20.

We have discussed many topics in this chapter or earlier chapters related to creating a dashboard, including the following:

- Dashboard permissions
- Dashboard folders and permissions
- Opening and searching dashboards
- Navigating a dashboard tab

Well, let's start with creating a dashboard.

Hands-on exercise for creating a dashboard

Let's create a dashboard with a component showing the number of accounts per sales representative in a horizontal bar chart, but before that, we need to create a report for the dashboard component data source. Assume you have all permissions required to create a report and a dashboard.

Creating a dashboard in Lightning is pretty cool; you just need to point and click to build the dashboard. Start with selecting a valid report for the dashboard:

1. Navigate to the **Reports** tab to create a new report.
2. A report is a basic requirement for a dashboard as it uses it as the data source for the dashboard component, so let's create the report:
    1. Click on the **New Report** button.
    2. Select the **Accounts** report type by clicking on the **Accounts & Contacts** category.
    3. Click on the **Create** button to continue.
    4. Select **All accounts** in the **Show** filter.
    5. Change the **Create Date Range** to **All Time**.
    6. Change the report format to **Summary**.
    7. Remove all columns and add only **Account Name** to the report.

8. Drag Account Owner to grouping drop zones.
9. Navigate to **Show | Details** to hide record details.
10. Save the report with the name `Account by Owner` to the **Unfiled Public Reports** folder. The following screenshot shows the report created:

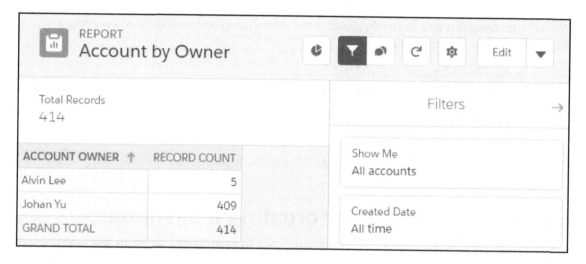

3. Navigate to the **Dashboards** tab and click on the **New Dashboard** button.
4. Enter Name as `Account Dashboard`.
5. Remove **Private Dashboards** from the folder by clicking on the cross icon and select a public folder; in my case, I have a dashboard folder called **Company Dashboards**.
6. Click on the **Create** button to continue.
7. Now you should see the matrix in nine columns and many rows.
8. Click on the **+ Component** button to start adding dashboard components.

9. Select the report created earlier in this exercise, **Account by Owner**, which is stored in the Public Reports folder. If you do not see the report here, you can flip through views (such as Recent, Private, and Public) and folders. Of course, you also can search by report (and folder) name. Consider the following screenshot:

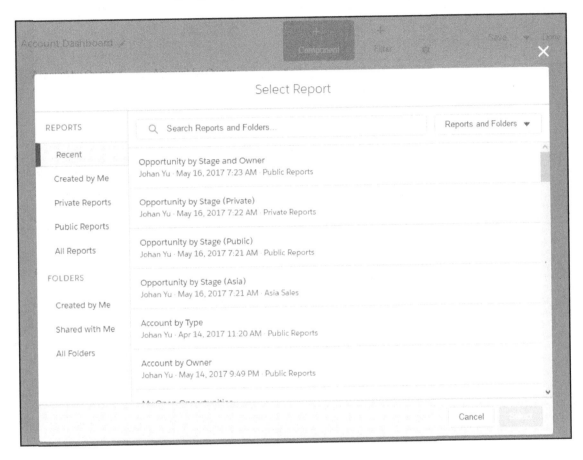

10. Select the report and click on the **Select** button.
11. By default, **Vertical Horizontal Bar Chart** has been selected; for this exercise, just keep that chart type and scroll down the window to enter **Subtitle** and **Footer**.
12. Enter **Subtitle** as All accounts and **Footer** as Date = all time.
13. Click on the **Add** button to continue.

14. By default, the component just added will occupy three columns and three rows. You can adjust the component to be smaller or bigger; let's change it to two columns by three rows. Keep the default component title as it is, which is the report title. Consider the following screenshot:

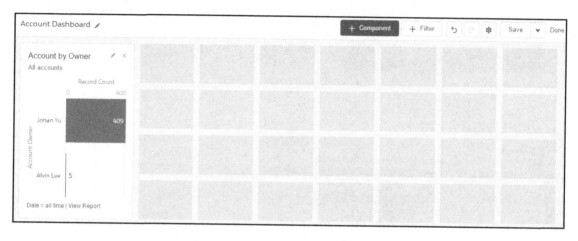

15. Click on the **Save** button and then hit the **Done** button.

16. Here is our first dashboard:

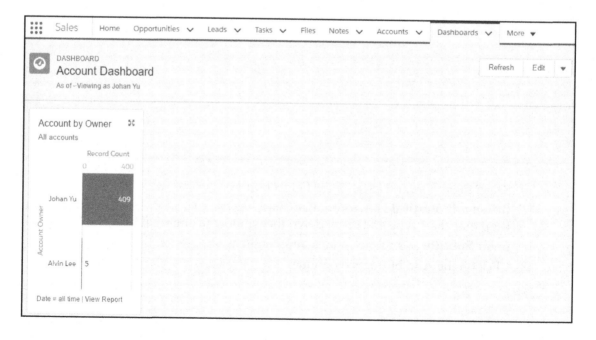

Let's continue by adding another dashboard component:

1. Click on the **Edit** button.
2. Click on the **+ Component** button to add another dashboard component.
3. Select the same report created earlier, **Account by Owner**.
4. Now select the **Donut** chart.
5. Add `All accounts` for **Subtitle** and `Date = all time` for **Footer**.
6. Click on the **Add** button.
7. The new component will be added below the existing component; drag it to the right of the existing component and keep the size as a 3 x 3 box.
8. Click on the **Save** button and then hit the **Done** button; here is what you will see:

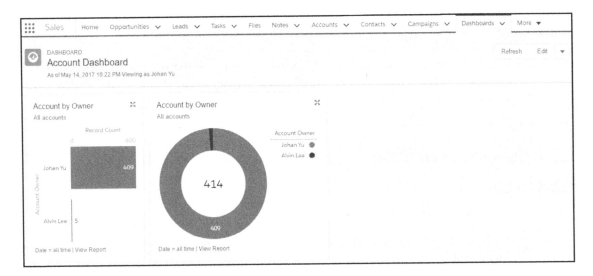

If you hover your mouse over both charts, you will get the details we saw in the report. Let's analyze this dashboard:

- Click on the chart or expand the icon to get a full screen of the chart size.
- Note the **View Report** link; clicking on this link will open the report.

- Hovering your mouse over the chart will get you more information on that chart slice.
- In this exercise, we proved that we can use the same report for more than one component in the same dashboard, and we can use it for a different type of chart.
- Notice this under the dashboard title, **As of May 14, 2017 10:22 PM -Viewing as Johan Yu**. This means that other users who view the dashboard will see the same as the user **Johan Yu,** with data refreshed on **May 14, 2017 10:22 PM**. If the object sharing is private, the user will see the dashboard with the data set where the user does not have the visibility.
- A dashboard is not the same as a report. When you open a report, it will show the current data, while for a dashboard, by default, it will show the data as of the latest refresh. Other users will be able to refresh the dashboard by clicking on the **Refresh** button, even the user who does not have permission to edit the dashboard. Once refreshed, other users will see the dashboard based on the latest refreshed data.
- When other users click on **View Report**, they will see the data as themselves (the logged-in user); the report generated is not related to the dashboard viewing user anymore; therefore, the number may not be the same as in the dashboard data.

Hands-on exercise for editing and maintaining a dashboard

There are two ways to edit a dashboard:

- Open the dashboard and click on the **Edit** button, as shown in the following screenshot:

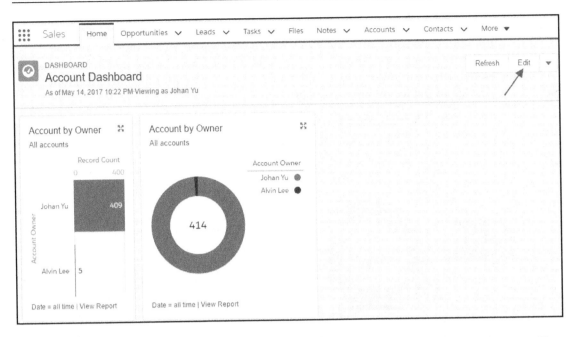

- In the **Dashboards** tab or **Search** result, find the dashboard and click on the **Edit** link under the arrow dropdown for the dashboard, as shown in the following screenshot:

Once you are in the **Edit** mode or the Dashboard Builder, you can add, delete, or modify existing components, the same as when you create a new dashboard. You can save the modified dashboard as a new dashboard by clicking on the **Save As** link under the arrow next to the **Save** button, or you can even delete the dashboard with the **Delete** link under **Save As**, as shown in the following screenshot:

OK, let's look at a hands-on exercise to edit the dashboard created earlier by adding a new component and then saving the dashboard as a new dashboard:.

1. Open **Account Dashboard**.
2. Click on the **Edit** button.
3. Click on the first component (leftmost) and change the size to four columns with three rows.
4. Move the second component accordingly to the right of the first component.
5. Add the new component by clicking on the **+ Component** button.
6. Select the same **Account by Owner** report.
7. Select the **Vertical Bar Chart**.
8. Change **Sort Rows By** to **Value Ascending**.
9. Add **Subtitle** as All accounts and Footer as Date = all time.
10. Click on the **Add** button.
11. Modify the component size to two columns with three rows and move it to the right of the second component.

12. Click on the **Save As** link under the arrow next to the **Save** button; if you click on the **Done** button, the system will ask if you would like to save or the discard changes.

13. Enter the name as `Account Dashboard copy`; leave the folder as the existing folder.

14. Click on the **Create** button. Refer to the following screenshot:

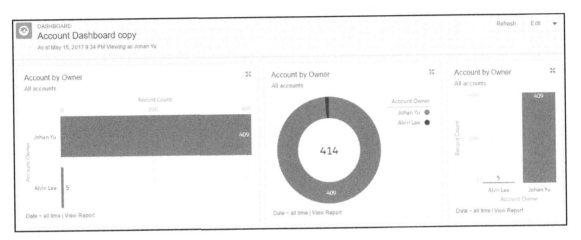

15. Now we are no longer in the edit mode or the dashboard builder; we are in the view mode. Note that there are a few buttons and links in the top-right section:

    - **Refresh**: Click on this button to refresh the dashboard data
    - **Edit**: Click on this button to edit the dashboard.
    - **Clone**: Click on this link to clone as a new dashboard without the need to edit, and save as a new dashboard
    - **New Dashboard**: Click on this to create a new dashboard without the need go back to the **Dashboards** tab
    - **Delete**: Click on this to delete the existing dashboard; the deleted dashboard will be moved to the Recycle Bin (as of the Summer '17 release, you need to switch to Classic to access the Recycle Bin)

Next, let's move the **Account Dashboard copy** dashboard from the **Company Dashboards** folder to a folder called **Asia Sales**:

1. Edit the dashboard.
2. Click on the gear icon **Edit Dashboard Properties** button.
3. Cross the existing folder, select the new folder, and then click on the **Save** button to close the properties window. This is shown in the following screenshot:

4. Click on the **Save** button again to save the changes for the dashboard.
5. Now the dashboard should be located in a new folder; you can double-check by clicking on the Dashboards tab, and it should be listed in the recent items.

The dashboard components

As mentioned earlier, one dashboard can contain up to 20 components, and each component can be present in the form of a chart, a matrix, or a table.

The two main steps to build a dashboard are as follows:

1. Select a report as the data source.
2. Select the component type.

Defining the dashboard components

There are 11 types of dashboard components available in Salesforce Lightning (as of the Summer '17 release):

- **Horizontal Bar Chart**
- **Vertical Bar Chart**
- **Stacked Horizontal Bar Chart**
- **Stacked Vertical Bar Chart**
- **Line Chart**
- **Donut Chart**
- **Metric Chart**
- **Gauge Chart**
- **Funnel Chart**
- **Scatter Chart**
- **Table**

The highlighted area in the following screenshot shows these:

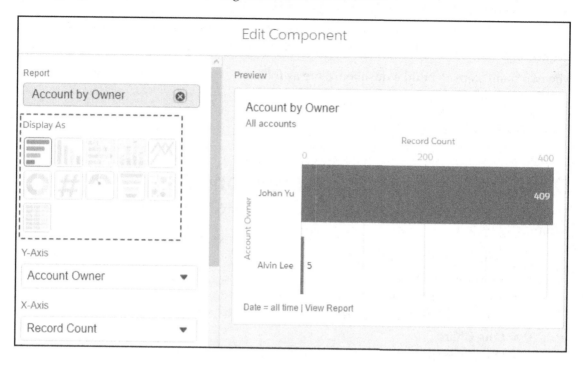

We will not discuss all the types of components, but let's discuss a few of them.

Tables

Tables are useful in presenting information in an easy-to-scan format. Charts give dashboard readers information at a glance, and tables give more details. Add a table to your dashboard to show the data in summary, as shown in the following screenshot:

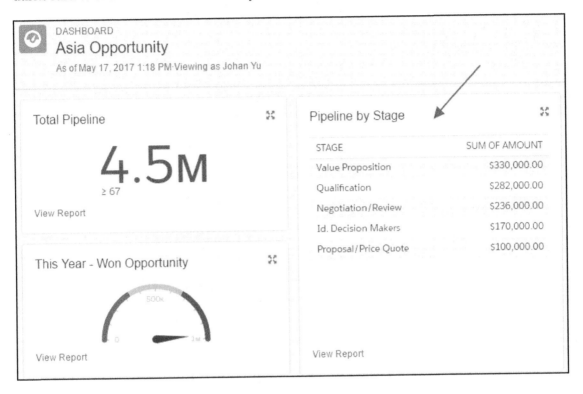

Funnel charts

Use a funnel chart when you have multiple groupings in an ordered set and want to show the proportions among them. Funnel charts are ideal to show the stages of your opportunities. Consider the following screenshot:

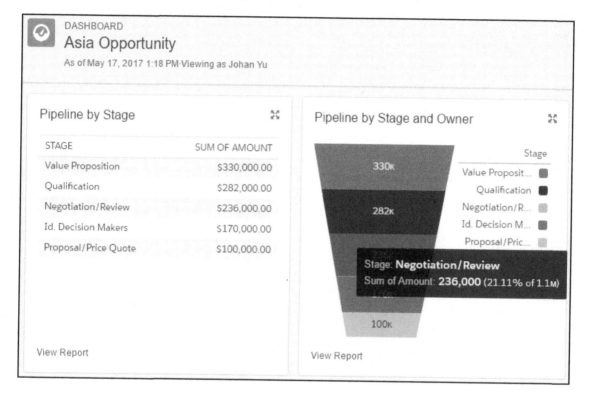

Gauge charts

Gauge charts added to Lightning Experience dashboards show percentages and the total by default. You can manually set the value for each segment range, and you also can change the chart color. Consider the following screenshot:

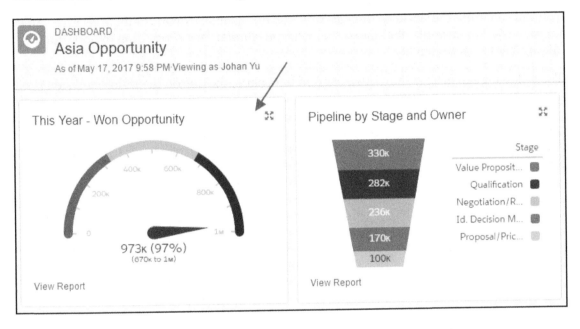

Stacked Bar charts

Stacked bar charts are great to compare absolute values between bars. To use a stacked bar chart, the report must have at least two groupings, and one of the groupings must be a number.

You can configure the stacked bar chart to 100%; this enables you to compare relative values for each bar. For example, the stacked bar lets you compare the proportion of opportunity among sales representatives.

The following screenshot shows two stacked bar charts; the one on the right-hand side is configured with **Stack** to **100%**:

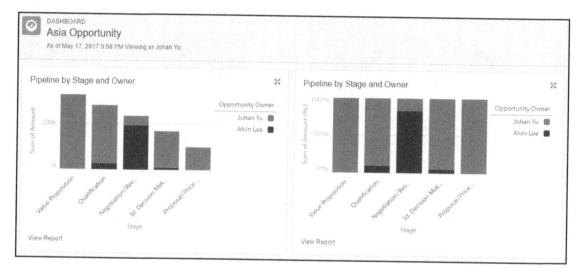

Scatter charts

Scatter charts are useful to show one or two groups of report data plus summaries. They are also useful in identifying trends across large datasets. To use a Scatter Chart, the report must have at least two summarized fields. Scatter charts will easily show the opportunity age with the opportunity stage. Consider the following screenshot:

Cumulative Line charts

Instead of a normal line chart, you can configure the line chart as a cumulative line chart. You can make your line charts on cumulative reports to highlight closed won opportunities over months. Consider the following screenshot:

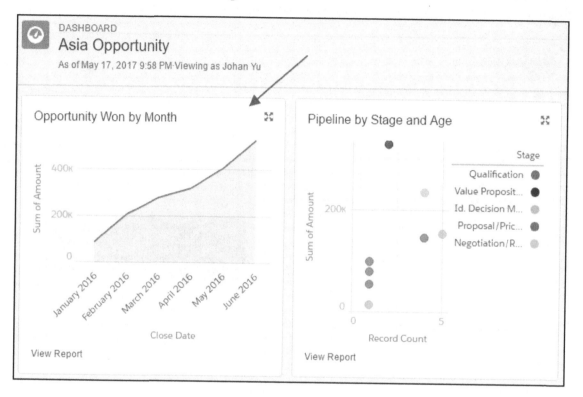

Combination charts

Combination charts plot two or more sets of data on a single chart, making charts *multimetric*. For example, the bar chart shows the pipeline **Amount** for each month, while the **Line Chart** shows the number of the pipeline for each month, adding the second y-axis on the right-hand side for additional measurement. This is shown in the following screenshot:

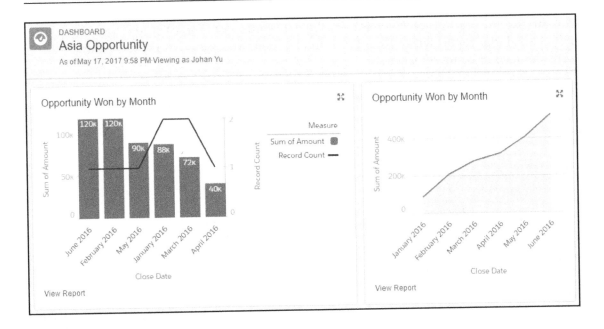

Reports as a data source

Salesforce gives you the flexibility to use any saved reports as the data source for the component. However, a component that uses the report saved in the **My Personal Custom Reports** / Private Report folder will not work for other users, unless the report is stored in a private report folder of the viewing user because the dashboard is viewed as the private report folder owner.

You can use any report type of a report as the data source, but for a **Tabular** format report, only the **Tabular** report with a **Row Limit** filter added can be used as the data source. Consider the following screenshot:

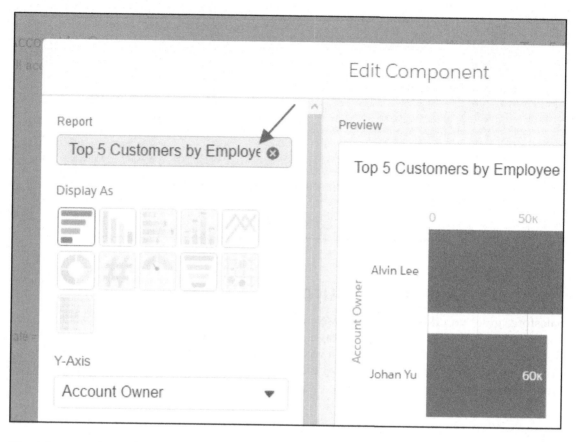

The takeaway from this section is not to assume that types of charts and features of the chart in a report and a dashboard are the same. They look similar, but they are not exactly the same.

Summary

In this chapter, we worked with reports, including opening a report, searching for a report, and adding a report to favorites. We also navigated reports and discussed each component available when running reports.

When you click on the **Reports** tab, you will be presented with the recently opened reports. You can click on the header to sort in finding a report. There is a menu under **REPORTS**. Under **REPORTS** would be the **FOLDERS** category, where you can check the folder that your create, the folder shared with you, and all folders you have access to.

The action button is available in the Reports tab for each report, and it is also available after opening a report depending on the user permission in general and user permission related to the specific report.

You also learned about subscribing to reports; for report delivery to emails, you need to have permissions to subscribe to a report, and there are up to five reports you can subscribe to.

In the next chapter, we will start working with dashboards, where a report serves as the data source for the dashboard component.

10
Learning Advanced Dashboard Configuration

In Chapter 9, *Building Dashboards in Lightning Experience*, we introduced dashboards, starting with opening a dashboard, navigating to the **Dashboards** tab, navigating to a dashboard, and looking at the items in the Dashboard Builder. You learned the basic structure of a dashboard and saw how it is related to the report, and how a dashboard is defined and stored on the Salesforce platform. We continued with the dashboard components, which are the heart and soul of dashboards in Salesforce. Finally, we created a dashboard from scratch and then enhanced it with dashboard filters and scheduled the dashboard for auto-refresh.

In this chapter, you will continue to learn and create an advanced dashboard using out-of-the-box functions offered by Salesforce. We will start with the dashboard filter and cover how to implement it and other use cases for the dashboard filter. We will continue with the concept of dynamic dashboards, and we will look into the dashboard drill down with filters preserved from the dashboard to report. We will end with looking for a prebuilt dashboard available in AppExchange and cover a hands-on exercise to install it.

The following topics will be covered in this chapter:

- Implementing the dashboard filters
- Using dynamic dashboards
- Dashboards and reports drill down
- Getting more from AppExchange

Implementing the dashboard filters

Have you ever had the need to analyze a dashboard based on different criteria? For example, we would like to look at the pipeline dashboard for the current year, current quarter, and current month.

For this example, it is not an issue to create three dashboards, but since the data source of the dashboard is driven by reports, this means that we would need to create three sets of reports for each dashboard, and if you have 10 components for the dashboard, you will need 30 reports to support this.

Therefore, instead of creating multiple dashboards, it would be better to consolidate and easier for the user to just have one dashboard only since all the components for the dashboard are the same. Also, consider the maintenance effort for 30 reports and three dashboards and compare this to one dashboard with 10 reports used as the data source.

The dashboard filter comes into the picture for this scenario; with just one dashboard, you can change the filter to include different records in the dashboard based on the selected filters.

Getting to know the dashboard filters

The dashboard filter is a great feature to filter the data in the dashboard component. All components will be filtered according to the filters selected. With the dashboard filter, you can use the same dashboard with different combinations of data.

Adding filters to a dashboard gives users the ability to have many results using a dashboard, so one dashboard serves the purpose of multiple dashboards. Without filters, you'd have to create multiple dashboards, with each dashboard having the same components with different filters. For example, add a filter in the industry field to track an account by industry. As admin, it is easier to maintain fewer dashboards.

If you have selected filters on a dashboard, the last filters selected by you will be applied by default when you reopen the dashboard. Salesforce will remember this for each user filter it applied for each dashboard.

To create a dashboard filter, you define a label for the filter, select the field that contains the type of information you want to filter, and then define how the filter returns the data. Each filter ideally contains more than one value, including the operator. Each filter can have up to 10 values maximum, and each dashboard can have up to three filters.

Hands-on exercise for adding a filter to a dashboard

Let's use the **Account Dashboard** created in `Chapter 9`, *Building Dashboards in Lightning Experience* for this exercise; we will add a filter based on **Industry** (a field in **Account**) with the option equal to:

- **Apparel** or **Education**
- **Energy**
- Not blank

This allows users to analyze the numbers of accounts related to the **Account Industry**:

1. Open and edit the **Account Dashboard** dashboard. If you come from the **Dashboards** tab, you can click on the **Edit** link directly; it is located under the arrow action menu, as shown in the following screenshot:

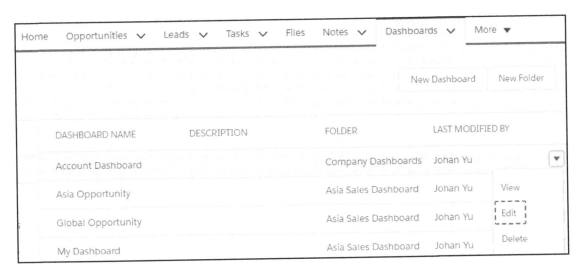

2. At this moment, we have two components in this dashboard; let's add another component, say, `Account by Type`:

3. Create a new report `Account by Type`:
   - Click on the **Reports** tab
   - Click on the **New Report** button
   - Select the **Accounts** record type and then click on the **Create** button
   - Change the filter to **Show** as **All accounts** and **Date Field Range** as **All time**
   - Change the report format to **Summary**
   - Drag **Type** into the grouping area
   - Save the report with the name as `Account by Type` and Report Folder to **Unfiled Public Reports**

4. Go back to the dashboard from the Dashboard Builder and click on the + **Component** button.
5. Select the report just created, **Account by Type**.
6. Click on the **Add** button. This is shown in the following screenshot:

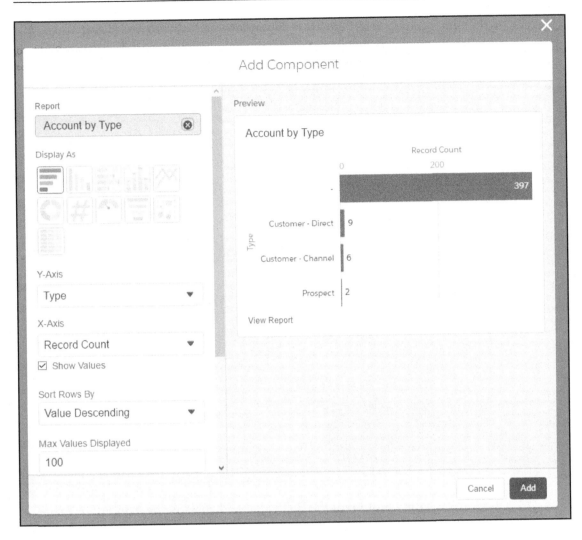

7. Move the new component added to the right of the second component.
8. Click on the **+ Filter** button to add a filter.
9. Select the field you would like used as a filter; in this exercise, select **Industry**.
10. In **Display Name**, type `Account Industry`.
11. Click on the **Add Filter Value** button.

12. In the filter options, select **equals** in **Operator**. For **Value(s)**, select **Apparel** and **Education** and in **Display Text**, enter `Apparel or Education`. Consider the following screenshot:

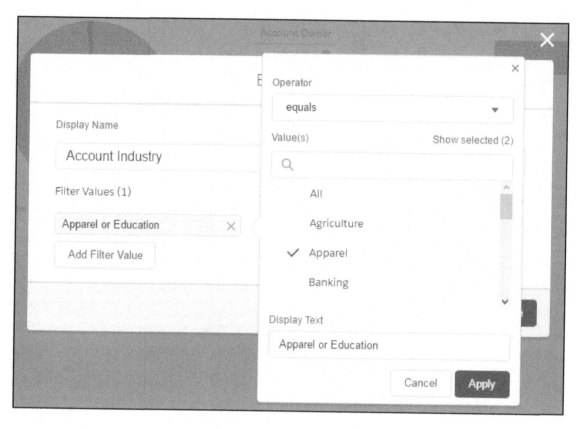

13. Click on the **Apply** button for the first value and click on the **Add Filter Value** button again to add the second filter value.

14. In the filter options, select **equals** in **Operator**. For **Value(s)**, select **Energy,** in **Display Text**, enter `Energy`.

15. Click on the **Apply** button for the second value, and click on the **Add Filter Value** button again to add the third filter value.

16. In the filter options, select **not equal to**. For **Value(s)**, leave it blank; in **Display Text**, enter `blank`.

17. Click on the **Apply** button for the third value and then click on the **Add** button. This is what it would look like:

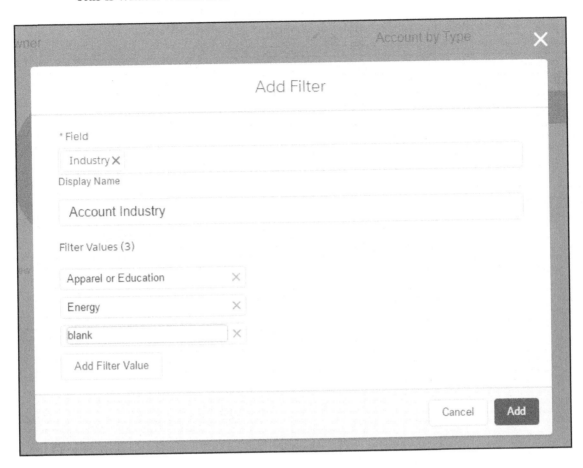

18. Back to the Report Builder, click on the **Save** button and then click on **Done** to exit the Dashboard Builder.

19. Now we have a filter called **Account Industry** in the dashboard with three values defined. Consider the following screenshot:

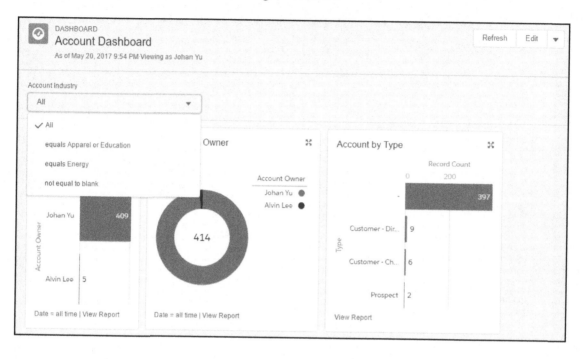

20. When you select the filter for **equals Apparel or Education**, the chart will be readjusted as the filter is selected, as shown here:

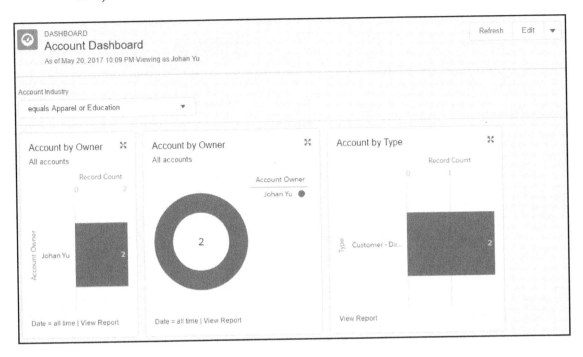

21. To remove or edit the filter, go to the Dashboard Builder by clicking on the **Edit** button in the dashboard; next, look for the pencil icon (**Edit Filter**), as shown in the following screenshot:

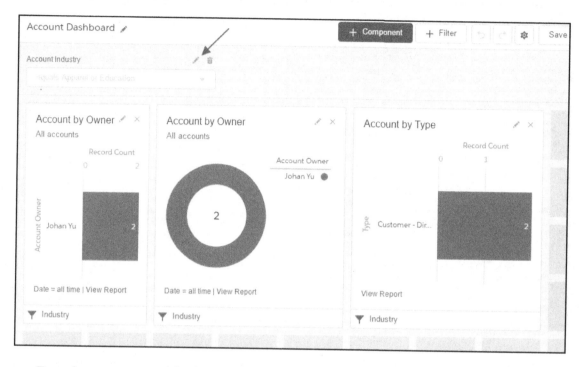

From here, you can add a filter by clicking on the **Add Filter Value** button or delete the value by clicking on the cross icon. To edit the existing values, click on the filter value name; for this example, let's click on **Energy** and then select **Electronics** and change the Display Text to `Electronics or Energy`. Click on the **Apply** button and then click on the **Update** button. Click on the **Save** button and then click on **Done** to exit the Dashboard Builder. Consider the following screenshot:

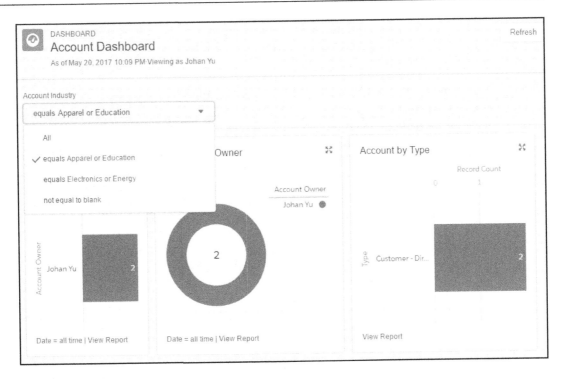

 You can have up to three filters in a dashboard. To add more filters, click on the **Add Filter** button in the dashboard edit mode.

Viewing a dashboard

In terms of runtime, as we discussed in `Chapter 9`, *Building Dashboards in Lightning Experience*, when you open a dashboard, it will show the data based on the latest refresh (manual or scheduled); while for a report, when you open a report, it always shows the current data.

The other difference between dashboards and reports in terms of the runtime is that a report always shows data visible to the running user, while in a dashboard, it can be configured to set the running user as follows:

- **Me**: The user who configures the dashboard, not the logged in user.
- **A specific user**: A user defined as a dashboard viewer; data visibility and reports visibility (used as the data source) will be based on this user. The dashboard creator is only able to select a user in a lower role hierarchy of the dashboard creator.
- **The logged in user**: The user sees the data as themselves. According to their own access to data, this is similar to reports, but there is also the option to enable **Allow dashboard viewers to change this (dynamic dashboard)**. The running user needs to have access to the reports; otherwise, the user will see an error message in each component, **The source report isn't available; it's been deleted or isn't in a folder accessible to the dashboard's running user.** Consider the following screenshot:

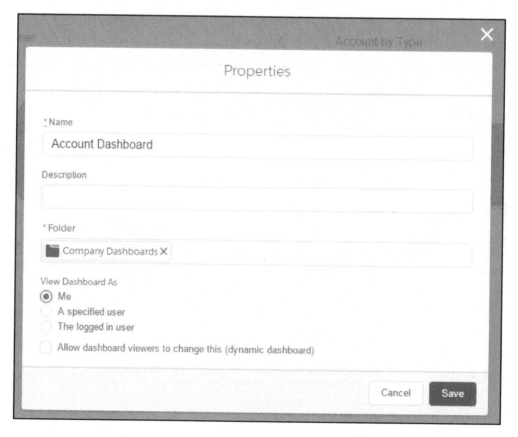

When a user creates a new dashboard or edits an existing dashboard, depending on the user permissions, the user may have different options available for **View Dashboard as**, such as the following:

- **Me** and **A specific user:** Only available when the user has the **View My Team's Dashboards** permission
- **The logged in user** (with allowing dynamic dashboard): This will be available only when a user has the **Manage Dynamic Dashboards** permission

Using a dynamic dashboard

Before we start with the definition of dynamic dashboards, let's understand whether there is a concept of a static dashboard. Yes, there is, but it is not called a **static dashboard**. So, there are two types of dashboards in Salesforce--normal dashboard and dynamic dashboard.

In summary, here is the difference between normal and dynamic dashboards:

Description	Normal dashboard	Dynamic dashboard
Viewing user	Viewing user is defined on dashboard creation, users cannot change the viewing user when opening the dashboard	Viewing user is the user who opens the dashboard. The user is able to change the viewing user (the user needs to have additional permission and the dashboard needs to be configured)
Number of dashboards	No limitation	There is a limit to the number of the dynamic dashboards, this limit is based on the edition subscribed
Permissions to create dashboard	No extra permissions	Needs additional **Manage Dynamic Dashboards** permission
Permissions to change viewing user	Not available	Needs additional **View My Team's Dashboards** or **View All Data** permission
Schedule a dashboard refresh	Available	Not available
Folder	Any folder	Only public folder, cannot store dynamic dashboard in personal/private folder

A normal dashboard

For a normal dashboard, the user will see a dashboard with the data visibility of someone else; it may be your manager or someone not directly related in your role hierarchy. Let's make a sample and see how it works in a normal dashboard. I will use following role hierarchy to explain this:

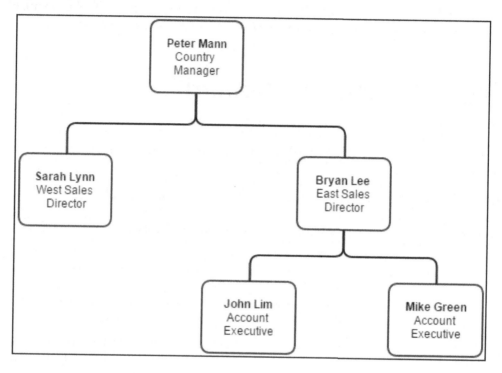

Let's say a normal dashboard is configured with a running user as **Peter Mann** - the **Country Manager**, with the role hierarchy located at the top. Any user who opens the dashboard will have the data visibility of **Peter Mann**:

- Even the user does not have visibility of the records.
- Even the user does not have access to the reports used as the source data for the dashboard components; for example, reports located in Peter's personal report folder or the folder that the user does not have access to.

Note that when the user clicks on **View Report** from a dashboard component, it will show the records visible for that user only, not as the dashboard viewing user. Therefore, reports generated may differ for each user.

A normal dashboard runs using the security settings of a specific user, which is the defined user. All users with access to the dashboard will see the same data, regardless of their own personal settings. One of the good use cases of using a normal dashboard is to show the dashboard as someone from top-level management in the company, such as the head of the business unit or the country head, so employees know the overall company performance. Also a good approach is to motivate team members by showing peer performance within a team.

What is a dynamic dashboard?

Dynamic dashboards offer users the ability to view the dashboard with data based on the running user data visibility, or data visibility of someone in the team or in your organization; this depends on the user permissions and dashboard setting. With a dynamic dashboard, the user can see a dashboard based on running user data visibility; this is much more simpler, without having to create separate dashboards for each user.

This is useful when you have the dashboard for each sales representative; when the sales representative logs in, they will see their own data, but when the manager logs in, they will see their team data. Also the manager will be able to see each of his team dashboards by changing the viewing user without the need to change the dashboard. Note that the manager needs to have the **View My Team's Dashboards** permission for this purpose.

Combining the dynamic dashboard with the dashboard filter discussed earlier will give the manager an overall view of the team pipeline or a view of the other statistics.

In `Chapter 2`, *Concepts and Permissions in Reports and Dashboards*, we discussed permissions related to dashboards. Some of the permissions are specifically related to dynamic dashboards only:

- The **Manage Dynamic Dashboards** permission
- The **View My Team's Dashboards** permission

The users with the **Manage Dynamic Dashboards** permission are able to create and edit dynamic dashboards. A dynamic dashboard is marked with **The logged in user** selected in **View Dashboard As**, and each user will see different data in the dashboard based on their data visibility. This is different from a normal dashboard, where all users see the same data based on one person's data visibility.

For users with the **View My Team's Dashboards** permission, when users open a dynamic dashboard with **Allow dashboard viewers to change this (dynamic dashboard)** enabled, they are able to select another user under their team from the role hierarchy, so all data in the dashboard will be refreshed with the visibility of that user. This includes user data and data shared with them and the data under that user's team. Furthermore, users with the **View All Data** permission will be able to select any users as dashboard viewers in the dynamic dashboard.

Limitations of the dynamic dashboard

The number of dynamic dashboards you can configure depends on your Salesforce edition; you can have up to five dynamic dashboards for the Enterprise Edition, up to 10 dynamic dashboards for the Unlimited and Performance Editions, and three for the Developer Edition. If you need additional dynamic dashboards, you can reach your account executive to purchase them.

You can't save a dynamic dashboard to a personal folder. The dynamic dashboard must be stored in a folder with shared access.

You cannot schedule a dynamic dashboard; dashboards have to be refreshed manually.

Hands-on exercise for creating a dynamic dashboard

Let's consider following activities for a hands-on implementation: change a normal dashboard to a dynamic dashboard and let the user choose the running user in the dashboard.

Before you start, make sure you have **Manage Dynamic Dashboards** and **View My Team's Dashboards** permissions; otherwise, you will not see the **Viewed Dashboard As** selection under the dashboard properties. You can reach out to your Salesforce administrator if you are not sure that you have this permission. The permissions are defined in your user profile setup or can be individually added to your user details using a **Permission Set**. This is shown in the following screenshot:

Again, let's use the **Account Dashboard** for this exercise. Before we change the dashboard to a dynamic dashboard, let's look at the dashboard again; note that the viewing user of the dashboard is **Johan Yu**, and the following screenshot is taken when logged in as Alvin Lee:

Perform the following steps for this hands-on exercise:

1. Navigate to the **Dashboards** tab, look for the **Account Dashboard** dashboard, and click on the **Edit** link under the arrow on the right-hand side of the dashboard name. Alternately, you can open the dashboard and then click on the **Edit** button.

2. Click on the gear icon; if you hover your mouse over, the label is called **Edit Dashboard Properties**.

3. Under **View Dashboard As**, at this moment, **Me** should be selected.

4. Change this to **The logged in user**, and select **Allow dashboard viewers to change this (dynamic dashboard)**.

5. Click on the **Save** button to close the properties window.

6. Click on the **Save** button again to save the dashboard changes and then click on **Done** to exit the Dashboard Builder.

7. Now you should see the **Change** link next to **Viewing as**; if you do not see it, refresh the dashboard or refresh the web browser. Consider the following screenshot:

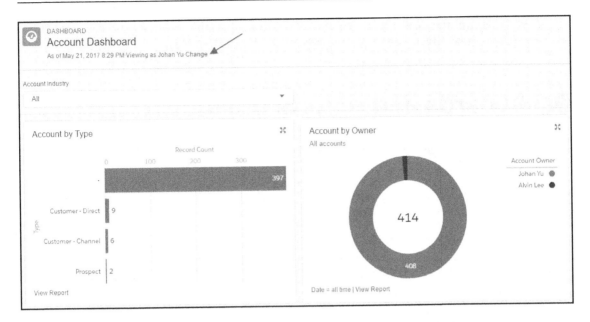

8. Click on the **Change** link; this will allow you to select other users as the dashboard viewing user. In my exercise, I'll select **Alvin Lee**, as shown in the following screenshot:

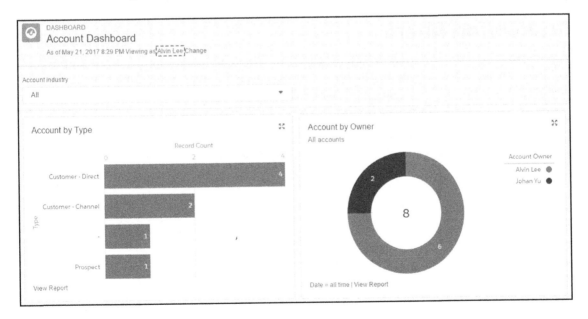

9. Note that the number of records shown in dashboard components changed. This is because **Alvin Lee** sees fewer accounts than **Johan Yu**.

Dashboards and reports drill down

As we have discussed in Chapter 9, *Building Dashboards in Lightning Experience*, a dashboard is built on components, and each component has a report used as the data source.

You can hover over each bar or portion of the chart to see more information, such as the percentage of the bar compared to the total.

When the user clicks on **View Report** from the component, it will bring the user to the report. However, you need to note that the report data will be based on the logged in user, while the dashboard data is based on someone set as a viewing user, so it would be not the same dataset for the dynamic dashboard.

Clicking anywhere in the chart or the expand icon will show one big chart, and you can still hover your mouse here, the same as in the dashboard view. Click on **View Report** from here and go to the same report used as the data source.

Preserving filters

When you have a dashboard with filters, select the filters and then on click **View Report** from the dashboard component. The report opens and is filtered in the same way as the dashboard, so you can keep analyzing data without missing a beat!

Filters conveyed from a dashboard to a report are called **Linked Filters**. You can remove **Linked Filters** from the report, but you can't edit them directly. **Linked Filters** don't persist after you leave the report. Consider the following screenshot:

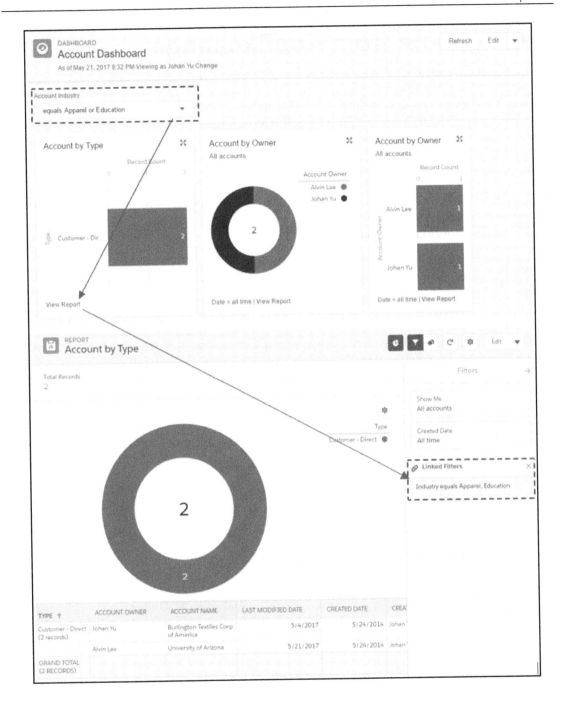

Getting more from AppExchange

If you are not familiar with AppExchange, it is a business app store hosted by Salesforce.com for Salesforce users. You can find thousands of apps to be installed into your Salesforce instance to meet or enhance your business needs. Some of the apps are free, while many have a license fee. They are built by Salesforce partners. In addition, there are some sample apps that have been provided by Salesforce Labs. Salesforce Labs does not support the apps they post on the AppExchange, but it offers many examples of Salesforce features that help admins learn how to use these features.

The app installed from AppExchange is considered a third-party app, which means it is not supported by the Salesforce Support team. For paid apps, usually, the developer will provide their support for their app.

 To reach Salesforce AppExchange, navigate to `https://appexchange.salesforce.com` and you will find many apps there, or you could search for them with the help of a keyword in the textbox.

To find apps related to the dashboard, type `dashboard` in the search textbox, and you will get many dashboard apps built by Salesforce Labs which you can install and use it for free, and there are apps built by Salesforce partners, which are either free or paid apps.

 It is always a good practice to try the app installed into a Sandbox before installing it in a production environment. Also, even if you install an AppExchange package, you can uninstall it without causing any problems for your other Salesforce organizations.

A few dashboard apps built by Salesforce Labs are as follows:

- **SALESFORCE CRM DASHBOARDS**
- **SALES ACTIVITY DASHBOARD**
- **SERVICE & SUPPORT DASHBOARDS**
- **SALESFORCE1 ADOPTION DASHBOARD AND REPORTS**

As you know, the dashboard needs to be supported with reports as the data source, so when you install apps related to the dashboard, it will also include the reports needed as the data source. If the standard presentations of dashboards or data filters or groupings do not match your organization, you can easily modify it and save it as new reports and dashboards. Consider the following screenshot:

Hands-on exercise for installing a dashboard from AppExchange

In this exercise, we are going to install "Salesforce CRM Dashboards" from AppExchange. Let's start:

1. Navigate to `https://appexchange.salesforce.com`.
2. Type `dashboard` in the search textbox in the top-right corner and press *Enter*.
3. Click on **Salesforce CRM Dashboards** from the search result.

4. Click on the **Get It Now** button as shown in the following:

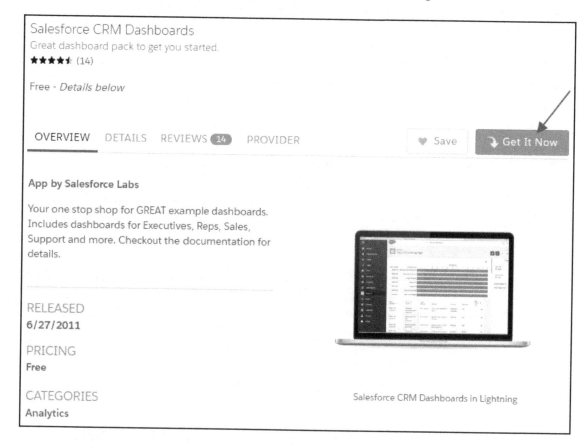

5. Click on the **Log in to the AppExchange** button to log in with your Salesforce credentials.

6. Now click on the **Install in production** or **Install in Sandbox** button, as shown in the following screenshot:

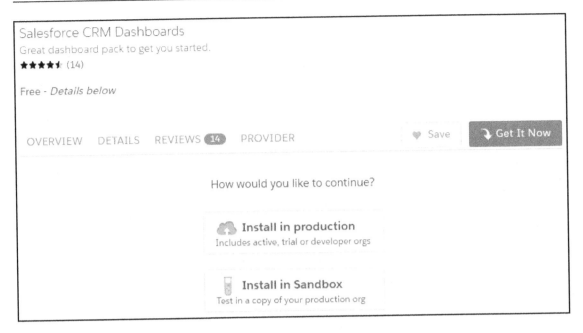

7. Check **I have read and agree to the terms and conditions.** and then click on the **Confirm and Install!!** button.

8. You may get a prompt to enter your Salesforce username and password.

9. Now you can select to install the app for **Admin Only**, **All Users**, or **Specific Profiles...** I will select **Admin Only** for this exercise and then click on the **Install** button.

10. Wait for a minute for installation; once finished, it will say **Installation Complete!**. Then, click on the **Done** button.

11. You will also be notified by email when the installation was done; for some big packages, you may need to wait for the email rather than see it complete on the screen.

12. This will bring you to the **Installed Packages** setup menu, and you will find the app here:

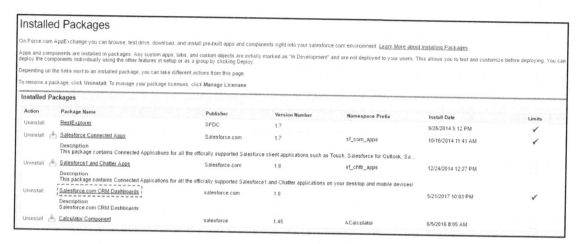

13. You can click on the package name **Salesforce.com CRM Dashboards** to see the package detail. You can uninstall from here or view the package components. Let's click on **View Components**.

14. Note that this package installs multiple dashboards in the multiple dashboard folders, including the reports too, as shown in the following screenshot:

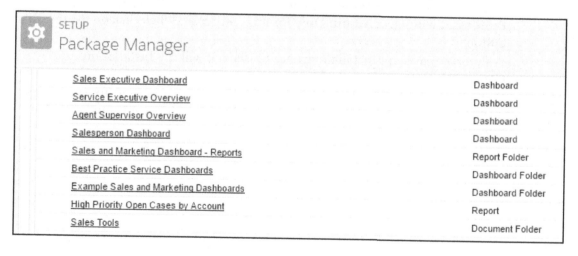

15. Let's open a **Sales Executive Dashboard** dashboard; you can search the dashboard name with a global search or go to the **Dashboards** tab to find the dashboard.

16. Open the dashboard and see the components provided; you can modify the dashboard components details, add new components, or remove components not relevant to your company. So, this is as per a normal dashboard and reports that you can modify as required.

Sales Year to Date dashboard

In this section, we'll build a complete Sales **Year to Date** (**YTD**) dashboard, which will include multiple components, dynamic dashboards, and filters. If you are not familiar with YTD, it is a period starting from the beginning of the year (either the calendar year or fiscal year) to the present day. in this sample, I'll use the calendar year. So, if today is 25 August 2017, the YTD will be 1 Jan 2017 - 25 Aug 2017.

Creating reports as a data source

Perform the following steps to create reports required to serve as the data source for dashboard components:

1. From the **Reports** tab, create a report folder called `Global Sales.`
2. Switch to Classic, share the report folder visibility to everyone, by adding **Public Group** as **All Internal Users** with **Viewer** access, and then switch back to Lightning Experience.
3. Create a report called `Pipeline for 120 days by Stage` with the the following details:
   - Select **Report Type** as **Opportunities**
   - Set **Opportunity Status** to **Open**
   - Select **Next 120 Days** for **Close Date** filter
   - Remove all columns, then add **Opportunity Name**, **Account Name**, **Amount**, **Opportunity Owner**, **Stage** and **Close Date** to the report
   - Change the report format to **Summary**, with group by **Stage**
   - Add a second level grouping **Close Date** as grouping, and change the **Close Date** grouping to **Calendar Month**
   - Summarize the **Amount** field with **Sum**
   - Hide the report **Details**
   - Save the report as `Pipeline for 120 days by Stage` in the report folder, **Global Sales**

4. Clone the preceding report as a new report called `Expired Pipeline`, store the report into the same report folder, **Global Sales** and update the cloned report with the following:
    - Change the **Close Date** filter to **All Time**
    - Add **Close Date** as a **Field filter**, select operation as **less than**, and filter value with **Today**, tick **Locked** for the filter, and then click on the **OK** button
    - Remove **Close Date** from the grouping, but add it to the report
    - Save the report

5. Clone the **Expired Pipeline** report as a new report called `Won Opportunities (YTD) by Sales Rep`, store the report into the same report folder, **Global Sales**, and update the cloned report with the following:
    - Change **Opportunity Status** to **Closed Won**
    - Change **Close Date** as the **Field filter** operation to **less or equal**, and then click on the **OK** button
    - Remove **Stage** from the grouping, and then add **Opportunity Owner** as the grouping
    - Save the report

6. Clone **Won Opportunities (YTD) by Sales Rep** report as a new report called `Won Opportunities (YTD) by Month`, and store the report into the same report folder, **Global Sales**. Update the cloned report with following:
    - Remove **Opportunity Owner** from grouping, and then add **Close Date** as the grouping, change the **Close Date** grouping to **Calendar Month**
    - Save the report

7. Clone **Won Opportunities (YTD) by Month** report as a new report called `Lost Opportunities (YTD)`, store the report into the same report folder, **Global Sales**, and update the cloned report with the following:
    - Change **Opportunity Status** to **Any**
    - Add **Stage** as **Field filter**, select operation as **equals**, and filter value with **Closed Lost**, tick **Locked** for the filter, and then click on the **OK** button
    - Delete **Opportunity Owner** from the grouping, and then add Lost Reason as the report grouping. **Lost Reason** is a custom picklist field; you need to create this custom field or change to other fields for this exercise
    - Save the report

8. Now, we have five **Summary** reports stored in the **Global Sales** report folder.

Creating a sales YTD dashboard

Continue with the following steps to create the dashboard:

1. From the **Dashboards** tab, create a dashboard folder called **Corporate Dashboard**.
2. Switch to Classic, share the dashboard folder visibility to everyone, by adding **Public Group** as **All Internal Users** with **Viewer** access, and then switch back to Lightning Experience.
3. Create a dashboard called **Global Sales (YTD)** and store it in the **Corporate Dashboard** folder.
4. Now, you should see a blank dashboard with nine boxes across the columns.

Let's add the first component to show the total amount of Won Opportunities as a Gauge chart:

1. Click on the **+ Component** button.
2. The system will ask you to select a report. Click on **All Folders**, and then click on **Global Sales**; you should see five reports created earlier.
3. Select the **Won Opportunities by Month (YTD)** report.
4. Select **Gauge Chart**, use the default value, and enter **Segment Ranges**.
5. Change the **Title** to Won Opportunities (YTD), and then click on the **Add** button.
6. Now the first component added to the dashboard, with the component size, will occupy 3x4 boxes (this is the default size).

Now, add the second component to show the total amount of **Won Opportunities by Sales Rep (YTD)**:

1. Click on the **+ Component** button.
2. The system will ask you to select a report. Click on **All Folders**, then click on **Global Sales**, select and **Won Opportunities by Month (YTD)**.
3. Select **Display** as **Vertical Bar Chart**, and **Sort Rows By Label Ascending**, and then click on the **Add** button.
4. The second component added to the dashboard, by default will occupy 3x4 boxes, and is located below the first component.
5. Move the component next to the right of the first component by dragging and dropping it.
6. Notice that we use the same report **Won Opportunities by Month (YTD)** for multiple dashboard components.

Let's add few more components using reports prepared earlier:

1. Add the third component:
    - Use the report **Won Opportunities by Sales Rep (YTD)**
    - **Chart Type** to use is **Horizontal Bar Chart**
    - Move the component next to the right of the second component

2. Add the fourth component:
    - Use the report **Pipeline for 120 days by Stage**
    - The **Chart Type** to use is **Horizontal Bar Chart**
    - On the **Y-Axis**, select **Close Date**, and **Sort Rows By Label Ascending**
    - Since the report has two groupings, by default we will have two groupings too in the chart. Resize the chart size to 5x7 boxes. The reason for making this chart bigger is to have a better visual of pipeline stage in the coming months

3. Add the fifth component:
    - Use the report **Expired Pipeline**
    - The **Chart Type** to use is **Horizontal Bar Chart**
    - On the **X-Axis**, select **Record Count**, and **Sort Rows By Label Ascending**
    - Add **Subtitle** as **This needs to be clean!** and **Footer** as **No record should be here**
    - Move the component next to the right of the fourth component, and set the chart size to 4x4 boxes

4. Add the sixth component:
    - Use the report **Lost Opportunities (YTD)**
    - The **Chart Type** to use is **Donut**
    - Move the component below the fifth component, and set the chart size to 2x3 boxes

5. Save the dashboard.

Let's see what we have now:

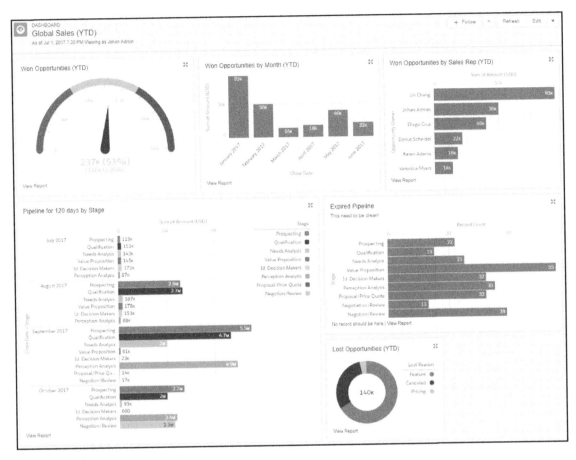

From this dashboard, there are many items management, and the sales manager need to focus and work on:

1. Sales YTD is **53%** of the target; we need to close at least another 47% won opportunities.
2. We had bad sales in **March** and **April**.
3. Award bonuses for top sales representatives and provide guidance for sales representatives at the lower end of the leaderboard.

4. Put more effort into monitoring and guiding big pipelines, such as the one on the **Perception Analysis** stage in **September 2017**.

5. For expired pipelines, sales need to work on them, if they should be closed at a loss or to reactivate them by changing the forecast **Close Date**.

6. Look at **Lost Opportunities** with the amount and percentage of **Lost Reason**.

Adding dashboard filters

Next, let's add filters, so we can analyze the data easier:

1. Edit the dashboard.

2. We would like to have a filter for the account's **Industry**.

3. Click on the **+ Filter** button and select the **Industry** field from **Account**:
   - First value, **equal** to **Agriculture**
   - Second value, **equal** to **Communications, Telecommunications**
   - Third value, **not equal** to `blank`
   - You can add more filter values, or combine the values if that makes sense

4. Click on the **Add** button and now we have the first filter added.

5. Let's add another filter, to analyze if the opportunity by Account's **Country**. We'll categorize them into US and International (not US).

6. Click on the **+ Filter** button again and select **Billing Country** from **Account**:
   - First value, **equal** to `United States`
   - Second value, **not equal** to `United States1`

7. Save the dashboard.

Once the filters are added, users can play around with them to get the dashboard with data set based on the filter options selected as shown in the following screenshot:

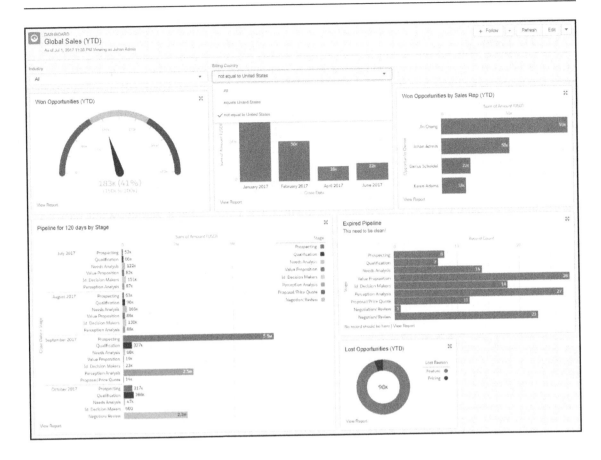

Adding a dynamic dashboard

Enabling a dashboard as a dynamic dashboard is pretty simple, as long as you have the permissions required, and have not used all the numbers of the dynamic dashboards given:

1. Edit the dashboard.
2. Edit the dashboard properties by clicking on the gear icon.
3. In the **View Dashboard As** option, select **The logged in user** and enable **Allow dashboard viewers to change this (dynamic dashboard)**.
4. Save the dashboard.

Refresh the dashboard, and now you should see the **Change** link next to **Viewing as** under the report name. With this, the sales manager is able to change the dashboard viewer user with any of the sales representative under the manager role hierarchy.

Summary

This chapter concludes the dashboard section in general in this book. We started with implementing a dashboard filter so that a dashboard could be used for multiple scenarios instead of creating a dashboard for each criterion.

We continued with a deep dive into dynamic dashboards, looked at how they are different from normal dashboards, covered how to create a dynamic dashboard, and finally discussed the limitations of using dynamic dashboards.

We covered drill down options in dashboards related to the dashboard filter and report filters and we explained how to get prebuilt dashboards from AppExchange, whether free or paid for. In the last topic of this chapter, we built a sample complete dashboard from scratch, using reports, dashboard components, dashboard filters, and enabling dynamic dashboards.

In the next chapter, we will discuss advanced tips and tricks related to reports and dashboards that may be useful for you to create awesome analytics in Salesforce.

11

Advanced Tips and Tricks for Reports and Dashboards

We discussed reports in detail from Chapter 4, *Creating and Managing Reports* to Chapter 8, *Working with Reports* then dashboards in Chapter 9, *Building Dashboards in Lightning Experience* and Chapter 10, *Learning Advanced Dashboard Configuration*, thus covering almost everything about reports and dashboards in Salesforce Lightning. In this chapter, we are going to share more advanced topics on reports and dashboards, and some tips and tricks related to reporting and dashboards.

We will start with a topic on how to implement collaboration using **Chatter** in reports and dashboards, including feed tracking, and posting dashboard component to **Chatter** feeds and groups. We will continue to learn tips on using URL parameters in the report to change filter values dynamically, without the need to edit the dashboard.

Field history tracking is another useful feature for the admin to implement tracking value changes within the fields tracked--just select the fields to track, and you can trace who changes a value and when, and what the original and the new values are, but for **Text Area (Long)** and **Text Area (Rich)** including **Picklist (Multi-Select)**, it will just track there is a change, not track the original and new value. We will end this chapter by looking at **Reporting Snapshot**, where we can store historical data in a custom object and then create a report for data analysis.

The following topics will be covered in this chapter:

- Reports and dashboards collaboration with **Chatter**
- Filtering reports via URL parameters
- Setting and using **Field History Tracking**
- Preparing a report on historical data with **Reporting Snapshot**

Reports and dashboards collaboration with Chatter

Salesforce offers **Chatter** as a collaboration platform in the system, similar to Facebook, where you can post messages, photos, and so on. You will also be able to create a group and collaborate within the group. Furthermore, with a **Chatter** feed, you can collaborate with other users at the record level, such as **Account**, **Opportunity**, and other objects; this includes reports and dashboards.

Enabling collaboration in a report

You can utilize a **Chatter** feed in a report to collaborate with your teams, for example, to give attention to the Sales Pipeline report or others.

Let's look back on the items available when you open a report--there is an icon called Collaborate next to **Filters**, as shown in the following screenshot:

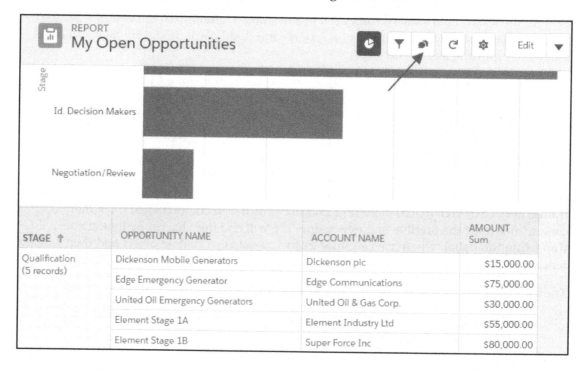

If you do not see this icon, your admin needs to enable the report for collaboration, following these steps:

1. Navigate to **Setup** | **Feature Settings** | **Chatter** | **Feed Tracking**.
2. Look for **Report**, and tick **Enable Feed Tracking.** You can select all fields here for tracking.
3. Click on the **Save** button. This is shown in the following screenshot:

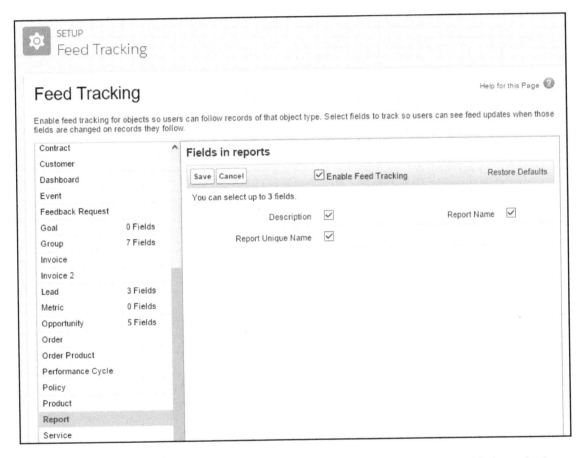

Now open a report, and you should see the **Collaborate** icon in the report. Click on the icon, and it will open the **Chatter** panel. By default, there are two tabs here: **Post** and **Poll**.

Because this is just **Chatter** post or poll, you can use **Chatter** style when posting, such as using @ to mention the username. Click on the **Share** button when you are done. This is shown in the following screenshot:

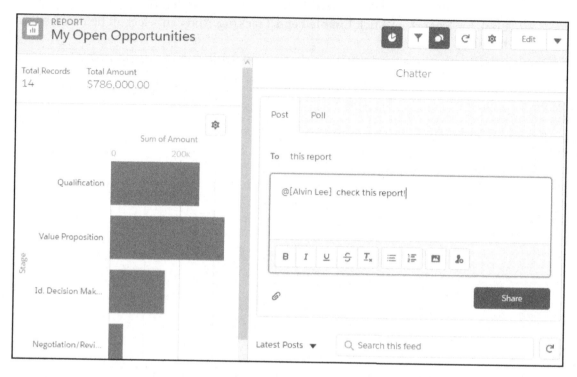

Similar to a normal **Chatter** post, the user mentioned will be notified. That user can just click on the Notifications icon at the top-right corner, next to the username, to open the post and comment on or like the post. Enabling a **Chatter** post for the report may look simple, but it is a powerful feature to serve as a collaboration tool among users within the report. This feature is pretty similar to **Chatter** posts in records, such as **Account**, **Opportunities**, and so on. The following screenshot shows the **Chatter** panel at the right-hand side:

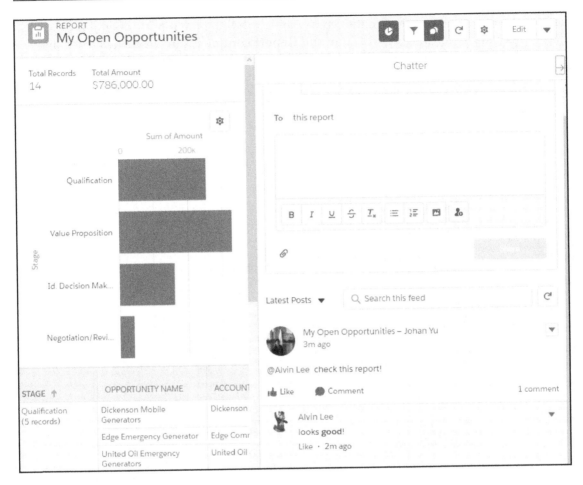

In the preceding screenshot, we only have the **Post** and **Poll** actions in the **Chatter** page. We can add or remove actions by navigating to **Setup** | **User Interface** | **Global Actions** | **Publisher Layouts.** Then edit the layout and select **Salesforce1 & Lightning Actions**.

Tracking report feed

If you remember, in an earlier exercise when enabling report for feed tracking, we also enabled tracking for these items:

- **Report Name**
- **Report Unique Name**
- **Description**

Let's do a simple exercise: change the report name by editing the report--open report properties and change the **Report Name** and **Report Unique Name**. Save the report, and let's see how the tracking works. Open the **Chatter** panel from the report by clicking on the Collaborate icon. This is shown in the following screenshot:

Dashboard collaboration and feed tracking

Similar to a report, you can collaborate using **Chatter** feed tracking in the dashboard. The Collaborate icon is located next to the Refresh button on the dashboard; if you do not see the icon, follow these steps:

1. Navigate to **Setup** | **Feature Settings** | **Chatter** | **Feed Tracking**.
2. Look for **Dashboard** and tick **Enable Feed Tracking;** select all fields here for tracking.
3. Click on the **Save** button.

These are the five items that you can track in dashboard feeds:

- **Dashboard Running User**
- **Dashboard Unique Name**
- **Description**
- **Title**
- **Using Grid Layout**

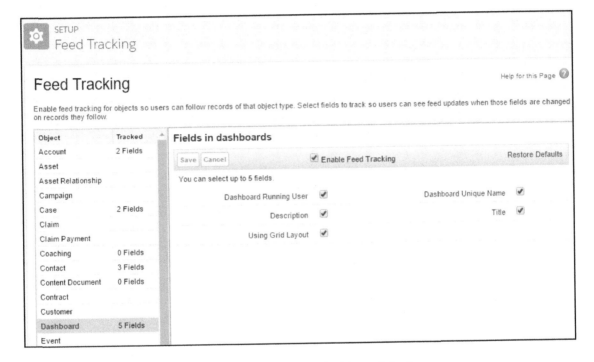

The preceding screenshot shows the items in the dashboard feed.

Let's have a quick hands-on exercise for dashboard collaboration and feed tracking:

1. Open our existing dashboard, **Account Dashboard**.
2. Click on the Collaborate icon to open the **Chatter** window. This is shown in the following screenshot:

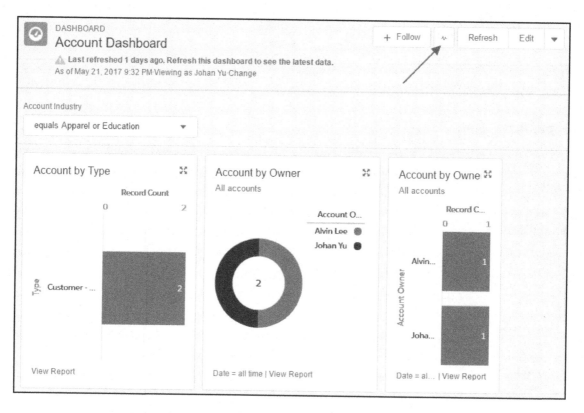

3. With both **Chatter** post and poll, you can mention other users to be notified. For this exercise, let's create a new poll to see whether users preferred the new dashboard design. Check the following screenshot:

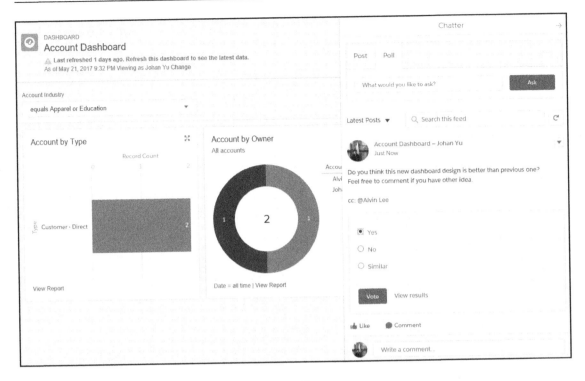

4. Users can like or comment on the poll too.

5. Let us add a **Description** for the dashboard; remember that we tracked **Description** in **Chatter** feed tracking earlier.

6. Edit the dashboard, edit the dashboard properties (gear icon), then add text to the **Description** text box. For this exercise, let us type `This dashboard contains all items related to Accounts`.

7. Click on the **Save** button to exit the report properties window. Click on **Save** again to save the dashboard, and then click on **Done**.

8. Open the **Chatter** panel again (Collaborate icon), and notice under **Post** that the change we made in **Description** is tracked as a post.

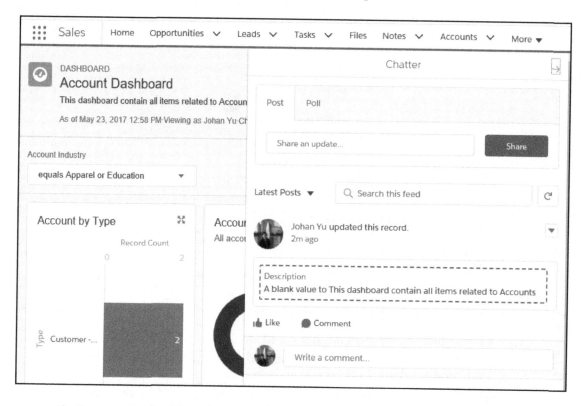

9. Because the feed here is part of **Chatter** feed, now let us open the **Chatter** tab. It should appear there too, as shown in the following screenshot:

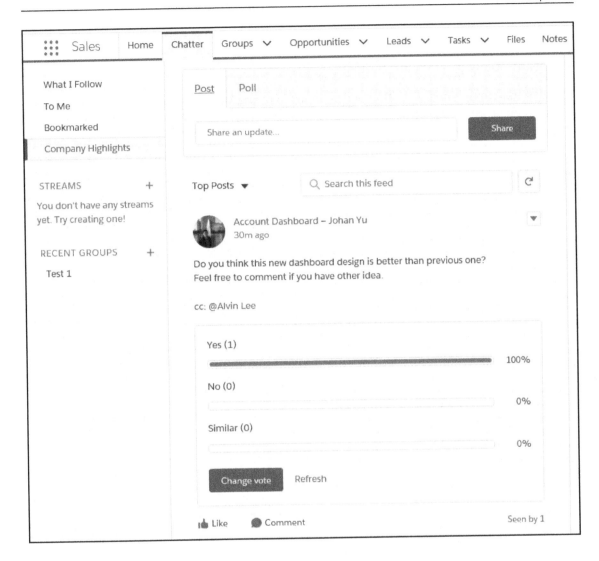

Following dashboards

As you may be aware in Salesforce, we can follow a record, such as an account or opportunity, or other records. So, when someone changes the record value, we'll be notified of the update in our **Chatter** feeds and via email (depends on each user's **Chatter** email setting). The same is true for the dashboard; by following a dashboard, the user will be notified of updates in the user's **Chatter** feed.

Your admin needs to enable feed tracking for the dashboard, otherwise, no users in the organization will be able to follow any dashboard. If feed tracking is not enabled for the dashboard, you will not see the button.

To make this clear, when we follow a dashboard, we are following the dashboard itself, not the components in that dashboard, so updated components will not appear on our **Chatter** feed. Consider the following screenshot:

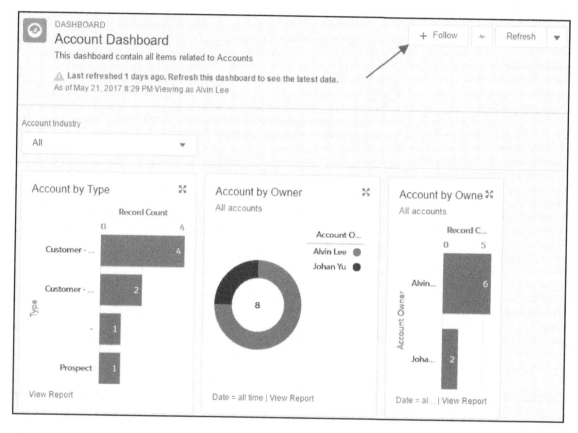

Click on the **+ Follow** button next to the Collaborate icon to follow a dashboard. This is the same as following records from objects, such as **Account**, **Opportunity**, and the like. When you follow a dashboard, you will be notified of changes to the fields being tracked for the dashboard, such as **Dashboard Running User**, **Description**, **Dashboard Unique Name**, and **Title**.

Let's look at the following sample. A user will see the post in the dashboard on his **Chatter** page, not because the user is mentioned in that post, but because the user follows the dashboard, the same way a user follows **Account**, or **Contact**, or other records:

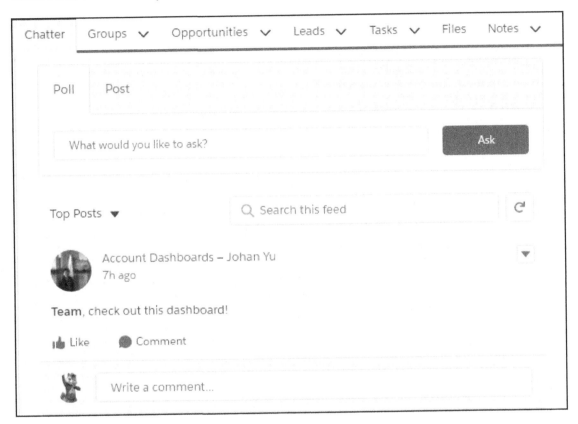

Posting a dashboard component snapshot

By posting a dashboard component snapshot to **Chatter**, you can get your team to respond or give feedback on a topic, such as a dashboard component that shows a drop in the opportunity pipelines or others. Once the dashboard has been enabled for feed tracking, your users can share dashboard snapshots to the dashboard's feed, to a **Chatter** group, or to the user's feed.

To enable dashboard component snapshot, navigate to **Setup** | **Feature Settings** | **Analytics** | **Reports & Dashboards Settings,** and look for **Enable Dashboard Component Snapshots**. If you don't enable feed tracking, users will not able to post dashboard components to the dashboard's feed. Posting components to a person's or group's feed allow someone without access to the dashboard to see the chart.

Snapshot post is a static image from a dashboard component at the time when it is posted. If the dashboard has filters applied, the snapshot image will be based on the component with the filters applied. Information on when the snapshot was posted and viewed by the user will be added to the Snapshot post.

These are the three options to post a dashboard snapshot:

1. **This dashboard**
2. **A group**
3. **My followers**

When a snapshot is posted to dashboard feed, all users who are able to open the dashboard will see the dashboard snapshot at a point in time as a **Post** in **Chatter**.

Let us have a quick hands-on exercise for posting a dashboard snapshot:

1. Open the dashboard.
2. Select the component that you want to take a snapshot of; the component will show as one big chart.
3. Click on the **Share** button in the bottom-right corner of the screen.
4. You can select to post in this dashboard, a group, or my followers. In this exercise, let us select **This dashboard**.
5. You can enter a message in the **Message** box.
6. Click on the **Post** button. This is shown in the following screenshot:

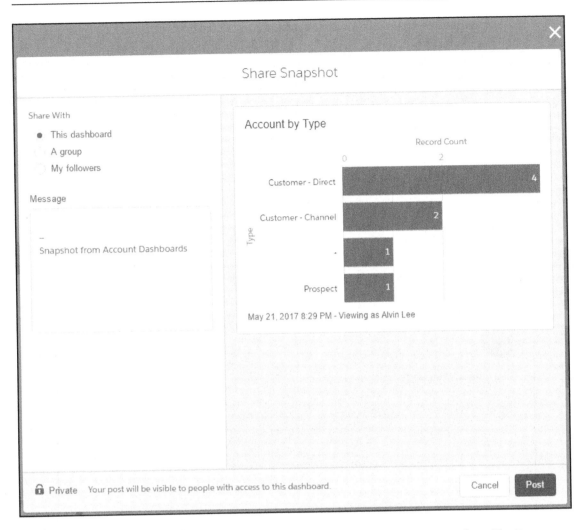

Posting a snapshot to a **Chatter** group will get attention from the users in that **Chatter** group. Snapshots posted to a **Chatter** group feeds can be seen by everyone in the group-- even the ones without access to the dashboard, so, don't post sensitive information. To post a snapshot to a **Chatter** group, follow these steps:

1. Open the dashboard.
2. Select the component of which you want to take a snapshot; the component will show as one big chart.
3. Click on the **Share** button in the bottom-right corner of the screen.
4. Select to post into **A group**, then type the group name.

5. You can enter a message in the **Message** box.
6. Click on the **Post** button. This is shown in the following screenshot:

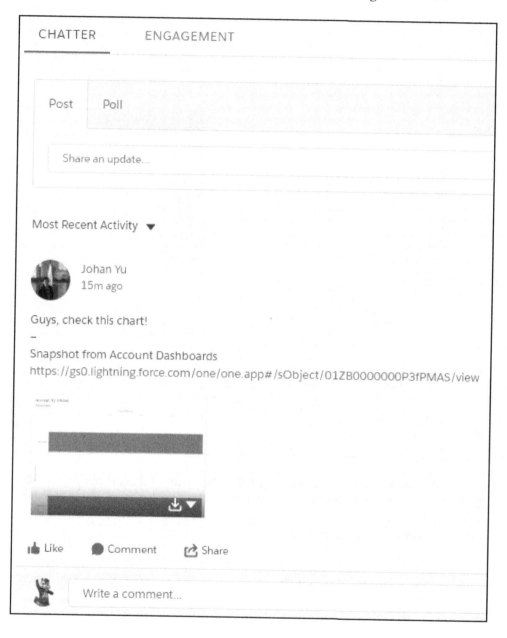

Filtering reports via URL parameters

If you are familiar with Classic, you can implement the report parameter by adding `pv` after the report URL. How do we do that in Lightning? Fortunately, Salesforce offers the same feature, but before we look at the sample and do some hands-on exercise, let us discuss how powerful this feature is.

With this feature, you can pass values in the report URL, as parameters act as filter values for the report. One of the uses is to create a custom button or link from the record page pointing to the report created, and with specific filters, you will be able to create a dynamic report based on the source record. For example, to generate a report for all opportunities related to an account.

Another usage of the report with a URL parameter is the ability to reuse the same report for different purposes, instead of creating two similar reports. For example, in the case of Pipeline for New Business and Pipeline for Existing Business with URL parameters, once the report is loaded, you can create two bookmarks with the URL parameters.

Using a parameter as a report filter will save us from creating many similar reports differentiated only by filters, or having to keep editing the report and changing the filter values.

Hands-on exercise for implementing a report filter via URL parameters

Use case: we would like to analyze certain **Account** fields, which are not visible in the Account page layout. The report will be filtered by **Account Name**, but instead of repeatedly editing the report to change the **Account Name** value, let us use a report filter with a URL parameter.

1. Create a simple **Tabular Account** report, and name it `Account Name Report`.
2. Select the **Show** field to be **All accounts**.
3. Set **Date Field Range** to **All Time**.
4. Add the filter, **Account Name contains** `blank`; click on **OK** to confirm the filter.
5. Click on the **Save** button, and click on **Run Report**.
6. Click on the **Reports** tab, then open the report again (it should appear at the top of the list).

7. The following screenshot shows the report generated, and get the report's URL. In my case, it is **https://gs0.lightning.force.com/one/one.app#/sObject/00OB0000001sBuoMAE/view**:

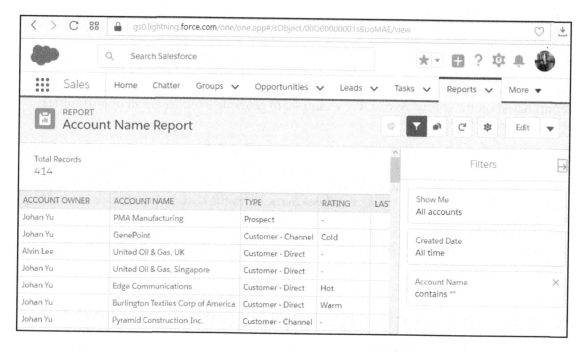

8. Okay, now we are going to add a parameter to the report's URL.
9. Let's say we would like to show all accounts that contain the name united.
10. Add united as the URL parameter, and hit *Enter* in the web browser: https://gs0.lightning.force.com/one/one.app#/sObject/00OB000000 1sBuoMAE?fv0=united. This is shown in the following screenshot:

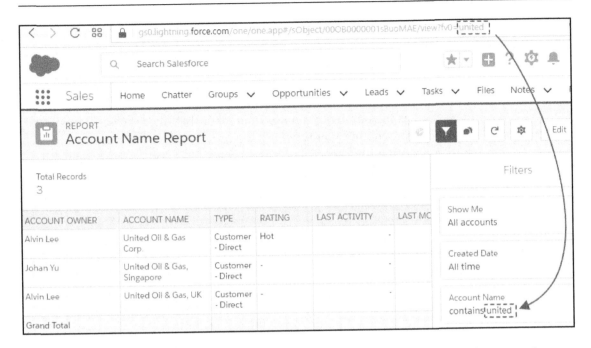

As you can see in the preceding screenshot, **united** added to the parameter becomes the filter value for the report. If you do not save the report, the report will stay as it is, but if you save the report, the report will have **united** stored permanently.

Let us analyze the preceding report and URL:

- Here is the original URL:
  `https://gs0.lightning.force.com/one/one.app#/sObject/00OB000000`
  `1sBuoMAE/view`
- Then we change the URL by adding a parameter as follows:
  `https://gs0.lightning.force.com/one/one.app#/sObject/00OB000000`
  `1sBuoMAE/view?fv0=united`
- We add `?` after the report ID, which is `00OB0000001sBuoMAE`; `&` denotes a new parameter in the URL. If you have multiple parameters, substitute `?` with `&` from the second parameter onwards.

- We add `fv0`, where `fv` stands for filter value, as the parameter name. The `0` is the numerical order in which the filter appears in the report; the first filter is 0, the second filter is 1, the third is 2, and so on and so forth. To set the value of the second filter in the report, specify `fv1` as the parameter name. Standard filters don't count in this order, and can't be filtered using URL parameters.
- We add `united` as the parameter name--remember that filter is case-insensitive, so it doesn't matter whether you type `united` or `United`. If you want to add more than one word with a space, such as `united oil`, you can just type as it is, but the browser will add `%20` in between to follow the URI encoded, so it will become `https://gs0.lightning.force.com/one/one.app#/sObject/00OB000000 1sBuoMAE/view?fv0=united%20oil`.

Now, what if I just need to change the filter value for the second parameter, but not for the first one? Well, that should not be an issue--you can just add `fv1` in the parameter (without `fv0`), for example: `https://gs0.lightning.force.com/one/one.app#/sObject/00OB0000001sBuoMAE /view?fv1=customer`. This is shown in the following screenshot:

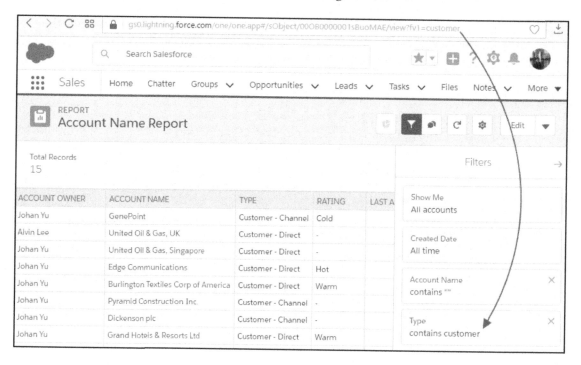

There are a few things to note related to filtering with URL parameters, which are as follows:

- URL parameters only support field filters manually added to the report.
- They do not support standard filters provided by the report, such as **Role Hierarchy**, scope, territory, **Opportunity Status**, **Probability**, and date filters.
- They do not support **Cross Filter** and **Row Limit** filters.
- The first field manually added as a filter will count the first parameter, which is fv0.
- If a chart is added to the report, the chart will be adjusted as the report filter is applied, including the filter that uses the URL parameters.
- You can't add, change, or delete the fields being filtered via URL parameters; you can only modify the value of existing filters.
- Parameters do not have to be added in the same sequence as the report filters, for example, we put can fv1 before fv0:
  https://gs0.lightning.force.com/one/one.app#/sObject/00OB000000 1sBuoMAE/view?fv1=customer&fv0=united ; here, fv1 is added as the first parameter, but fv1 is for the second filter. Then we add fv0, which is the first filter, as the second parameter. Use ? only before the first parameter, then use & to separate all other parameters.

Setting and using field history tracking

Tracking field history is an out-of-the-box Salesforce feature to track value changes in a field. You can select up to 20 fields per object to track; contact Salesforce Support if you need to track more fields. For field types, **Text Area (Long)**, **Text Area (Rich)**, and **Picklist (Multi-Select)**, history tracking does not track the original value and new value when a record is updated, but only tracks that a change has occurred for the field. This feature is simple, but powerful for audit purposes.

Salesforce retains history for up to 18 months; however, if you need to archive for a longer period, contact your Salesforce Support to acquire Field Audit Trail and define a policy for how long you wish to retain field history tracking. This payable feature will allow you to extend the archive for up to 10 years.

As an admin, you can enable field history tracking by yourself with a few clicks--select certain important fields to track for both standard and custom objects.

Remember, with field tracking the field value is not tracked until the object is enabled and the fields are selected for tracking. This means that if you enable tracking the **Account Name** today, you will not be able to track **Account Name** changes made before today.

History tracking is not just to track when you edit a record, but also when you create a new record, including records that are created when a **Lead** is converted. The field history entry will be marked as **Created** when you create a new record, or **Created by lead convert** when the record is converted from a **Lead** record; both, the old value and the new value will be blank.

History tracking on standard objects

History tracking supports both standard and custom objects. But not all standard objects are supported by field tracking; only the following standard objects support history tracking: **Accounts**, **Articles**, **Assets**, **Campaigns**, **Cases**, **Contacts**, **Contracts**, **Contract Line Items**, **Entitlements**, **Leads**, **Opportunities**, **Orders**, **Order Products**, **Products**, **Service Contracts**, and **Solutions**.

To enable history tracking on a standard object, such as **Account**, perform these steps:

1. Navigate to **Setup** | **Object and Fields** | **Object Manager** | **Accounts** | **Fields & Relationships**, and click on the **Set History Tracking** button.
2. Check the **Enable Account History** checkbox.
3. Select the fields you want to track.
4. Notice that **Description** will be tracked for changes only. This is because **Description** is a **Text Area (Long)** field, the same when you track fields with the type of **Text Area (Long)**, or **Text Area (Rich)**, and **Picklist (Multi-Select)**.
5. Click on the **Save** button to save the changes.

History tracking on custom objects

For custom objects, you need to enable tracking in the object details before selecting the fields to track. Let's say we have a custom object named `Claim`. Perform the following steps:

1. Navigate to **Setup | Objects and Fields | Object Manager**.
2. Click on the **Claim** object link and click on the **Edit** button.
3. Enable **Track Field History** in optional features, and click on the **Save** button. This is shown in the following screenshot:

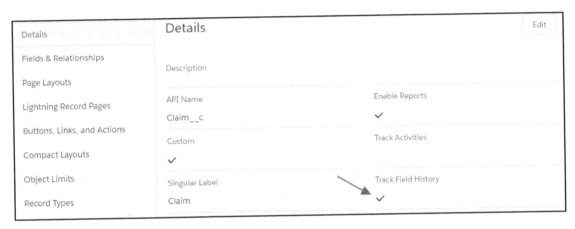

4. Select **Fields & Relationships** from the menu on the left-hand side.
5. Click on the **Set History Tracking** button, and select the fields you want to track.
6. Do the same with the standard object, for the **Text Area (Long)**, **Text Area (Rich)**, and **Picklist (Multi-Select)** fields--it will track changes only, not the old and new values.
7. Click on the **Save** button to save the changes.

History objects

When you enable **Field History Tracking** for an object, at the backend Salesforce will create a new object. The object name will end with **History**, for example, **AccountHistory**, **ContactHistory**, and so on for the standard object, and for the custom object it would be **__History**, for example, `Claim__History`.

When any changes happen to a tracked field in a record, Salesforce will create a new record in this object. For example, if you have five tracked fields in an object, and three of them change in one transaction, Salesforce will create three records in this object.

As a developer or admin familiar with SOQL, you can look into the object to query for the following:

- `CreatedById`: User who makes the change
- `CreatedDate`: Date of change
- `OldValue`: Shows the old value
- `NewValue`: Shows the new value
- `ParentId`: (for custom object), the record ID related to the changes
- `ObjectId` (for example: `AccountId` or `ContactId` for standard object)

You cannot create, update, or delete records in this object manually, you can only query. For a good reason, the storage usage for history objects is not counted as data storage.

Reading the history tracking value

Once you enable history tracking, there are two ways to see the tracking value, not including using an API query. These two ways are discussed next.

The history related list

Add a field history information-related list to the object page layout. This information will be visible to all users assigned to the particular page layout, just in case you have multiple page layouts.

To add the history related list to the object page layout, open the page layout editor. In this exercise, let us take the **Account** object, so the related list for this would be **Account History**. Select **Account History** in **Related Lists**, and drag it to the page layout. This is shown in the following screenshot:

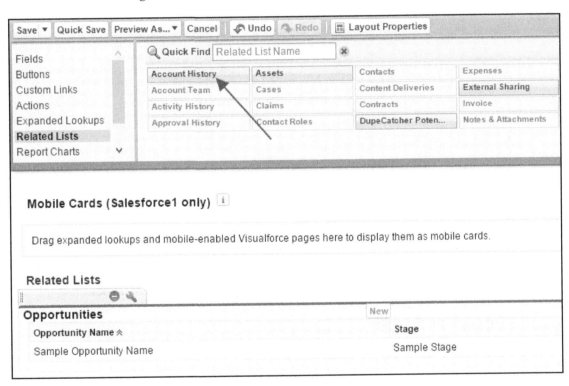

Once the history related list is added to the page layout, any update to the fields tracked will be shown here, as seen in the following screenshot under the **Related** tab (left arrow); but you can also add it as a related list in the Lightning component (right arrow):

Let us analyze the preceding screenshot:

- The history is sorted by date in descending order
- The first history shows when the record was created
- When updating more than one field in one transaction, it will track as two different items, but with the same date and time; see changes in **Account Owner** and **Account Number**
- Because **Description** is a long text area field, it will not track the original and new value, but just track that a change occurred

All objects will have the same label, and end with history, for example, **Account History**, **Contact History**, **Claim History**, and so on. But for opportunity object, it is an exception--it is called **Opportunity Field History**. Consider the following screenshot for the sample of **Opportunity Field History**:

The same is true for an API object name--it will be called **Opportunity Field History** instead of **Opportunity History.** The **Opportunity History** object is used to store **Opportunity Stage** information.

History reports

Another option to get a history tracking value is using a report. The user just needs to have the **Run Report** permission, and the permission to access the object to run the report created.

To create the report, start by selecting a custom report type such as **Account History** report, as shown in the following screenshot:

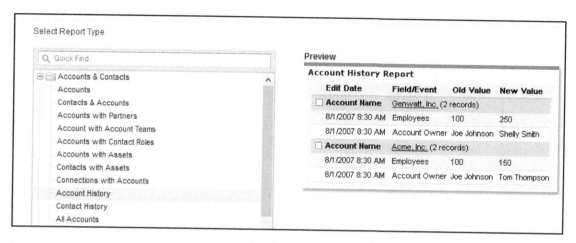

By default, it will show **My accounts**, but you can modify it like a normal report. Add a filter, add groupings, change the report format, and add/remove fields of the report. If you look at the left panel for field availability, only fields from the **History Data** group will contain historical data, while other fields will show live data in Salesforce if you bring that field to the report. Consider the following screenshot for fields under **History Data**:

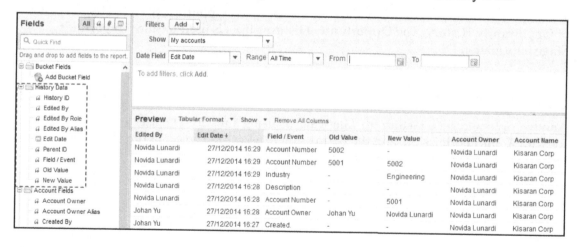

If you notice in the preceding screenshot, `Parent ID` for the **Account History** report type is **Account ID**. This will be the same for other objects; for example, if this is **Contact History**, the **Parent ID** would be Contact ID.

For a custom object, once you enable **Track Field History** in the object details, create a new custom report, and notice the report type ending with `History` is available for you to use, such as `Claim History`. Similar to the aforementioned **Account History**, you can use this report type as a normal report. Consider the following screenshot for the report:

HISTORY ID	PARENT ID	ACCOUNT NAME	EDITED BY	EDIT DATE ↓	FIELD / EVENT	OLD VALUE	NEW VALUE
017B000002TtGNh	001B000000SW0QO	Electric Inc Limited	Alvin Lee	5/24/2017 9:10 PM	Account Number	-	8001
017B000002TtGfz	001B000000SW0QO	Electric Inc Limited	Johan Yu	5/24/2017 9:10 PM	Account Owner	Johan Yu	Alvin Lee
017B000002TtGcL	001B000000SW0QO	Electric Inc Limited	Johan Yu	5/24/2017 9:09 PM	Description	-	-
017B000002TtGcK	001B000000SW0QO	Electric Inc Limited	Johan Yu	5/24/2017 9:09 PM	Account Name	Electric Inc	Electric Inc Limited
017B000002TtGYa	001B000000SW0QO	Electric Inc Limited	Johan Yu	5/24/2017 9:08 PM	Created.	-	-
017B000002TtGVC	001B000000SW0QJ	Big Inc. Limited	Johan Yu	5/24/2017 9:07 PM	Description	-	-
017B000002TtGVB	001B000000SW0QJ	Big Inc. Limited	Johan Yu	5/24/2017 9:07 PM	Account Name	Big Inc.	Big Inc. Limited
017B000002TtGWA	001B000000SW0QJ	Big Inc. Limited	Johan Yu	5/24/2017 9:07 PM	Created.	-	-

Limitations of using field history tracking

Some of the limitations have been explained previously, but let us summarize them here:

- By default, only a maximum of 20 fields can be tracked
- For **Text Area (Long)**, **Text Area (Rich)**, and **Picklist (Multi-Select)** type of field, you cannot track the original and new value
- Not all standard objects can be tracked; for example, **User**, **Task**, **Event**, **Campaign**, and **Quote**
- Not all fields can be tracked; for example, the **Formula** field, **Roll-Up Summary**, auto-number fields, **Created By**, **Last Modified By**, and **Expected Revenue** fields on **Opportunity**

Reporting on historical data with Reporting Snapshots

Can we have a report on data trending in Salesforce? Does Salesforce only report current data? Field history tracking will store old and new values whenever value changes in fields are detected. But to use it for trending would be too difficult, unless you export the data to an external database and analyze it with live data--it will not include deleted data either (if any).

So, is there any other way to store historical data in Salesforce so that we can easily use it for reporting? Yes, if you are using Salesforce Enterprise Edition or later, you can configure **Reporting Snapshot** to store historical data.

The same as field tracking, do not expect the old historical data to be available before you configure the **Reporting Snapshot**. Only historical data for a specific **Reporting Snapshot** will be available after it has been properly configured and scheduled.

Each Salesforce edition has a limited number of **Reporting Snapshots** that can be created and scheduled, so use it wisely, or you can contact Salesforce Support to acquire more.

Configuring a Reporting Snapshot

Only users with the **Manage Reporting Snapshots** permission will be able to create and configure a Reporting Snapshot.

The major steps to configure and implement a **Reporting Snapshot** are summarized as follows:

1. Create a **Source Report** as follows:

   Create a report with the **Tabular** or **Summary** report format. The number of records created in the target object depends on the report format and the number of records returned in the report result.

   For a **Tabular** report, it will be one-to-one, meaning each record in the report will create a record in the target object.

   For a **Summary** report, it could be a **Group Summary** or a **Grand Summary**. A **Grand Summary** will always create only one record in the target object, while a **Group Summary** will create a number of records in the target object--as many as the number of groupings. The following screenshot shows options of **Grouping Level**:

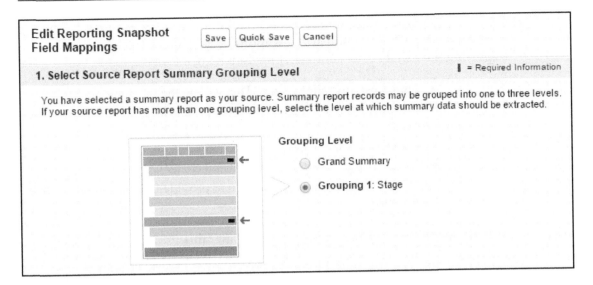

Edit Reporting Snapshot Field Mappings

[Save] [Quick Save] [Cancel]

1. Select Source Report Summary Grouping Level

▌ = Required Information

You have selected a summary report as your source. Summary report records may be grouped into one to three levels. If your source report has more than one grouping level, select the level at which summary data should be extracted.

Grouping Level

○ Grand Summary

◉ Grouping 1: Stage

> The maximum number of records that will be stored is 2000 per snapshot run.

2. To create a target object, create a custom object as the target object to store the data returned from the report. Make sure the target object is not included in the workflow.

3. Create fields in the target object: By default, a **Reporting Snapshot** will give us information about three things, which we can capture in the target object fields: **Reporting Snapshot Name**, **Reporting Snapshot Running User**, and **Execution Time**. It is a good practice to create similar field names, or the represented data will be created from the **Source Report**. You need to create additional custom fields to capture the data being collected in the **Source Report**.

4. Create the **Reporting Snapshot** : Navigate to **Setup** | **Feature Settings** | **Analytics** | **Reports & Dashboards** | **Reporting Snapshots**. Click on the **New Reporting Snapshot** button, and enter the following information:

   - **Reporting Snapshot Name**: This will be the job name
   - **Running User**: The report result depends on data visibility of this user
   - **Source Report**: Select the report created in step 1
   - **Target Object**: Select the custom object created in step 2
   - **Description**: It is a good practice to provide information for future reference

   We'll discuss this further in hands-on exercise after this.

5. Map fields from **Source Report** to target object: If your **Source Report** is the **Summary** format, you need to select the grouping level. An applicable **Source Report** field will be available for each target object--it is based on the field type.

6. Set a schedule: Optionally, you can enable the emailing of a **Reporting Snapshot** to yourself or other users. But it is mandatory to schedule the frequency and time when the **Reporting Snapshot** should run; otherwise, the **Reporting Snapshot** is not active. Select **Frequency** on a **Daily**, **Weekly**, or **Monthly** basis, and pick an available preferred start time. The selection here is similar to scheduling a report for the future run.

Hands-on exercise for creating a Reporting Snapshot

Create a history report of opportunity by stages with an amount.

Creating a Summary report

We will not go through each step to create a report, as it has been covered in detail in earlier chapters. This report needs to be in a **Summary** format--group by **Stage**, add the **Amount** column, and summarize it with **Sum**. See the next screenshot, and make sure you get a similar one.

You can store the report in any folder as long as the running user is able to access the report. But, as a good practice, create a new report folder purposely only for **Reporting Snapshot**.

Let us name this report as Opportunity by Stage (for Snapshot):

REPORT		
Opportunity by Stage (for Snapshot)		

Total Records	Total Amount	
40	$4,511,000.00	

STAGE ↑	RECORD COUNT	AMOUNT Sum
Prospecting	1	$5,000.00
Qualification	6	$282,000.00
Value Proposition	2	$330,000.00
Id. Decision Makers	6	$170,000.00
Proposal/Price Quote	1	$100,000.00
Negotiation/Review	4	$236,000.00
Closed Won	20	$3,388,000.00
GRAND TOTAL	40	$4,511,000.00

Creating a custom object

This custom object will be used to store all values when the snapshot is run on schedule. Navigate to **Setup** | **Objects & Fields** | **Object Manager** | **Create** | **Custom Objects** to create a new object; let us name the object as Opportunity Snapshot. Set the record name data type to **Auto Number**.

Creating custom fields

From the custom object created previously, create the following fields to store values from the report and snapshot running information, and make sure the fields created have the correct field type. Consider the screenshot for fields that need to be created:

FIELD LABEL	FIELD NAME	DATA TYPE
Created By	CreatedById	Lookup(User)
Currency	CurrencyIsoCode	Picklist
Execution Time	Execution_Time__c	Date/Time
Last Modified By	LastModifiedById	Lookup(User)
Opportunity Snapshot Name	Name	Auto Number
Owner	OwnerId	Lookup(User,Group)
Record Count	Record_Count__c	Number(16, 2)
Running User Id	Running_User_Id__c	Text(255)
Snapshot Name	Snapshot_Name__c	Text(255)
Stage	Stage__c	Text(25)
Total Amount	Total_Amount__c	Currency(16, 2)

Fields & Relationships (11)

In this exercise, we will capture the group summary (this is defined by the report used as **Source Report**, which is in the **Summary** format), so we just need a few custom fields to store the summary information, which, for this exercise, are **Record Count** and **Total Amount**.

But if you use a **Tabular** report as the **Source Report**, it will capture the report detail. You may need to create more fields, as you need to capture from the **Tabular** report. Each row in the report will create one record in the target snapshot object.

Creating Reporting Snapshots

This is where we define the **Reporting Snapshots** configuration as follows:

1. Navigate to **Setup** | **Feature Settings** | **Analytics** | **Reports & Dashboards** | **Reporting Snapshots**.
2. Click on the **New Reporting Snapshot** button.
3. Enter the following information:
   - **Reporting Snapshot Name**: Let us name it `Opportunity Snapshot`
   - **Description**: This is optional, but it is always a good practice to put a description for the snapshot
   - **Running User**: This user will determine data visibility when the snapshot is run
   - **Report Source Name**: Selects the report we created in Step 1, **Opportunity by Stage (for Snapshot)**
   - **Target Object**: Selects the object we have created in Step 2, **Opportunity Snapshot**
   - Click on the **Save** button to continue. Check the following screenshot:

Identification	Edit Delete		
Reporting Snapshot Name	Opportunity Snapshot	Next Run	5/26/2017 11:00 AM
Reporting Snapshot Unique Name	Opportunity_Snapshot	Last Run	5/25/2017 11:26 AM
Description	To get daily Opportunity stage information	Created By	Johan Yu, 5/24/2017 9:58 PM
Running User	Johan Yu	Last Modified By	Johan Yu, 5/26/2017 7:33 AM
Source Report	Opportunity by Stage (for Snapshot)	Target Object	Snapshot Opportunity
Group Column	Stage		

Mapping fields from Source Report to target object

Once **Reporting Snapshots** are created, click on the **Edit** button in the **Field Mappings** section.

- Select the grouping level to **Grouping 1: Stage**.
- **Map Summary Fields from Source Report to Target Object.** This is shown in the following screenshot:

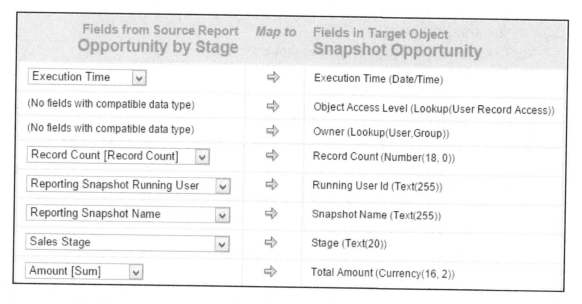

Fields from Source Report Opportunity by Stage	Map to	Fields in Target Object Snapshot Opportunity
Execution Time [v]	⇨	Execution Time (Date/Time)
(No fields with compatible data type)	⇨	Object Access Level (Lookup(User Record Access))
(No fields with compatible data type)	⇨	Owner (Lookup(User,Group))
Record Count [Record Count] [v]	⇨	Record Count (Number(18, 0))
Reporting Snapshot Running User [v]	⇨	Running User Id (Text(255))
Reporting Snapshot Name [v]	⇨	Snapshot Name (Text(255))
Sales Stage [v]	⇨	Stage (Text(20))
Amount [Sum] [v]	⇨	Total Amount (Currency(16, 2))

- Click on the **Save** button to continue.

Scheduling a Reporting Snapshot

Once the **Reporting Snapshot** is created, click on the **Edit** button in the **Schedule Reporting Snapshot** section.

- Optionally, you can enable the email sent to you or to other users based on **Public Groups**, **Roles**, **Roles and Subordinates**, and **Users**. For this exercise, we will select email **To me**.

- Set the schedule run frequency as **Daily**, **Weekly**, or **Monthly**. For this exercise, we select **Daily Every day,** as we would like to see the daily trend.
- Start date, End date, and **Preferred Start Time**: Enter the current date as the start date for one year, then select a preferred time of late night.

The following screenshot shows options available when scheduling **Reporting Snapshot**:

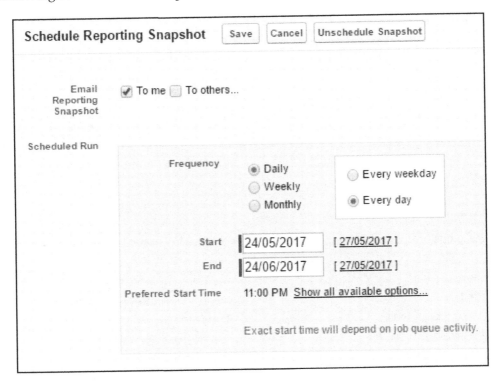

Summary and schedule

Let us see what we have so far in the following screenshot:

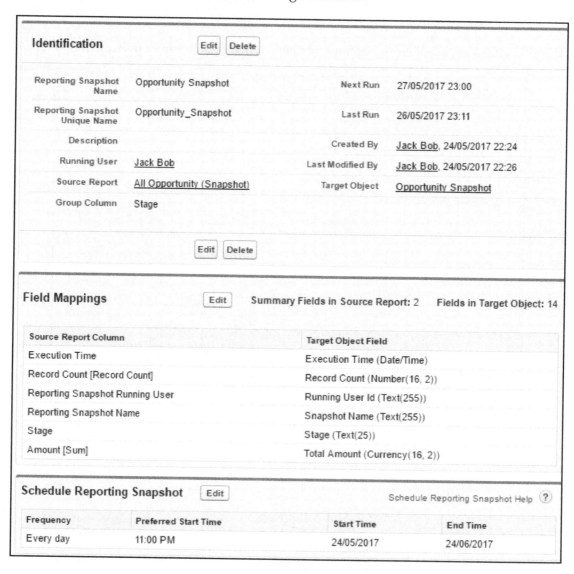

We have done all the configurations needed to implement a **Reporting Snapshot**. After this, what we can do is just wait until the **Preferred Start Time**. This is a limitation, as we cannot test straight away. But you can run the **Source Report** manually to make sure it shows you the summary information you want to collect.

As we had enabled emailing of **Reporting Snapshot**, once the snapshot schedule finishes for the day, we will get an email from Salesforce with the subject `Reporting Snapshot:` *`Name`* `- Status -` *`Status`*. The email content will describe when the snapshot was run, the status of the snapshot run, how many records were inserted into the target object, the number of failure records, and a link to the **Reporting Snapshot** log. Here is a sample of the email:

Wed 24/5/2017 11:11 PM

noreply@salesforce.com on behalf of ⬛⬛⬛⬛⬛⬛⬛⬛⬛⬛⬛⬛⬛⬛⬛⬛⬛⬛

Reporting Snapshot: Opportunity Snapshot - Status - Success

To ⬛⬛⬛⬛⬛⬛⬛

The reporting snapshot Opportunity Snapshot ran from 24/05/2017 23:11 to 24/05/2017 23:11. Below are details about the reporting snapshot:

8 records were inserted into the target object from the source report

0 records failed to load into the target object from the source report

The following fields on the target object could not be mapped: null

The status of the reporting snapshot is: Success

You can obtain further details by viewing the reporting snapshot's run detail page, or by clicking this link: https://ap1.salesforce.com/0A890000000M2WS. If you are not currently logged into salesforce.com, you will be asked to do so to view the reporting snapshot's run detail page.

Thank you,

salesforce.com

History and monitoring a Reporting Snapshot

To look for past scheduled runs for the snapshot, open the particular **Reporting Snapshot**, and scroll down to the **Run History** section, just below where we schedule it in **Schedule Reporting Snapshot**. Consider the following screenshot:

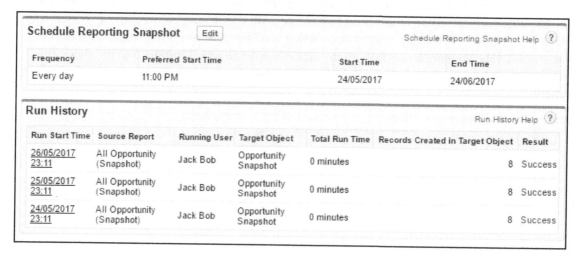

If you have multiple **Reporting Snapshots** scheduled, you can monitor them by navigating to **Setup | Environment | Jobs | Scheduled Jobs**. Look for items of the **Reporting Snapshot** type. Consider the following screenshot:

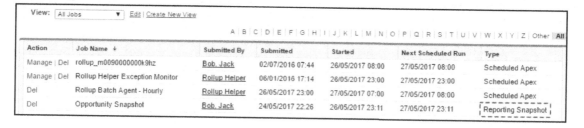

As an admin, this page will show you all the **Reporting Snapshots** scheduled, and when the next scheduled run for each snapshot is.

Reporting on historical data

Once the snapshot is run, it will copy the report result into the target custom object. You can create a normal report to analyze data in that custom object; just make sure that **Enable Reports** has been enabled for that custom object.

Let us see how the data is copied into the target object by creating a report:

STAGE ↑	EXECUTION TIME	RECORD COUNT	TOTAL AMOUNT	RUNNING USER ID
Closed Lost (3 records)	24/05/2017 23:11	3.00	USD 9,900.00	00590000000OjrD
	25/05/2017 23:11	3.00	USD 9,900.00	00590000000OjrD
	26/05/2017 23:11	4.00	USD 109,900.00	00590000000OjrD
Closed Won (3 records)	24/05/2017 23:11	25.00	USD 1,092,612.92	00590000000OjrD
	25/05/2017 23:11	25.00	USD 1,092,612.92	00590000000OjrD
	26/05/2017 23:11	25.00	USD 1,092,612.92	00590000000OjrD
Id. Decision Makers (3 records)	24/05/2017 23:11	5.00	USD 208,807.20	00590000000OjrD
	25/05/2017 23:11	5.00	USD 208,807.20	00590000000OjrD
	26/05/2017 23:11	5.00	USD 208,807.20	00590000000OjrD
Needs Analysis (3 records)	24/05/2017 23:11	34.00	USD 565,387.00	00590000000OjrD
	25/05/2017 23:11	35.00	USD 575,387.00	00590000000OjrD
	26/05/2017 23:11	35.00	USD 575,387.00	00590000000OjrD
Negotiation/Review (3 records)	24/05/2017 23:11	2.00	USD 117,500.00	00590000000OjrD
	25/05/2017 23:11	2.00	USD 117,500.00	00590000000OjrD
	26/05/2017 23:11	1.00	USD 17,500.00	00590000000OjrD
Perception Analysis (3 records)	24/05/2017 23:11	2.00	USD 8,499.00	00590000000OjrD
	25/05/2017 23:11	3.00	USD 28,499.00	00590000000OjrD
	26/05/2017 23:11	3.00	USD 28,499.00	00590000000OjrD

For this example, with this report, we can analyze how **Record Count** and **Total Amount** by **Stage** changed over a period of days.

Summary

This chapter shared many tips starting with setting up collaboration in reports and dashboards using **Chatter** feeds and groups. We continue with tips for using parameters in a report, which is done by adding parameters to the web browser URL. This parameter overwrites the existing value defined in the report, and with this, we can change the report filter value temporarily without the need to keep editing the report. We continued by introducing **Field History Tracking**, as how to take advantage by simply enabling a field for history tracking. We do not need developers for this, and it can be done within minutes. We ended the chapter by looking at a hands-on exercise to use **Reporting Snapshot** to store daily or weekly data in a custom object.

In the next chapter, we will discuss accessing reports and dashboards from the Salesforce1 mobile app, which supports both iOS and Android devices. It also supports offline mode for users who need to read, edit, and add data to Salesforce when they do not have an internet connection.

12
Dashboards and Reports in the Salesforce1 Mobile App

This chapter will discuss how to access your reports and dashboards using the default Salesforce mobile app called **Salesforce1**. Salesforce1 is an app to experience Salesforce from any mobile and tablet device, and brings all your **Chatter**, CRM, custom apps, and business processes together in a unified, modern experience for any Salesforce user. With the power of the Salesforce1 platform, you can now customize and build any app, and instantly deploy that functionality through the Salesforce1 app. And the best part for customers is that this app is available for free--you just need to enter your Salesforce username and password.

We will not go through the Salesforce1 app in detail: installation, permissions, configuration, notification, action, approval, event, and navigation. But we will discuss, in depth, topics such as accessing the dashboards and reports with the Salesforce1 mobile app, the offline mode when you do not have access to the internet from your device, and the access report and dashboard using a mobile web browser.

Salesforce1 is available for both iOS and Android devices; however, all the screenshots used in this book have been taken from an iPhone or iPad. Usually, Salesforce updates the app version in every release. This book is written based on the Salesforce1 app version 12.3.

The following topics will be covered in this chapter:

- Introduction to the Salesforce1 app
- Working with dashboards in the Salesforce1 app
- Sharing dashboard snapshots to **Chatter** feed
- Working with reports in the Salesforce1 app
- Accessing your reports and dashboards offline
- Limitations of the Salesforce1 mobile app

Introduction to the Salesforce1 mobile app

The Salesforce1 mobile app is an enterprise class out of the box mobile app built by Salesforce.com. It is available for all Salesforce users including the **Chatter Free** users. This app is available for both iOS and Android platforms; you can download and install it for free from the App Store for iOS devices, and from Google Play for Android devices.

This app supports both smartphones and tablet devices. Salesforce1, also available for users to use supported mobile web browser with supported devices, gives the same user experience as the installed app; for this option, you do not need to install the app on your mobile device.

The app will work for you out-of-the-box, and respect your Salesforce configuration, security, and customization, and is implemented without any efforts to reconfigure it. The only exceptions are AppExchange products that are not certified for Salesforce1 and any custom Visual Force pages not designed or configured for use in Salesforce1. This app gives you real-time access to the same Salesforce.com information as you see in the office using a web browser.

Prior to the Salesforce1 app, Salesforce built a few different mobile apps, such as Salesforce Classic, Salesforce Touch, Logger & ForcePad, and **Chatter** Mobile. The Salesforce1 mobile app combines all of these into one single platform as a unified mobile experience across iOS and Android smartphones and tablets.

The Salesforce1 app is automatically enabled for all existing and new customers unless it is turned off by your admin. When you log into the Salesforce1 app, the branding, navigation, notifications, and the offline setting are controlled in your Salesforce configuration. The following screenshot is a sample of Salesforce1 app captured from an iOS device:

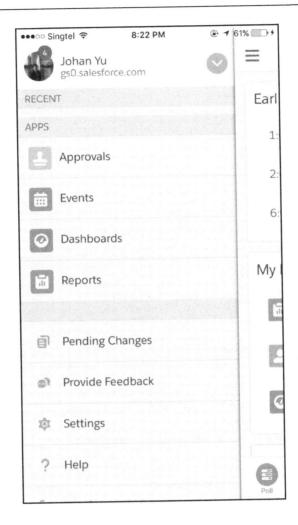

Working with dashboards in the Salesforce1 app

To access the dashboard in the Salesforce1 app, tap on the navigation menu, and scroll down to the **Dashboards** menu under the **APPS** section. If you do not see the **Dashboards** menu there, add it like this: navigate from **Setup** | **Apps** | **Mobile Apps** | **Salesforce1 Navigation**, select **Dashboards**, and add the selected items. The following screenshot shows how to configure **Mobile Navigation**:

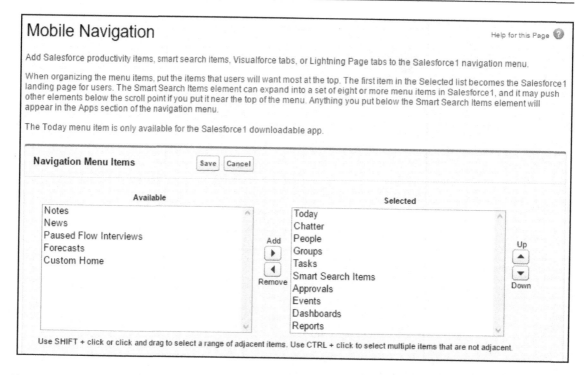

You can search the dashboard with the dashboard name, and you should be able to find all the dashboards you have access to as in the Salesforce web page.

Here are a few items related to the dashboard for Salesforce1:

- All the components in the dashboard will be available when you open the dashboard in the Salesforce1 app too.
- For a mobile device, the dashboard will be displayed as a column. The first dashboard would be the one located at the top left, the next one will be located below (not to the right) of the top-left component, and then followed by all the other components.
- For a tablet device, the dashboard will be displayed in two columns; the first dashboard would be the one located at the top left, followed by the right component, which was originally located below the first dashboard. This will continue to show all the components for the dashboard. Consider the following screenshot:

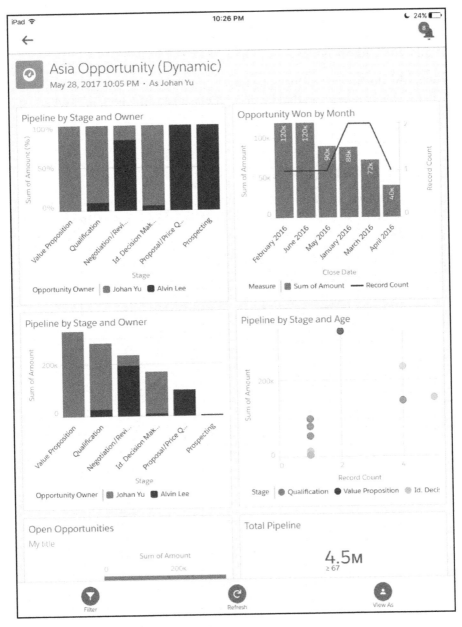

At the minimum, you need to have a **Run Report** permission to open the dashboard, and you also need to have access to the dashboard folder, which is the same as what you need to open the dashboard from the web page.

The menu visibility of dashboards in the Salesforce1 app does not depend on tab settings in the user's profile. Once you tap the dashboard's menu, it will open a list of the recent dashboards that you had opened.

When you open the dashboard in the Salesforce1 app, the same way as in accessing the web, you will be able to see when the dashboard was last refreshed, and who is the viewing user.

Refreshing a dashboard

You can also refresh the dashboard from a mobile app. Tap the **Refresh** icon at the bottom of the dashboard, and it will prompt you to confirm the dashboard refresh. This is shown in the following screenshot:

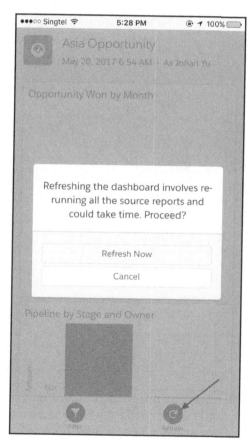

The dynamic dashboard

When you open a dynamic dashboard in the Salesforce1 mobile app, and if you have permission to run the dashboard as someone else, you will be able to do the same in the mobile app. Tap on the **View As** icon, and select a user. This is shown in the following screenshot:

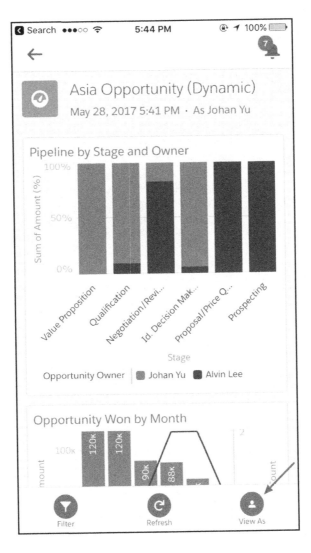

The dashboard filters

When you open the dashboard with filters configured in the Salesforce1 app, you will be able to filter the dashboard as well from the mobile app. Tap on the **Filter** icon, and select the filters defined. This is shown in the following screenshot:

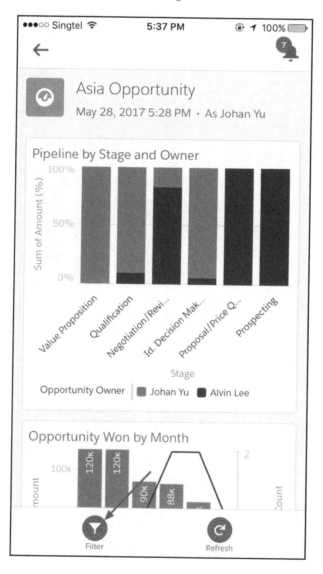

Sharing a dashboard snapshot to Chatter feed

If you remember, in `Chapter 11`, *Advanced Tips and Tricks for Reports and Dashboards*, we explained the ability to post dashboard snapshots to the dashboard feed or user/group feed from Salesforce in web browsers. You can do the same from the Salesforce1 app. You can post the dashboard snapshot to your feed, and mention another user or **Chatter** group as follows:

1. Open the dashboard from the Salesforce1 app.
2. Select the dashboard component by tapping on it; notice the blue dash line around the component--the expand icon will appear at the top-right corner of the chart. This is shown in the following screenshot:

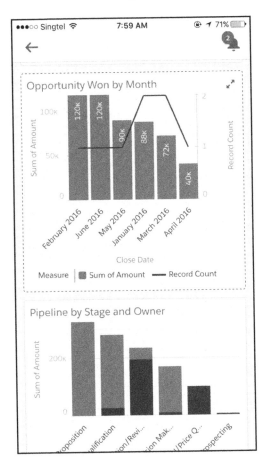

3. Tap on the expand icon to open the chart in full screen.
4. Look for the **Share** icon at the bottom of the dashboard.
5. Tap on the **Share** icon, then enter the text as you want in the share window. You can mention users or a **Chatter** group by tapping the head icon, or enter text starting with @. The user will get an email if the **Chatter** email notification is enabled for **Mentions me in a comment**. Consider the following screenshot:

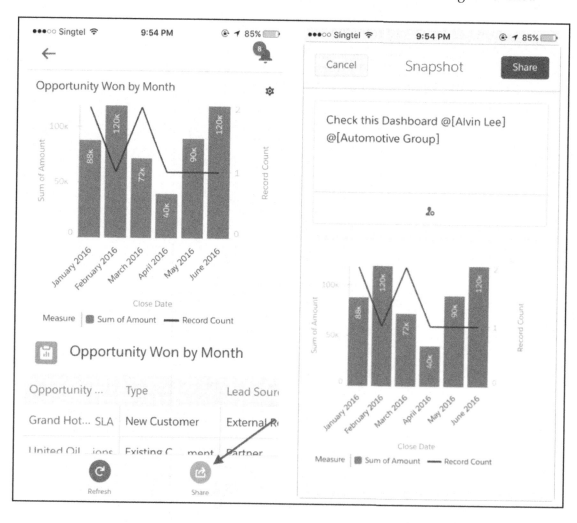

6. When other users see your **Chatter** page, they will see the dashboard snapshot in your **Chatter** feed. This is shown in the following screenshot:

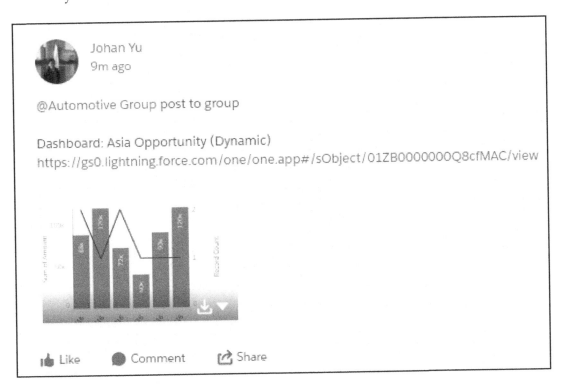

Changing the component chart types

We can't create a dashboard from scratch in Salesforce1, and it doesn't seem that you need to create a dashboard on the go, but you can change the component chart in the Salesforce1 app, although you may not be able to save it. Let's discuss this in detail:

1. Open the dashboard from the Salesforce1 app.
2. Tap on the dashboard component; the expand icon will appear at the top-right corner of the chart.
3. Tap on the expand icon to open the chart in full screen.
4. Look for and tap on the gear icon, which is located below the notification icon.
5. The system will offer you the opportunity to change the chart type for easy analysis of the data.

6. Tap **Done** when finished. The chart will change, but will not be saved.

7. You will see a stacked bar chart option when you have multiple groupings in the source report. This is shown in the following screenshot:

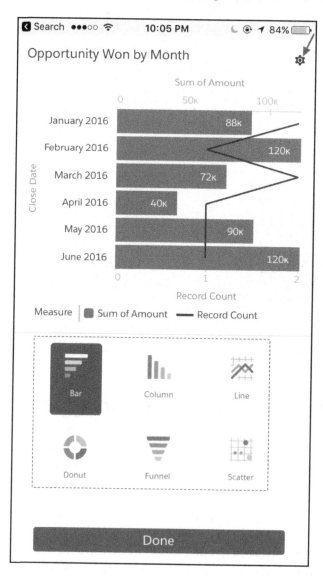

Chart details and reports

When the dashboard opens in the Salesforce1 app, the same as it opens in the browser, you can also tap a segment of the chart to get more information for that segment of the chart.

When you expand the dashboard, you will see the report under the chart; you can still tap a segment of the chart for more information. Not just that, the report below the chart will also be filtered with a group of the charts tapped, as seen in the following screenshot:

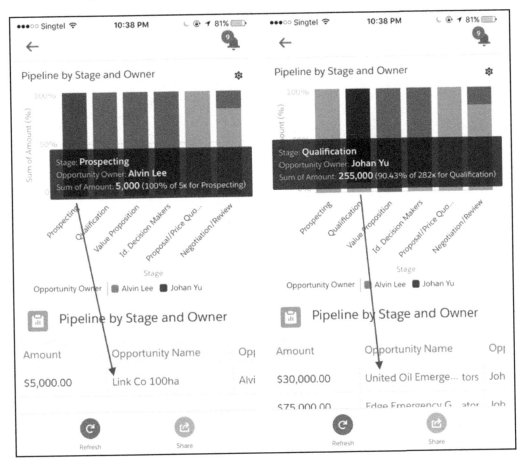

Notice in the preceding screenshot, when we tap the bar, the records shown below the chart are refreshed; from there, you will also see more information about the bar, such as: **Sum Amount**.

Working with reports in the Salesforce1 app

There are a few options to access reports in the Salesforce1 mobile app. Let us discuss them in detail.

Report menu items

If you do not see the **Reports** menu in the Salesforce 1 app menu, make sure to add it-- navigate to **Setup | Apps | Mobile Apps | Salesforce1 Navigation**, select **Reports**, and add the selected items. This is shown in the following screenshot:

Account Own...	Account Name	Las
Johan Yu	GenePoint	5/2
Alvin Lee	United Oil & Gas, UK	4/1
Johan Yu	United Oil & Gas, ... pore	5/2
Johan Yu	Edge Communications	5/4
Johan Yu	Burlington Textiles ... rica	5/4
Johan Yu	Pyramid Constructi...Inc.	5/1
Johan Yu	Dickenson plc	5/2
Johan Yu	Grand Hotels & Re... Ltd	5/4
Johan Yu	Express Logistics a... port	5/4
Alvin Lee	University of Arizona	5/2
Alvin Lee	United Oil & Gas Corp.	5/6

Account by Type (8:29 PM, Singtel, 66%)

When you open a report in the Salesforce1 mobile app, the report format will be ignored. **Summary** and **Matrix** format reports will be presented just as columns, similar to **Tabular** reports. If the report has a chart added, it will not be visible when the report opens in Salesforce1.

In the **Tabular** format report, the first column will be frozen, so, when you scroll to the right to see more columns, the first column will stay visible. For **Summary** and **Matrix** reports, the first column (not the group fields) will be frozen, while fields used as a group will be the last columns.

You can sort the report by tapping on the column header; by default, it will be sorted in the ascending order--you can tap the header again to change it to sort in the descending order.

Drilling down from dashboards

As you know, a report is the data source for the dashboard. When you select and expand the dashboard component in the Salesforce1 mobile app, you can drill down into the report used as the data source. When the report opens, it shows the chart above the report. If the original report has a chart added, the original chart will not show in the Salesforce1 mobile app.

You can filter data in the report based on dashboard grouping by tapping on the group in a chart of the report, except for the **Table** and **Matrix** components. When you tap on an item of the chart, it will prompt you to show more information on that segment, and the report generated will be automatically refreshed and filtered with the segment selected. This is shown in the following screenshot:

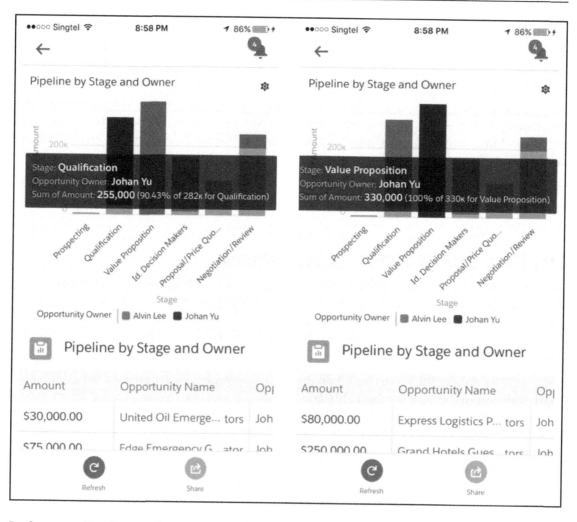

In the preceding image, the two screenshots have been taken from the same report. In the left one, **Stage** as **Qualification** is selected, and the report following it has been auto-filtered with **Owner** as **Johan Yu** and **Stage** as **Qualification**. In the one on the right, the bar for **Stage** as **Value Proposition** is selected, and the report has been auto-filtered with **Stage** as **Value Proposition**.

Drilling down to records

When the report column is the name of an object, you can tap on it to open the record detail, such as **Account Name**, **Opportunity Name**, **Opportunity Owner**, and so on. From the record detail page, tapping on the arrow at the top-left will bring you back to the report.

Accessing offline

The Salesforce1 app supports offline access. You can read, create, and edit existing records that you recently accessed. When you get an internet connection again, the data added or modified will auto-sync back to Salesforce. Records pending sync will be marked with a green triangle and white arrow. However, offline access is not possible for Salesforce mobile web browsers.

To enable offline support for the Salesforce1 app, navigate to **Setup | Apps | Mobile Apps | Salesforce1 Offline**, tick **Enable Caching in Salesforce1**, and tick **Enable offline create, edit, and delete in Salesforce1**. This is only for the Salesforce1 app installed on your devices, not for the Salesforce1 mobile browser app.

When the offline setting is enabled, you will also be able to access the reports and dashboards recently opened in the offline mode, including a drill down to the record detail.

Limitations of the Salesforce1 app

There are a few limitations in accessing the dashboards and reports from the mobile app, but since this app is useful for on the go access, you may not need the full features of dashboards and reports on a small screen device.

Here is a summary of some of the limitations of this app:

- Inability to create and edit dashboards and reports
- Inability to modify dashboard components
- The report format is ignored
- Charts added in reports are not made available
- **Chatter** feeds are not available

Summary

We started this chapter with an introduction to the Salesforce1 mobile app, continued working with dashboards using the Salesforce1 mobile app, explained dashboard refresh, opened dynamic dashboards, and dashboard filters using the Salesforce1 mobile app. We also discussed how to post dashboard snapshots to **Chatter** feed for collaboration.

Next we discussed reports in Salesforce1, how to open the report, including the additional filter feature when drilling down the report from a dashboard component. We summarized the limitations of accessing the dashboard and filter from the mobile app.

This is the last chapter in this book. Thanks for reading and learning. We hope it will help you in your daily job as a Salesforce system administrator or as a business user to fully utilize the reporting and dashboard features in Salesforce Lightning.

Index

Made in the USA
Columbia, SC
22 June 2023

18729169R00220